Text, Discourse and Corpora

Corpus and Discourse

Corpus linguistics provides the methodology to extract meaning from texts. Taking as its starting point the fact that language is not a mirror of reality but lets us share what we know, believe and think about reality, it focuses on language as a social phenomenon, and makes visible the attitudes and beliefs expressed by the members of a discourse community.

Consisting of both spoken and written language, discourse always has historical, social, functional and regional dimensions. Discourse can be monolingual or multilingual, interconnected by translations. Discourse is where language and social studies meet.

The *Corpus and Discourse* series consists of two strands. The first, *Research in Corpus and Discourse*, features innovative contributions to various aspects of corpus linguistics and a wide range of applications, from language technology via the teaching of a second language to a history of mentalities. The second strand, *Studies in Corpus and Discourse*, is comprised of key texts bridging the gap between social studies and linguistics. Although equally academically rigorous, this strand will be aimed at a wider audience of academics and postgraduate students working in both disciplines.

Research in Corpus and Discourse

Meaningful Texts
The Extraction of Semantic Information from Monolingual and Multilingual Corpora
Edited by Geoff Barnbrook, Pernilla Danielsson and Michaela Mahlberg

Corpus Linguistics and World Englishes
An Analysis of Xhosa English
Vivian de Klerk

Evaluation in Media Discourse
Analysis of a Newspaper Corpus
Monika Bednarek

Idioms and Collocations
Corpus-based Linguistic and Lexicographic Studies
Edited by Christiane Fellbaum

Working with Spanish Corpora
Edited by Giovanni Parodi

Historical Corpus Stylistics
Media, Technology and Change
Patrick Studer

Conversation in Context
A Corpus-driven Analysis
Christoph Rühlemann

Studies in Corpus and Discourse

English Collocation Studies
The OSTI Report
John Sinclair, Susan Jones and Robert Daley
Edited by Ramesh Krishnamurthy
With an introduction by Wolfgang Teubert

Text, Discourse and Corpora

Theory and Analysis

Michael Hoey, Michaela Mahlberg, Michael Stubbs and Wolfgang Teubert

With an introduction by John Sinclair

continuum

Continuum
The Tower Building   80 Maiden Lane
11 York Road   Suite 704
London SE1 7NX   New York, NY 10038

British Library Cataloguing-in-Publication Data
A catalogue record for this book is available from the British Library.

ISBN: 978-08264-9171-8
       978-08264-9172-5

Library of Congress Cataloging-in-Publication Data
A catalog record for this book is available from the Library of Congress.

Typeset by RefineCatch Limited, Bungay, Suffolk
Printed and bound in Great Britain by Athenaeum Press Ltd, Gateshead, Tyne & Wear

In memory of John Sinclair, without whom none of this would
have been possible.

Contents

Contributors

Michael Hoey is Baines Professor of English Language at the University of Liverpool. He is an Academician of the Academy for Social Sciences and chief advisor to Macmillan Publishers on dictionaries. He co-edits (with Tony McEnery) a series of corpus linguistics monographs for Routledge. His single-authored monographs include *On the Surface of Discourse* (George Allen and Unwin, 1983), *Patterns of Lexis in Text* (OUP, 1991), *Textual Interaction* (Routledge, 2001) and *Lexical Priming: A New Theory of Words and Language* (Routledge, 2005). He has also written over 60 articles. He has lectured by invitation at universities or conferences in 40 countries.

Michaela Mahlberg is Lecturer in English Language at the University of Liverpool. For her first degree she studied English and Mathematics at the universities of Bonn and Exeter, and she completed her PhD in English Language at the University of Saarbrücken. She worked at the universities of Bari (Italy), Birmingham (UK), Saarbrücken (Germany) and Liverpool Hope University College (UK), and she also taught at Tuscan Word Centre Courses. She has recently published the monograph *English General Nouns: a Corpus Theoretical Approach* (John Benjamins, 2005). She is the Editor of the *International Journal of Corpus Linguistics* published by John Benjamins.

John M. Sinclair was Professor Emeritus of Modern English Language at the University of Birmingham, where he spent most of his career. His education and early work was at the University of Edinburgh, where he began his interest in corpus linguistics, stylistics, grammar and discourse analysis. In his later life he divided his time between Italy, where he was President of The Tuscan Word Centre, and Arisaig in Scotland. He holds an Honorary Doctorate in Philosophy from the University of Gothenburg, and an Honorary Professorship at the Universities of Jiao Tong, Shangai and Glasgow. He was an Honorary Life Member of the Linguistics Association of Great Britain and a member of the Academia Europæa. He was the Founding Editor-in-Chief of the Cobuild series of language reference materials. His main current project was as consultant to Learning and

Teaching Scotland in the preparation of language corpus resources for Scottish schools. Sadly, John died while this book was in production.

Michael Stubbs has been Professor of English Linguistics at the University of Trier, Germany, since 1990. He was educated at the universities of Cambridge and Edinburgh, and was then Research Associate at the University of Birmingham (1973–74), Lecturer in Linguistics at the University of Nottingham (1974–85) and Professor of English at the Institute of Education, University of London (1985–90). He has also been Chair of the British Association for Applied Linguistics (1988–91) and Honorary Senior Research Fellow at the University of Birmingham (1994–99). He has lectured in several countries around the world, most recently Italy, Denmark, Norway, Sweden and Finland. His main current research areas are English phraseology and corpus semantics. His most recent book is *Words and Phrases* (Blackwell, 2001).

Wolfgang Teubert is Professor of Corpus Linguistics at the University of Birmingham. He studied German and English Language and Literature at the University of Heidelberg, and there he earned his DPhil for his thesis on the valency of nouns. From 1971 to 2000 he was working, as researcher, head of department and senior research fellow, at the Institut für Deutsche Sprache in Mannheim. From grammar he moved on to lexicology, critical discourse analysis, language change and finally to corpus linguistics. In the 1990s he was involved in a number of EC-funded European projects studying the feasibility of a corpus approach to multilingual human language technology. Today he is trying to find a theoretical foundation of corpus linguistics in the framework of social constructionism, systems theory and hermeneutics.

Introduction

John Sinclair

Empirical linguists are often criticized for having their eyes and ears so close to their data that they do not tackle any wider issues. They are always at risk of having their scholarly reports greeted with cries of 'So what?' and indeed such a judgement is a professional hazard for all of us. The findings from careful data analysis are often so fascinating to the researcher that he or she forgets that the rest of the world wants an evaluation of the data and not merely a report on it.

This collection is nowhere in danger of the 'So what?' judgement. The authors show, in a number of different ways, how a base of empirical observation of data – in this case mainly text corpora – can be used as a foundation for a broad range of intellectual exploration. Hoey develops his concept of 'priming' to move from the factuality of a corpus to the personal skills of individuals; Teubert works from the usage of words representing key concepts to extended social critiques; Stubbs looks at the observed or implied philosophical bases of corpus linguistics, relating it to the famous duality of rationalism and empiricism. And Mahlberg, while supporting each of her colleagues, extends the methodology significantly in order to make statements about literary texts that will be of interest to a wider audience than corpus linguists.

The tight, empirical world of the corpus student is opened out substantially by the papers in this book, and the broad relevance and significance of knowledge derived from a corpus is clearly demonstrated in a set of highly original studies.

Both Hoey and Teubert give central importance to people's language experience, but bring out different aspects of it. Hoey builds on the structural side, and Teubert on the semantics. They are thus complementary in their explorations of the way in which previous communicative events shape current ones. For Hoey, each instance of a word, a structure, a pattern in use leads to all the participants in the event adjusting their expectations in the light of that shred of experience. They will be more prepared to receive the same kind of textual signal on a future occasion. Adjustment, which Hoey calls 'priming', is a direct connection between experience and expectation, and as repeated instances crop up in further encounters, the adjustment is proportionate to the frequency of the events.

While Hoey makes it clear that priming remains a psychological notion, a descriptor for individual behaviour, he shows that it can be used in a loose sense in corpus linguistics; although a corpus cannot be primed, the individuals whose communicative experiences form the texts that make up the corpus are primed to behave as they do, and so the corpus is a record both of the routine and regular primings and the instances that go against the anticipated primings.

In his first chapter Hoey applies the apparatus of priming onto literary text, for which it would seem to be eminently suited; both the regularities of everyday language encounters, and the strikingly unusual combinations that are found in literary texts are explained in the theory of lexical priming. Hoey begins with an explication of the first lines of *'The time has come,'* the Walrus said, *'to talk of many things . . .'* – the supremely ironic verse of Lewis Carroll. He teases out the implications of *the time has come* in particular. Then he turns to the use of the word *call* in Michael Moorcock's novel *The Eternal Champion,* and shows how the clever deployment of this word controls the reader's evaluations of the central character of Erekosë. Thirdly Hoey turns to a short poem of Philip Larkin which is itself about expectations, and illustrates the skill of the writer in creating the world of the newborn lamb.

In his second contribution to the book, Hoey argues that the same psychological mechanisms that set up lexical primings can also be used in the building of personal grammars (and, since all language experience is shared, the basic information for the creation of general grammars). He cunningly uses a halfway house as the focus of his data – the numerals, which are sort-of-adjectival and sort-of-deictic, but not really either. As individual words they have – surprisingly to some observers – clear patterns of collocation, and as class members they share another set of co-occurrence patterns, here 'colligation', with the other numerals. The exposition of how children first encounter numerals in their written form is simultaneously surprising and obvious – the hallmark of a good arrangement of corpus evidence.

Teubert also bases his arguments on textual experience that precedes the events under examination, and he sees the meaning of a word, phrase or sentence as the accumulation of its previous occurrence. This adds a diachronic dimension which is not really part of Hoey's argument, and it focuses not on the experience of the individual but on the available language experience of a society. Meaning is always provisional, always changing; there is a Darwinian flavour to Teubert's view that it is the right of each member of a speech community to use a word in whatever way they please, but if the usage is not adopted by the other members of the speech community then it simply disappears – only the fittest survive.

Teubert's second contribution is a detailed workout of his theoretical position in relation to two words that resonate through the ages – *work* and *property*. Following his intertextual theory of the acquisition of meaning, he studies the development of the concepts of work and property from the early notion of personal labour and physical possession to the tussle between socialist and capitalist ideologies in the last two centuries.

For this task Teubert sets up an extremely specific corpus of papal encyclicals dealing with industrial relations. It should be noted that in his earlier, more general paper he does not use a corpus at all, but 'googles' the words and phrases that interest him. While controversies rage over the reliability, representativeness and impartiality of Google searches, Teubert demonstrates that for sketching out the way in which words are currently being used it is a simple and powerful tool. So in his two contributions Teubert shows both conventional corpus analysis, using a specially compiled small corpus, and the flexibility of directly searching the internet.

Stubbs opens up the debate still further, and considers what kind of theory would be appropriate for language, given the insights in recent years of generative grammar and corpus linguistics, approaches which are almost diametrically opposed. His first paper is in the philosophy of science, what might fashionably be called 'metatheory', though Stubbs commendably avoids the term. What, he asks, are the irreducibly different components of a theory of language? He rejects dualisms and monisms and develops a strong case for a four-component framework, adapting the model proposed by Juhan Tuldava.

Stubbs returns to the coal-face of practical corpus analysis in his second paper in the book, and gives several worked examples using different methodologies and models. The chapter includes a short guide to Fletcher's PIE database, which Stubbs has helped to shape into one of the most useful corpus resources currently available; it is somewhat forbidding at the start, however, and these clear examples, leading to telling points of interpretation, both guide and encourage anyone making use of PIE (Phrases in English).

Mahlberg, as befits the originator, compiler and editor of the book, takes a judicious middle path. Like Teubert, she takes a phrase that resonates with political and social colour, but instead of googling, she makes a corpus from a year's journalism and follows its usage carefully. Like Stubbs, she makes a detailed analysis of concordances taken from the corpus, and formulates interesting interpretations; because of the sectionalizing of her corpus she is able to relate the occurrence of the phrase to precise sections of the *Guardian*.

In her second paper, Mahlberg links with Hoey's literary concerns. It is important to note that corpus experts are now able to engage with literary text despite, in general, pinning their faith on often-repeated events. It is a defining characteristic of literary texts that their language is at least to some degree unexpected, unprimed as Hoey might put it. Evidence of the routine behaviour of language users is found in corpora, and a distinctive literary text is just not worth including in a general corpus because it will disappear below the waves since its textual patterns are not echoed in other texts. It is thus a challenge to turn a corpus resource into a tool for literary interpretation, and Mahlberg is leading the way in this with her finely observed analysis of Dickens' style. Hoey and Mahlberg illustrate the two main ways in which the corpus and the unique literary text can profitably meet; Hoey sets the phrasing of a poem against the normative phraseology of a large corpus, while Mahlberg makes a corpus of her author's work and seeks the regularities and the distinctive traits of patterning. As well as following Hori in assembling a substantial corpus of Dickens' writings (conveniently, Charles Dickens was a prolific writer) she compiles an intermediate corpus of nineteenth-century novels by other authors, so that the comparisons can be subtle and precise. And, to give yet another dimension, she contrasts one novel, *Bleak House*, with the Dickens canon as well as the other reference points.

In another innovative move, Mahlberg calls on long n-grams (e.g. 8-grams) to sort out the characteristic phraseology. Stubbs introduces the technique as one of his contrasting approaches, and Mahlberg shows how valuable it is to be able to trace the longish repeated strings in a literary composition. N-grams are among the very earliest computational objects to be used in textual studies, going back 50 years at least. They are immensely powerful in that they uncover strong patterns of coselection, but they are dreadfully limited by their rigidity of definition; since the remarkable variability of language patterns is as notable as their extent, variation is the most obvious first step away from the physical events, but n-grams are hopelessly pinned to actual forms in actual sequences.

Mahlberg makes use of 5-grams following her study of 8-grams (and above); she wisely sees such data purely as entry points into the study of the phraseology, but points out that even evidence as inflexible as this can be brought directly into service, for example in finding key differences between Dickens and his contemporaries.

All in all, the papers in this book offer a series of broad and penetrating insights into language, based on strictly disciplined studies of an impressive range of data, using an equally impressive range of methodologies. This is the cutting edge of corpus linguistics at the present time, and the book gathers together papers which are at the same time representative and highly original.

The papers gathered together here form a large part of the record of an unusually interesting event that took place in Saarbrücken in September 2004. The event centred on a short intensive course in corpus linguistics, jointly organized by The Tuscan Word Centre and the University of Saarbrücken, and included in the middle a 'Teachers' Day', where the course tutors, reinforced by some guest lecturers, turned their attention to a large audience of local teachers who had gathered. It is encouraging to note that the Teachers' Day is now an annual event.

The empirical side of corpus linguistics was represented by coordinated sessions in a laboratory, where participants had hands-on experience of conducting queries and interpreting the results. This was the base on which the talks built, making a powerful synthesis; the reader should remember that during the course the accent was on the practicalities of data handling, and the originals of these chapters were indications of what can be done with corpus evidence in the hands of leading researchers.

It is clear from every page in the book that the authors offer a variety of routes from the data to interpretation and understanding of the central mechanisms of language. Teubert articulates the chilling verdict that society hands down to the vast majority of the text that we produce: 'Only those contributions count which leave a trace in subsequent texts of this discourse community'. For certain this book will leave more than a trace in subsequent texts to do with almost all aspects of the description of languages.

1 Lexical priming and literary creativity

Michael Hoey

Introduction

In this chapter, I shall try to show how claims I have made elsewhere about lexical priming might impact on discussions of literary text. Corpus linguistics, by its very nature, tends to concern itself with regularities and has therefore not much concerned with issues of how the new and unexpected might be explained. I want to show that a corpus-based theory such as lexical priming can not only account for linguistic and literary creativity (at least in so far as the latter is a matter of linguistic creativity) but can actually provide a fuller description than has sometimes been provided by non-corpus linguists in the past. My objective is not to illuminate the texts as literary artefacts, though in at least one of the cases there is, I think, some illumination to be had, but to show how the novelty of language can be described. I am going to look at fragments of three literary texts. The first is a sentence from Lewis Carroll's *Through the Looking Glass and What Alice Found There*, the second, the opening paragraph of a novel by Michael Moorcock, and the third, a verse from a poem by Philip Larkin. The choice of the three texts was largely (but not entirely) arbitrary. The Carroll verse was thrown up during an investigation of the phrase 'The time has come', the Moorcock analysis arose as a result of an invitation to contribute to a volume on apocalypses[1] and the Larkin verse was chosen because it was the subject of a famous early article by John Sinclair.[2] They do, however, reflect a reasonable range of literary artefacts, one being a verse written for children, one a fantasy novel, and one a poem written by a highly regarded modern poet.

1 Lexical priming: some claims

In Hoey (2003, 2004a, 2004b, 2005), I argue that the existence of colloca-tion undermines certain assumptions about the separability of grammar and lexis and requires a psychological explanation. The explanation I have offered is that each time we encounter a word (or syllable or combination of words), we subconsciously keep a record of the context and co-text of

Contextualized

Dynamic

the word, so that cumulatively as we re-encounter the word (or syllable or combination of words) we build up a record of its collocations. We are, I argue, primed by each encounter so that when we come to use the word (or syllable or combination of words) we characteristically replicate the contexts in which we had previously encountered it.[3] Once this is recognized to account for collocation, we can see that the same processes will account for a number of other phenomena in the language. So, I argue, in addition to collocation, we are primed to recognize and replicate:

- the grammatical patterns a word appears in and the grammatical functions it serves, including the grammatical categories it realizes (its colligations);
- the meanings with which it is associated (its semantic associations);
- the pragmatics it is associated with (its pragmatic associations);
- the genres, styles, domains and social situations it occurs in and/or is restricted to;
- the patterns of cohesion it forms in a text (or their absence) (its textual collocations);
- the textual positioning of the word, e.g. whether it typically begins or ends the sentences it appears in or whether it has a tendency to appear at the beginning of paragraphs or speaking turns (its textual colligations);
- its place in the larger semantics of the text, e.g. its association with contrast relations, problem-solution patterns, narrative climax (its textual semantic associations).

Dynamic

Just as was claimed for collocation, it is claimed that all these features are subconsciously identified each time we encounter a word and that these encounters *prime* us so that when we use the word, we will characteristically use it with one of its typical collocations, in its usual grammatical function, in the same semantic context, in the domain we have come to associate it with, as part of the same genre, in a familiar social context, with a similar pragmatics and to similar textual ends. Crucially, once a priming has been created, it is itself subject to further priming. So, to quote an example from Hoey (2005), *winter* is primed to collocate with *in*, and the combination *in winter* is in turn primed to occur with BE. This I term nesting. Also crucially, a priming may be negative as well as positive. Thus it may be noted that a particular verb rarely, if ever, for example, occurs with a human subject (a negative semantic association) or that a particular noun rarely occurs as head of a nominal group.

The notions of colligation and semantic association are shared with Sinclair (2004), though he uses the term 'semantic preference' for the latter. The notion of pragmatic association certainly overlaps with and may be subsumed in Sinclair's notion of semantic prosody.

This is not the place to offer detailed evidence in support of the above position; this has in any case been attempted in Hoey (2005). The application of this position to the literary texts I have chosen will, however,

Important theoretical points

provide some explanation of the claims I have made. Before I can begin my exploration of literary language, however, there are four important points I ① must make. The first is that lexical priming is a property of the person, not the word. It is convenient sometimes to say, for example, that a word is primed to occur with a particular collocate but this is shorthand for saying that most speakers are primed to associate the word with that particular collocate.

The second point follows from the first: because lexical priming is ② a product of an individual's encounters with the word, it follows inexorably that everyone's primings are different because everyone's linguistic experience is necessarily unique. We cannot claim in advance of the evidence that all speakers are primed the same way; this is another reason why a statement that a word is primed to take a particular collocate is an oversimplification. It is nevertheless an oversimplification I shall resort to occasionally, for the sake of preventing my sentences from becoming prolix.

The third point follows from the second: the existence of a priming for ③ an individual cannot be demonstrated directly from corpus evidence, because a corpus represents no one's experience of the language. The *Relative* corpus I frequently work with, for example, is entirely made up of texts from the *Guardian*. Even if somewhere there existed a person who had painstakingly read every sentence of the *Guardian* every day throughout the period the data were assembled, the corpus would still not fully reflect that person's primings, in that s/he would also have encountered other language in their lives, spoken and written, that would also have contributed to their primings. What such a corpus does do is permit a more detailed account of how a person might be primed by regularly reading the *Guardian*; it also points to an account of how a *Guardian* journalist might be primed.

The position just articulated applies with equal force to a general corpus. ③c Another corpus I work with is the Bloomsbury corpus created for the Macmillan Dictionary series. This is a general corpus, aiming to reflect the varieties and range of types of English, spoken and written, in the UK and the United States. That it does well, but even so the combinations of talk and texts that it includes can have been no one person's experience. Indeed it would have been a worse corpus if it had reflected well any one person's experience of the language, since there is no one whose experience is remotely representative of the language in all its uses. I conclude therefore that a corpus, even a general corpus, can only point indirectly to the relative likelihood of a language user being primed in a particular way.

The fourth and final of my important points follows partly from the third but is also an expansion of the observation that for every word we encounter, we note the genres, styles, domains and social situations in which it occurs. It is that the claims that might be made about a word's likely primings for a particular set of members of a speech community must be limited to the genre(s) and domain(s) from which the evidence has been drawn. For this reason, indeed, specialized corpora may be more revealing than general corpora about the primings that people may have, since a general corpus may on occasion iron out the primings associated with particular genres or domains.

not absolute only likely results —

Given all of the above, it will be apparent that corpora are for me only a way of **accessing the likely primings of a reader**. I make use therefore of a number of different corpora, the objective always being to get enough data to permit an exploration of possible primings. None of my claims are dependent on the frequency of a word or phrase in a corpus as a whole; the only issue is whether the data set used is large enough to permit the recognition of a priming. Nevertheless, it may be helpful to list the corpora I have at different points used and which I have referred to informally above:

- For some parts of the Moorcock analysis, I used a 4.5 million-word corpus made up of a variety of genres, including fiction, made up in part of *Guardian* features and in part of written components of the British National Corpus (BNC), constructed for me by Mike Scott.
- For the Larkin analysis I used a 98.5 million-word corpus made up of just over 95 million words of *Guardian* newspaper text, slightly more than 3 million words of BNC written text and approaching a quarter of a million words of spoken data collected over many years by my students; all but the spoken component was again created for me by Mike Scott. I shall refer to this as the *Guardian* A corpus.
- For the Carroll analysis I used a slightly different corpus (the previous two having been lost in a hard disk crash), yet again constructed for me by Mike Scott and made up of *Guardian* newspaper text. This comprised over 128,300,000 words. I also used this corpus to supplement the other two analyses. I shall refer to this as the *Guardian* B corpus.
- For the Moorcock analysis, I also used the Bloomsbury corpus. Commercial considerations do not permit me to be precise about its characteristics, but in general terms it is a large, carefully balanced corpus containing a wide range of separate components, including fiction.

Fairclough used this —

My corpus analysis throughout was done with the aid of WordSmith (Scott 1999), and indeed could not have been done without it.

2 The first literary example: ' "The time has come," the Walrus said . . .'

The sentence I choose to focus on as my first example of literary text is the famous line from 'The Walrus and the Carpenter' in Lewis Carroll's *Through the Looking Glass and What Alice Found There.*

'The time has come,' the Walrus said,
'To talk of many things:
Of shoes – and ships – and sealing-wax –
Of cabbages – and kings –

And why the sea is boiling hot –
And whether pigs have wings.'

To explore this sentence, I began by generating a concordance of 93 lines of *time has come* from the Bloomsbury general corpus, which I later supplemented with a concordance generated from the *Guardian* B corpus. Obviously neither corpus is ideal for the purpose in that Carroll was writing in the late nineteenth century whereas the Bloomsbury corpus is a collection of contemporary English and the *Guardian* corpus is entirely made up of writing that appeared in the *Guardian* newspaper in the early 1990s. Nevertheless, on the basis of these data, it would appear that we are characteristically weakly primed to expect *time* to occur with *has come* (collocation). In the Bloomsbury data there are 93 instances of *time has come* in approximately 80,000 lines of *time* (0.1 per cent). This suggests that we all recognize this as a combination of words that occurs in the language, though we may differ as regards the number of encounters we have had with the combination and some of us may only have it as a receptive priming, i.e. one we recognize but do not seek to replicate, rather than as a productive one.

It is not important how strong a priming is; once it exists, it may be subject to further primings. To judge by the corpus data, in which 72 of the 93 instances of the phrase occur with *the* (77 per cent), most speakers are primed for *time has come* to occur with *the*. This then is another instance of collocation priming. Actually the sequence of primings may well be different for different people. One person may indeed, as suggested here, first become primed for the co-occurrence of *time* and *has come* and then subsequently be primed to associate *the* with *time has come*. Another, however, may initially be primed to recognize the whole phrase *the time has come* and subsequently encounter instances which might weaken the certainty of the inclusion of *the* in the phrase. It is inherent in the position that I am presenting that there is no 'right' sequence in which primings might occur. Each person is uniquely primed by a unique set of encounters with the word or group of words in question, and the routes by which we come to approximate each other's primings for that word or group of words are likely to be various.

Taking the 72 instances of *the time has come* as our data set, we next can note that 25 of them (more than a third) have a semantic association with private verbs, i.e. verbs expressing feelings and internal states. In particular they occur with the lemmas THINK, FEEL, DECIDE and BELIEVE:

THINK	+ *the time has come*	10	(= 14% of the 72 instances)
FEEL	+ *the time has come*	5	(= 7%)
DECIDE	+ *the time has come*	4	(= 6%)
BELIEVE	+ *the time has come*	3	(= 4%)

I have formulated this priming in terms of semantic association, but it could be formulated grammatically. Since it is my contention that both our semantics and our grammars are a product of the intersection of all our individual primings, the possibility of formulating a priming in more than one way is unsurprising, though each formulation may account for slightly differing sets of data. We could also formulate the above priming in terms of pragmatic association. *The time has come* is also, it would appear, characteristically primed for pragmatic association with expression of opinion; 37 (51 per cent) of the 72 instances in my data set exemplify this. Though this overlaps with the semantic association with private verbs, it is not simply a restatement of the same priming because not every inner state expressed by a private verb is sensibly characterized as an opinion and not all instances of expression of opinion utilize private verbs, as in the following example:

Opinion + private verb.

> It could very well be that the **time has come** to examine the Syrian motivations in a fundamental way and to see whether it is at all possible to go forward (with the negotiations), perhaps in a different way.

As it happens, though, the Lewis Carroll sentence we are considering does not conform to these primings.

It is perhaps unsurprising in the light of the fact that private verbs are more associated with speech than writing to find that *the time has come* is associated with verbs of speech, whether in direct or indirect speech, as in:

> '**The time has come** for Russia to come back to the heart of Europe,' he **said**.

> He has **said the time has come** for Japan to put some of its military – perhaps a corps from its Self-Defence Forces – at the disposal of the United Nations for peace-keeping operations.

> '**The time has come**,' he **concluded**, 'for others to consider their own response to the tragic conflict of loyalties with which I have myself wrestled for perhaps too long.'

In the Bloomsbury corpus, 19 of the lines are from the spoken components of the corpus and these have to be disregarded, since normally there is no need to articulate the act of saying in speech. Of the remaining 53 lines, 38 (72 per cent) are either in indirect speech sentences containing a verb of speech or are in direct quotations, sometimes of more than one sentence's length, with a verb of speech at the beginning, during or at the end of the quotation. In the *Guardian* B corpus, this is true of 66 of the 126 lines (52 per cent). The discrepancy here is because the Bloomsbury corpus contains fiction components. The Lewis Carroll sentence of course is an instance of a direct quotation within a fiction, with a verb of speech dividing the quotation into two:

> 'The time has come,' the Walrus said,' to talk of many things'

A more surprising priming, at least to me, is the fact that *the time has come* appears to be associated semantically for many speakers, at least weakly, with acts of speech/communication that explain what it is that the time has come for (13 out of the 72 instances in the Bloomsbury concordance: 18 per cent; 35 out of 126 in the *Guardian* concordance: 28 per cent) (the latter inflated a little by several quotations from the same source), as in:

the time has come to declare failure

It may be that my surprise at the existence of this semantic association is the result of this being a weaker priming for me than it is for other people, though it would be unwise to assume that the strength of my (or anybody else's) intuitions match in any neat way against the strength of our primings. In any case, Lewis Carroll's sentence conforms to this likely priming:

'The time has come,' the Walrus said, 'to talk of many things'.

Moving on to the colligations of the cluster, my intuitions tell me that *the time has come* can be followed by *for* plus a nominalization or a non-finite clause (*the time has come for a reshuffle, the time has come for us to resign*), with *when*-clauses (e.g. *I think the time has come when we can indulge ourselves*) and non-finite clauses (*the time has come to look the worst in the eye*). All of these are attested in the data set but the distribution amongst these possibilities is uneven:

the time has come	+ *for* + nominalization/non-finite clause	20 (= 28%)
the time has come	+ *when*-clause	4 (= 6%)
the time has come	+ *to*- non-finite clause	54 (= 75%)

I checked these results with my supplementary set of data from the *Guardian* B corpus (126 lines of *the time has come*), and the results were rather different:

the time has come	+ *for* + nominalization/non-finite clause	57 (= 45%)
the time has come	+ *when*-clause	5 (= 4%)
the time has come	+ *to*- non-finite clause	61 (= 48%)
the time has come	+ other patterns	3

There seems to be little doubt that *the time has come* is characteristically primed for colligation with non-finite clauses beginning with *to* and there appears to be only a weak priming for *when*-clauses, but the evidence is apparently contradictory as regards the typical strength of the priming of *for* + nominalization. It may be that the difference is a reflection of the presence of a considerable amount of spoken data in the Bloomsbury corpus or it may be that the *for* structure is one that journalists are particularly primed with. (Even *when*-clauses, of course, are quite strongly primed in comparison with *while*-clauses or *after*-clauses which do not occur in either set of data.) The Lewis Carroll sentence is of course an instance of the *to*-construction:

'**The time has come**,' the Walrus said, '**to** talk of many things'.

non-finite

Importantly, as noted briefly above, the evidence is that priming does not stop at the clause boundary. It is my claim that as we encounter words and combinations of words (and, in principle, syllables – not all languages function like English in terms of their marking of textual features), we subconsciously recognize their textual uses, such as their characteristic textual positioning (their textual colligations), their contribution to the cohesion of the text (their textual collocations) and their function in terms of the developing textual semantics (their textual semantic associations). When we consider these for *the time has come*, the original data suggest the probability of a strong positive positional priming for the following textual colligations:

Sentence-initial (no quotation marks) + *the time has come* 29 (= 40%)
Quotation-initial (quotation marks) + *the time has come*   23 (= 32%)

Sentence/quotation-initial position was defined strictly as the first ideational element in the sentence or quotation. If a private verb preceded *the time has come*, the instance of *the time has come* was not included in the count. Had all such cases been included, the proportions would have been still higher. As it is, 72 per cent of the instances in my Bloomsbury data are utterance-initial, either beginning a written sentence or beginning a quotation from someone's speech.

In the *Guardian* B corpus, the proportions are as follows:

Sentence-initial (no quotation marks) + *the time has come* 32 (= 25%)
Quotation-initial (quotation marks) + *the time has come*   31 (= 25%)

The proportions may be lower, but still exactly half of all instances from the *Guardian* data are sentence or quotation initial, again excluding instances preceded by a private verb. These two sets of data point to a strong textual colligation, and it is one that our chosen Carroll sentence conforms to; the sentence is quotation-initial and verse-initial.

The next textual priming we have is a negative priming. *The time has come* never forms cohesive links with other sentences in the text in either of my sets of data. When we encounter the phrase, we expect no repetitions of *time* or *come*. This is an example of negative textual collocation. Again, the Carroll sentence conforms: there are no further references to time or its coming in the poem.

Finally, *the time has come* is primed for textual semantic association with a description of a major change in the world the text is describing – suggested solutions to problems, shifts in the political landscape and the like. Obviously it is less easy to count such large-scale patterns and what will be included for one investigator might well be excluded by another. But in my judgement, and exercising that judgement cautiously, 26 (that is, over a third) of the 72 instances of *the time has come* in the Bloomsbury data are used in this way. The Carroll sentence, interestingly, appears not to conform to this priming, but since the accompanying young oysters are eaten during the Walrus's talk with the Carpenter, it may conform in the eyes of the reader.

Let us now look again at the sentence. If we match it against the primings listed, we will see that it conforms to a good proportion, though not all, of the associations mentioned:

Table 1.1 Primings for use with *time has come*, and the primings actually used by Carroll

	'The time has come,' the Walrus said, 'to talk of many things'
primed to collocate with *the*	✓
primed to collocate with THINK	✗
primed for semantic association with PRIVATE VERBS	✗
primed for semantic association with SPEECH/COMMUNICATION ACTS	✓
primed for pragmatic association with EXPRESSION OF OPINION	✗
primed for colligation with non-finite clause	✓
primed for textual colligation with sentence/quotation-initial position	✓
negatively primed for textual collocation with cohesion	✓
primed for textual semantic association with major change	✗?

We could of course have started at the other end and considered the phrase *to talk of many things*. The verb phrase *to talk* would appear to be weakly primed to occur with *COME* for many speakers of English (6 instances out of 1,891 cases in the *Guardian* and 15 out of 4,264 cases in the Bloomsbury corpus) though there is only a single case of *the time has come to talk*. *To talk* collocates with *of* in both sets of data (70 out of 4,264 cases in the Bloomsbury corpus: 2 per cent; 103 instances out of 1,891 in the *Guardian*: 5 per cent) (the discrepancy certainly a reflection of the relative formality and totally written nature of the latter). We could obviously have noted in addition that *said* is primed to occur in the vicinity of quotation marks in fictional texts.

3 Overriding one's primings

We have found that Lewis Carroll's sentence conforms to most of the primings that native speakers of the language are likely to have and overrides a few. This is quite normal. Fluency is the result of conformity to one's primings. Creativity, in both the Chomskyan and literary sense, is the result either of making new selections from a semantic set for which a particular word is primed or of overriding one or more of one's primings. In this chapter, our concern is with exploitation of the effects of overriding the primings associated for most people with a particular word or cluster. There is in fact one instance in the Lewis Carroll sentence of a more radical choice not to make use of an existing priming, and that relates to the subject of *said*. Carroll has made a choice of subject for *said* different from that which would be prompted by the average person's priming in the context.

The verb *said* is of course strongly primed, for presumably all speakers of the language, for semantic association with HUMAN BEING as subject. Although NAMED HUMAN BEINGS are the most common semantic association for *said*, the pattern *the x said* is not where the novelty of Carroll's sentence lies. In my data I attest *the actress said, the man said, the princess said, the gunman said* and *the Chancellor said*, amongst very many others, though the dominant priming for *the * said* in newspaper writing is for semantic association with ORGANIZATION, as in *the school said, the company said, the magazine said*, etc. The novelty lies of course in the choice of the word *Walrus*. '*The time has come*,' *the Walrus said*, not the Prime Minister, the postman, the lecturer, Mrs Robinson, Sherlock Holmes or any other figure that comes under the general heading of a human being, fictional or real. Furthermore, the choice of a capital for *walrus* does not conform to the pattern for choices in the pattern *the * said*.

Looked at from the perspective of the language in general, Lewis Carroll has re-analysed the semantic set of items that is primed to co-occur with *said* – the set, he is in effect saying, is that of ANIMALS, not HUMAN BEINGS specifically. But we should not in fact be looking at the sentence from the point of view of the language as a whole. Primings are specific to particular genres, styles and domains, and Carroll, in overriding the more general priming, is in fact conforming to a genre-specific priming, namely that of *said* in young children's fiction and folk/fairy tales. The following are just a few instances from the small children's library that my wife and I have:

'Now what's for dessert?' **said the bear**. (from *It's the Bear!* by Jez Alborough, Walker Books)

'I thought so,' **said Owl**. (from *Winnie the Pooh: A Very Grand Thing*, adapted from the stories by A. A. Milne, Egmont)

Elephant said 'I can look up in the trees' (from *Giraffe is Tall!*, Alligator Books)

'Lift the latch and come in,' **said the wolf** in his sweetest voice. (from *Little Red Riding Hood: a Good Night, Sleep Tight Storybook*, by Christine Deverell, Grandreams Books)

'Sssss,' **said the** slippery, slithery snake. (from *Round and Round the Garden and other Action Songs*, compiled by Caroline Repchuk, Parragon Books)

Although all of these instances post-date Carroll's and so do not in themselves demonstrate the likelihood of Carroll or his readers being primed for animal as subject of *said*, Perrault's Red Riding Hood, which uses the Wolf as sayer, predates the Alice books by the best part of a century. Nevertheless, it is probable that at least some of Carroll's readers have first encountered this extension of the normal priming of *said* in the pages of the Alice books. For such readers, the extension would represent what I term a 'crack' in their priming – linguistic data that do not square with the primings they have so far formed for *said*. The crack could be mended either by extension of the primings or by assignment of the new evidence to a different genre or speech situation. A third option, of particular interest to literary stylisticians, is that of setting up a temporary priming that will last just for the duration of the work or will apply to the writings of the particular author. Temporary primings would account for the same data as were once handled as author-specific generative grammars by linguists such as Levin (1962) and Thorne (1972).

In the case of *the Walrus said*, Carroll has primed his readers well in his previous book *Alice's Adventures in Wonderland*, from which the following representative sample comes:

'Ahem!' **said the Mouse** with an important air

'Ugh!' **said the Lory**, with a shiver

'Found WHAT?' **said the Duck**

'In that case,' **said the Dodo** solemnly, rising to its feet . . .

'Speak English!' **said the Eaglet**

If, however, *Through the Looking Glass and What Alice Found There* is the first book by Carroll that the reader encounters, there are still ample examples of the same pattern within the book to temporarily prime the reader, e.g.:

The Horse, who had put his head out of the window, quietly drew it in and **said**, 'It's only a brook we have to jump over.'

A Goat, that was sitting next to the gentleman in white, shut his eyes and **said** in a loud voice, 'She ought to know her way to the ticket-office, even if she doesn't know her alphabet!'

'What do you call yourself?' **the Fawn said** at last

Indeed, the set is extended in the Looking-Glass book to cover all living things:

'What's the use of their having names?' **the Gnat said**

'We can talk,' **said the Tiger-lily**

'It isn't manners for us to begin, you know,' **said the Rose**.

So we can account for creative uses of language by reference either to the establishment of new primings or the overriding of existing ones, the former of course necessarily presupposing the latter.

4 Michael Moorcock – some subtle overridings

We have been considering genre-specific and temporary primings so far. We turn now to cases where the overriding does not lead to the establishment of new primings for the reader (unless of course, as with Shakespeare, the overriding is so often repeated that it results in a new priming for the reader). We are particularly concerned with the circumstances in which overriding of primings may occur and their possible effects, along with the constraints that may be placed on such overriding. To this end I shall look at two very different literary works. The first is a fantasy novel by Michael Moorcock, who makes subtle use of the opportunity to override his readers' primings, and the second is (part of) a poem by Philip Larkin. In the latter case, the issue starts to become not one of how primings have been cleverly utilized but one of whether the notion of lexical priming can adequately account for what Larkin has written.

The book of Michael Moorcock's with which we shall be concerned is *The Eternal Champion* (1970). The plot is simple and bleak: humans on a parallel earth call to their aid an eternal champion, Erekosë, to help them rid the world of the Evil Ones, the Eldren. He does so, almost wiping them out. At the last, he realizes that they were not evil after all and that it was the humans who were truly evil. So he switches side and wipes out the human race:

> Two months before I had been responsible for winning the cities of Mernadin for Humanity. Now I reclaimed them in the name of the Eldren . . . I destroyed every human being occupying them . . . Not merely the great cities were destroyed. Villages were destroyed. Hamlets were destroyed. Towns and farms were destroyed. I found some people hiding in caves. The caves were destroyed. I destroyed forests where they might flee. I destroyed stones that they might creep under . . . It was fated that Humanity should die on this planet
>
> (Moorcock 1970: 157)

As a reader, the questions that arose for me were twofold. Firstly, how does Michael Moorcock manage to portray sympathetically a hero who commits two great acts of genocide? And secondly, how does he manage to portray the human race such that we do not see them as evil at the outset and yet we see them as evil at the end? My answers to these questions centre on what I shall claim to have been the skilled overriding of the reader's primings in early paragraphs of the novel, such that what the reader sees the text as saying and what his/her primings might suggest it is saying are in conflict.

The very first paragraph of the novel is the following:

They called for me. That is all I really know. They called for me and I went to them. I could not do otherwise. The will of the whole of humanity was a strong thing . . . Why was I chosen? I still do not know, though they thought they had told me.

(ibid. Prologue, p. 8, italics in the original)

The call is literal:

> Then, between wakefulness and sleeping, I began every night to hear voices . . . At first I dismissed them, expecting to fall immediately asleep, but they continued, and I began to try to listen to them, thinking, perhaps, to receive some message from my unconscious . . . I could not recognize the language, though it had a peculiar familiarity.

(ibid. Chapter 1: 'A Call Across Time', p. 9)

Given that the calling is literal in the above passages (and is focused on in the title of the first chapter), it seemed worth looking at how we are likely to be primed for *called*. I began with a small corpus of 4.5 million words (drawn, as noted above, from the BNC and the feature sections of the *Guardian*). In this there were 41 instances of *called* used as active verb in the pattern *x (have/has/had) called y*, where both *x* and *y* are human beings (or in the latter case, very occasionally animals) and with no sequence-dependent intervening particles/prepositions such as *on*, *for* or *to*. In a concordance of 2,715 lines of *called* drawn from the fiction sections of the Bloomsbury corpus, I found that there were 194 instances of *called* (7 per cent of instances) used in this way.

Although far from the most common use of *called* in the fiction sub-corpus (*a horse called the Prince of Wales* and *Victor Hugo called me sister* would appear to illustrate the most common usages for *called* in these data), these figures show that *x called y* is likely to be in the primings of most speakers. In other words *called* is typically colligationally primed to occur with SUBJECT and OBJECT. This combination SUBJECT + *called* + OBJECT is typically primed to be used with the sense of summoning. In the original sample of 41 lines, over two-thirds had the sense of summoning, either by phone or more directly. Examples are:

> On one occasion **he called a player** into his office, took his hat from the hat-stand and threw it on the floor

> After taking an overdose he told his neighbour what he had done and **she called an ambulance**.

Summoning is exactly what 'they' are doing in Moorcock's first paragraph and yet he has not written:

They CALLED me. That is all I really know. They CALLED me and I went to them. I could not do otherwise.

(ibid. Prologue, p. 8, modified)

In the BNC/*Guardian* data, there are 31 instances of *called* used as active verb with *to*, i.e. *x called to y*, where *x* and *y* are human subject and human (and, again, occasionally animal) prepositional object (excluding idioms and instances of *to* + verb). In the Bloomsbury fiction there are 58 such cases (2 per cent of the sample). So we can infer that *called* is also typically primed for speakers to occur with *to*.

Of the 31 instances in the BNC/*Guardian* data, 29 have the sense of shouting to someone and 15 have the sense of summoning from a distance, and impressionistically the same patterns of usage seem to be true of the Bloomsbury data, e.g.:

> As I waited, **Ryan** came out of a near-by block and **called to me**: 'Can I have a word with you, old boy?'

> God heard the boy crying, and **the angel of God called to Hagar** from heaven and said to her, 'What is the matter, Hagar?'

Given that the opening paragraphs describe the hero being called by people from another planet and in another century, the characteristic primings of *called to* would seem entirely appropriate to Moorcock's purposes:

> *They called TO me. That is all I really know. They called TO me and I went to them. I could not do otherwise. The will of the whole of humanity was a strong thing . . . Why was I chosen? I still do not know, though they thought they had told me.*
>
> (ibid. Prologue, p. 8, modified)

So, as before, the question arises, why did Moorcock not use this expression?

We have seen that Moorcock could have used *called* or *called to* without inappropriateness. But he used *called for*, so we need to look at what the characteristic primings of this word combination are. There were 42 instances of *called for* in the BNC/*Guardian* corpus and there are 37 (1.4 per cent of instances) in the Bloomsbury corpus. So, once again, it would appear that most speakers are likely to be primed for *called* to occur with *for*. But only five in the BNC/*Guardian* sample were used with any sense of summoning, and two of these were calling for beer! (The latter, as it happens, will in due course give us a clue as to why Moorcock used *called for*.)

So for what are we typically primed to use *called for*? The two sets of data point in slightly different directions. In the BNC/*Guardian* corpus, 69 per cent of the instances (29 out of 42) refer to the solving of a problem, the improvement of a situation or the rectification of some injustice, pointing to a textual semantic association. In the Bloomsbury corpus, with its inclusion of fiction, the proportion is 16 out of 37, still high at 43 per cent, though less markedly so than data drawn from non-fictional sources.

> Why were we silent when **General Morillion called for military action** to stop the killing in Srebenica?

> '**You called for me**?' said Romanov. The Chairman nodded. 'I have just returned from the Kremlin,' he said. 'The General Secretary has entrusted us with a particularly sensitive project of great importance

to the State.' Zaborski paused. 'So sensitive in fact that you will report only to me.'

No sooner had it been evacuated than **the Labour MP for the constituency called for a public inquiry**.

So from the very first four words of Moorcock's novel, the primings of *called for* would appear to lead us to expect a Problem–Solution pattern *Yes* (Winter 1977; Hoey 1979, 1983, 2001). This suspicion is supported by the results of a search in the *Guardian* B corpus for *call* for*. In the corpus 12,166 instances of this combination were found, and, using Scott's pattern tool in WordSmith (Scott 1999), *help* was shown to be the sixth most common word to appear immediately after *call* for*. Furthermore, *aid* is the fiftieth most common choice in the position of two words to the right of *call* for*, e.g. *called for renewed aid*. Clearly, then, *call* for* is typically primed for semantic association with HELP. So Erekosë is a potential source of Help/aid; in Propp's terms (1928/1968), he is a hero or a donor. The very first words of the book type him in such a way that even his subsequently being the direct cause of genocides cannot affect this initial characterization. The first sentence also types the callers. They are encoded as having done the calling. They are therefore being characterized as having identified a problem and of seeking help.

So what kind of people call for help? Of the 29 cases of *called for* associated with problems, etc. in the BNC/*Guardian* sample, 24 are associated with leaders, representatives or campaign groups (or with laws created by leaders, etc.). So in newspaper writing at least, *called for* is also primed for a semantic association with LEADERS in subject function.

They [leaders] called for me [hero] [for help in solving a problem].

Just 64 sentences later, we learn that the callers are the king and his daughter, the leaders of all humanity. Leaders make laws to protect their people, representatives represent their people, campaign groups try to improve things on behalf of the people. They are all, in theory, altruistic.

The Bloomsbury data reveal another characteristic priming for *called for*, which chimes closely with the previous one. The prepositional object of *called for* is a servant or junior colleague, and/or some (act or object of) service. Of the 37 instances in this second fiction-based data set, 18 (almost exactly half) fit this description:

He opened his door and **called for the maid**.

Romanov immediately **called for the young researcher**

Miranda replaced the receiver and **called for her secretary**.

I called for champagne.

she called for Maria to bring the tea.

So, assuming we have been primed by our previous experience of fiction to associate *called for* with the meanings and purposes described above, Erekosë – the hero being called for – is capable of being understood as a servant summoned by his master, or at very least as a junior being summoned by his superior.

My questions about Moorcock's book were: how does he manage to portray sympathetically a hero who commits two great acts of genocide, and how does he manage to portray the human race such that we do not see them as evil at the outset and yet we see them as evil at the end?

The answer to the former question would seem to be, in part, that Erekosë is set up as a servant and as a source of help. The answer to the latter would appear to be, at least in part, that humanity is portrayed as having a problem which the leaders are trying to solve by calling for help. These effects of the choice of *called for* rather than *called* or *called to* are hard to equate with an evil humanity led by paranoid leaders who call up an immensely destructive force for whom power is right.

> *They called for me. That is all I really know. They called for me and I went to them.*
>
> (ibid. Prologue, p. 8)

In the light of my interpretation of the evidence for the primings of *called for*, it is perhaps worth attending to the clause that follows the second use of *called for*, namely *I went to them.* Examining this turns out to be less easy than it appears. The clause represents a comparatively rare choice. When I searched initially for *x* (human) *went to them* (human) in the *Guardian* A corpus, I found only four instances of the cluster. Intriguingly, in all four cases the person who does the going is dependent upon on them for help, support, leadership or business.

> In the beginning it was Muslims driven out by Serbs who went to them for shelter.

I then looked at the Bloomsbury corpus and found a further five instances of *x* (human) *went to them* (human). Again, in four out of the five cases the person who is described as going is dependent upon on them for help, support, leadership or business. On the assumption that this apparent priming for *went to* might not be sensitive to the plurality of the object pronoun, I then searched for *x* (human) *went to him* and found in the *Guardian* A corpus seven instances of the pattern. Once more, in four out of seven cases the person who goes is dependent on him for help, support, leadership or business. In the Bloomsbury corpus, there were a further 28 instances of *x* (human) *went to him*, and in this larger sample, the same semantic association was apparent in 11 out of 28 cases (39 per cent). On the same lines, I searched in both corpora for *x* (human) *went to her*. In the *Guardian* A corpus, I found five instances and, by now predictably, four conformed to the priming we have been considering, and in the Bloomsbury corpus, there were 18 instances, six of which (33 per cent) conformed. (Interestingly but irrelevantly for current purposes, another ten were associated with acts of intimacy that followed, an unexpected gender difference.)

On the basis of this scanty but consistent evidence, it would seem that we may be primed to use *went to them/him/her* when the people represented by the pronoun have the power to help us or simply have power over us. So in the sentence *They called for me and I went to them*, Erekosë is twice portraying himself (or being portrayed, to be more accurate) as summoned by people of greater power and going as supplicant or servant.

> *They called for me. That is all I really know. They called for me and I went to them. I could not do otherwise.*
>
> (ibid. Prologue, p. 8)

submissive

He may also be suggesting a special kind of weakness in the very words with which he notes that he was summoned. Consider the following from my data:

> A founding member, he eventually became leader of the Italian Communist Party in his early thirties, fighting ludicrous factionalism as buttons were busily being sewn on so many black shirts. Given a 20-year sentence for his belief (from England, only this paper was at his trial) he would continue to write to his mother, unaware that she had perished while he was inside. Gramsci died two days after his release. His father on his death bed, a couple of weeks later, would read the martyr's words over and over again: 'I could not do otherwise . . . sons must sometimes cause great grief to their mothers if they wish to preserve their honour and dignity as men'.

Since this is the only instance in my two corpora of the sentence *I could not do otherwise*, it can by itself only be weakly suggestive of how we might be primed for this sentence. What the example hints at, though, is that Erekosë is appropriating to himself the attributes of (perhaps) martyrdom and special heroism. A search for the sentence on the internet using Google threw up 10,000 instances. Inspection of the first 50 of these (discounting one morally unpleasant site and one page that would not open) showed that at least 28 were associated with actions driven by conscience; a proportion of the remaining 22 might have been interpreted in such a manner at a stretch. Given that the facts of the narrative show him to be in fact a genocidal monster, once again we have evidence of the skill with which Moorcock has exploited the reader's primings to mislead them into a different reading of his characters from that which their actions would seem to warrant.

5 Philip Larkin – poetry and priming

Having shown, I hope, the principles whereby creative language might be handled using corpus linguistics, I want to conclude by looking at a poem that John Sinclair wrote about over 40 years ago (Sinclair 1966). In an article entitled 'Taking a Poem to Pieces', he provided a ground-breaking contribution to stylistics which showed how the grammatical tools of the time could confidently and thoroughly account for the language choices made by Philip Larkin in his poem *First Sight* and contribute to an understanding of the poem.

The question here is: what can priming theory (and more generally corpus linguistics) say today about the poem? Unlike Sinclair, for reasons of space and the complexity of the analysis, I shall only attempt an analysis of the first four lines of the poem he analysed. The first verse reads as follows:

FIRST SIGHT

Lambs that learn to walk in snow
When their bleating clouds the air
Meet a vast unwelcome, know
Nothing but a sunless glare.
Newly stumbling to and fro
All they find, outside the fold,
Is a wretched width of cold.

Firstly, the title uses a common collocation. In the *Guardian* A corpus it occurs 433 times, of which 365 appear in *at first sight* and 30 occur with a possessive, so Larkin's title may be thought to allude to both – the first sight belongs to the lambs and turns out to be misleading. Secondly, there are 161 sentence-initial cases in my data where *first sight* is part of the first phrase of the sentence, most characteristically as a part of *at first sight*. Of these 21 are text-initial, i.e. more than one every eight instances. In the larger *Guardian* B corpus, there are 531 occurrences of *first sight*, of which 197 are sentence-initial and 28 are text-initial, a ratio of one text-initial for every seven sentence-initial instances. The average length of the texts would need to be seven or eight sentences long for these proportions to be explicable in chance.

With this in mind, I examined the source texts of 100 lines illustrating sentence-initial instances of *first sight*. The 100 lines included all the text-initial instances but were otherwise randomly chosen.[4] The average length of the source texts was 46 sentences and the median average was 36. Not one text was as short as seven or eight sentences. Taking just the 28 text-initial instances into account, the average length of the source texts was 40 and the median average was 28.5.

From the above figures, we can conclude that *first sight* is greatly more likely to begin a text than can be accounted for by chance. Exactly how much more likely will depend on which figures one uses in the calculation, but if we take the lower ratio of 1:8 and the medianaverage of the text-initial instances, it is 3.5 times more likely; if we take the higher ratio of 1:7 and the mean average of the sentence-initial instances, it is 5 times more likely. Larkin therefore fully conforms to our probable textual colligational priming in this respect.

The first word *lambs* occurs as subject 87 times in my data. Discarding non-finite forms, the subjects occur with the present tense 50 per cent more often than with the past, which suggests that for many users of the language *lambs* is colligationally primed to occur with the present tense. *Lambs* also collocates with *ewes* and *ewe* and with *bleating*. Both occur in the poem. One in five of the instances of *lambs* as subject (18 cases) occurs in association with the semantic set of weather/season. All but two of these are clauses in the present tense. So Larkin's choices conform to our primings.

We look now at *learn*. There were 1,239 instances of *learn* in my data, excluding all non-finite uses, modal uses and phase uses (*help x learn*), of which 51 per cent of all cases occur with first- or second-person pronouns. Of the remainder, 247 occur with CHILDREN or with *young x* (20 per cent) and 15 occur with ANIMALS/CREATURES (1.2 per cent). These percentages rise to 41 per cent and 2.5 per cent if the pronouns are discounted. Given the relative rarity of children and animals being talked about in newspaper data, these look like primings. To check, though, I ran a parallel analysis of 100 instances of the word *make* and found that *make* does not occur with either CHILDREN or ANIMALS in this sample – a trustworthy result for CHILDREN, at least. So it looks as if *learn* is indeed typically primed for occurrence with *young* and ANIMALS – *lambs* seem to fit the bill.

I also searched on *learn* to walk* and found 11 instances. Therefore *learn** and *walk* seem to collocate. I then examined 186 instances of *walk* in* where *in* was either postmodification or an adjunct. Twelve of these occurred as part of the semantic association *walk in* WEATHER. Out of 1,357, 122 (9 per cent) of the instances of *snow* occur in prepositional phrases with *in*, so it would appear that *in* and *snow* collocate. Of these instances of *in . . . snow*, 24 occur with verbs of movement (and three express lack of movement, e,g. *stuck*), i.e. one in five of *in . . . snow* occur with verbs of movement. Once again Larkin has not deviated from his and our primings, though notice that he in each case uses what is likely to be for many of us a less dominant priming rather than using the most dominant.

Another instance of Larkin conforming to a priming but taking a less favoured option within that priming occurs with the words that begin the next clause – *when their*. Of 15,949 instances of *when* used as a subordinator, 6,322 (40 per cent) are followed immediately by a pronoun (43 per cent if *there* is treated as a pro-form). So *when* is for most people strongly primed colligationally to be followed with a pronoun, but when the priming is followed by a pronoun there is no special priming for possessive pronouns.

Yet another instance of this is *bleating*, which collocates with *lambs* and *sheep*. Of 75 instances in my data, six occur with *lambs* and 11 with *sheep*. Together they account for 18 per cent of all instances of bleating. There is also some evidence of colligation, though of course the data set is small: of the 17 lamb/sheep cases, six occur with a possessive construction (with *of* the dominant choice). So *bleating* collocates with *lambs* and there is weak evidence for a colligational priming for possessive. But there are no instances in my data of *bleating* as subject, so here Larkin has overridden his and our most probable priming.

On *cloud the air*, my analysis breaks down for lack of relevant data. I have 88 instances of *cloud* the X*, one of which is *cloud the air*, used, however, non-literally. The fact that *cloud the air* occurs metaphorically is, however, tentative evidence of the co-occurrence having existed before as a literal expression.

We have already seen that *meet* is in the tense for which we are primed. There were 86 instances of *meet a* in my data and 59 per cent of these involved meeting something evaluated for good or ill, with negatives occurring more positively. Larkin conforms to the strong evaluative priming and the weak negative priming.

A vast has, for most people, an extremely strong colligational priming for being followed by a noun (or more accurately by words that are themselves strongly primed to occur as nouns). We are therefore compelled into one of two analyses of the word *unwelcome* that follows. Either this is an instance of a word being used in a way that overrides its normal priming – i.e. a word whose dominant priming is for use as an adjective is being used as a noun – or it is an instance of a delay in the fulfilment of the priming which leads us to expect *unwelcome* to be followed by a noun (75 per cent of the time).

The argument for the former is that the punctuation invites such a reading and *unwelcome* matches the negative priming referred to above. The arguments for the latter, however, are more powerful as I shall show and they pivot around *vast*.

Vast is for the majority of speakers strongly primed for the indefinite article, according to my corpus data. There are 5,395 instances of *vast* in my data and 25 per cent of these (1,324 instances) occur with *a*. It occurs 38 per cent of the time with *the*, but over half of these are the phrase *the vast majority*. There is no equivalent dominant phrase with *a*.

The phrase *a vast* is strongly primed to be followed by a further epithet/ descriptor. Of all instances of *a vast*, 11 per cent are followed by an immediate second epithet and a further 3 per cent by a coordinator followed by an epithet. For the purposes of comparison I looked at ten adjectives drawn from the beginning of the dictionary (omitting those with prefix *a-*). I looked at what followed *an abandoned, an abject, an able, an abnormal, an abortive, an abrasive, an abrupt, an absent, an abominable* and *an absolute*. Of 842 instances of these adjectives, only 2 per cent were followed with another epithet and 3 per cent by coordination and epithet. I then looked at *a massive, a huge* and *a gigantic*, which are close in meaning to *a vast*. Although a following epithet is more common among these, it still only occurs less than 6 per cent of the time, with coordination accounting for a further 2 per cent. So the priming of *a vast* for following epithet is twice as strong as that of its near-synonyms.

Given this priming, there is a tendency to want to interpret *unwelcome* as a following epithet. This tendency is further reinforced by the semantic characteristics of the epithets that tend to follow, of which 24 per cent have the suffix -*less* or the prefixes *un-* or *in-*, or belong to the semantic set of emptiness (e.g. *a vast, featureless field, a vast, inaccessible service, a vast, vacant area*).

If *unwelcome* is a following epithet, we expect a noun to follow, as I said, but what follows is not a noun; it is the verb *know*. The phrase *know* nothing* occurs 374 times in my data so there is a strong collocation here. The phrase *nothing but* occurs 1,074 times, so there is a strong collocation here too. But they do not occur together all that much. There are only 12 instances of *know* nothing but* (as opposed to 170 of *know* nothing about* and 76 of *know* nothing of*). Furthermore, *know* in the phrase *know nothing but* in my data always means 'has experienced nothing but'. This, I suggest, is Larkin's trick. We saw it with the title, we saw a hint of it with *clouds the air* and we have it here. He conforms to the primings but tweaks the meanings.

Sun and *glare* collocate strongly. So the morpheme sun is primed for *glare*. *Sunless* on the other hand is primed to occur with, amongst other things, words of vision (*gloom* is in my data). Here then we have priming of *sun* having forced an unexpected choice from the semantic set of vision.

We are left with *glare*. We noted earlier that *unwelcome* expects a following noun. The only available noun is *glare*. *Glare* has no strong priming for preceding adjectives, but when they do occur there is a strong priming for negativity. It is possible to defer the conformity to a priming, usually with coordination. Here the evidence points slightly in the direction of this being the case.

> i.e. Meet a vast unwelcome
> Knowing nothing but a sunless ⟩ glare

As it happens, this is the only place where my corpus-linguistic analysis comes to a conclusion in principle different from that of Sinclair's; he favours treating *unwelcome* as a deviant noun. The point, though, is that priming, based on collocation, colligation and semantic association permits a corpus-driven account of how Larkin's poem is constructed and where he deviates from the norms established for us all in our primings.

Some brief conclusions

In the previous section, like Sinclair all those years ago, I took (part of) Larkin's *First Sight* to pieces and showed, once again, that literary language is susceptible to the linguistic analysis available for less prestigious output. I hope more generally in this chapter also to have shown that it is possible to make use of the different types of lexical priming as uncovered indirectly in the hidden patterns in corpora to account for how literary writers manage to say something new, for how they are creative as well as natural. In so doing, I would claim tentatively that I have also shown how non-literary creativity might be explained, both of the kind described in Carter (2004) where ordinary people do interesting things with language, and of the kind described by Chomsky (1957 *et seq.*), where linguists were set the task of accounting for any sentence of the language, however improbable. More work will need to be done on these kinds of creativity, however, before firm conclusions can be drawn, and more particularly careful consideration will need to be given to the relationship between lexis and grammar. With this in mind, the next chapter concerns itself with this relationship and with the ways in which grammatical primings might be acquired.

Notes

1. An earlier version of the analysis of the Moorcock paragraph was originally undertaken for a literary volume, *Imagining Apocalypse: Studies in Cultural Crisis* (2000) (ed.) David Seed, London: Macmillan. The analysis has been rewritten and updated for this volume and reinterpreted in the light of my claims about lexical priming.
2. I was privileged to give the fourth John Sinclair Open Lecture in 2004 and my analysis draws on the text of that lecture.
3. Henceforth, whenever I refer to the priming of a word, I should be understood as including in that reference the priming of a syllable or combination of words.
4. One text was excluded because it was a compilation of smaller texts and no principled decision could be reached as to whether it should be treated as a single text or not.

References

Carroll, L. (1899) *Through the Looking Glass and What Alice Found There.* London: Macmillan and Co Ltd (Electronic Text Center, University of Virginia Library).
Carter, R. (2004) *Language and Creativity: The Art of Common Talk.* London: Routledge.
Chomsky, N. (1957) *Syntactic Structures.* The Hague: Mouton.
Hoey, M. (1979) *Signalling in Discourse.* Birmingham: ELR Discourse Analysis Monographs No 6.
—— (1983) *On the Surface of Discourse.* London: George Allen and Unwin.
—— (2001) *Textual Interaction.* London: Routledge.
—— (2003) 'Why grammar is beyond belief', in J.-P. van Noppen, C. Den Tandt and I. Tudor (eds), *Beyond: New Perspectives in Language, Literature and ELT.* Thematic Issue. *Belgian Journal of English Language and Literatures*, New Series 1. Ghent, Belgium: Academia Press, pp. 183–96.
—— (2004a) 'The textual priming of lexis', in S. Bernardini, G. Aston and D. Stewart (eds), *Corpora and Language Learners.* Amsterdam: John Benjamins, pp. 21–41.
—— (2004b) 'Lexical priming and the properties of text', in A Partington, J. Morley and L. Haarman (eds), *Corpora and Discourse.* Bern: Peter Lang, pp. 385–412.

—— (2005) *Lexical Priming: A New Theory of Words and Language*. London: Routledge.

Larkin, P. (1988) 'First Sight' in *Collected Poems*, ed. with an Introduction by Anthony Thwaite. London: Faber and Faber.

Levin, S. (1962) *Linguistic Structures in Poetry*. The Hague: Mouton.

Moorcock, M. (1970) *The Eternal Champion*. London: Mayflower.

Propp, V. ([1928] 1968) *Morphology of the Folktale* (trans. Laurence Scott, 2nd edn). Austin: University of Texas Press.

Scott, M. (1999) *WordSmith Tools, Version 3*. Oxford: Oxford University Press.

Sinclair, J. M. (1966) 'Taking a poem to pieces', in R. Fowler (ed.), *Essays on Style and Language*. London: Routledge, pp. 68–81.

—— (2004) *Trust the Text: Language, Corpus and Discourse*. London: Routledge.

Thorne, J. P. (1972) 'Generative grammar and stylistic analysis', in J. Lyons (ed.), *New Horizons in Linguistics*. Harmondsworth: Penguin, pp. 185–97.

Winter, E. O. (1977) 'A clause relational approach to English texts.' *Instructional Science* (special edition) 6: 1–92.

2   Grammatical creativity: a corpus perspective

Michael Hoey

Introduction

In the previous chapter, it was argued that a lexical priming perspective on
creative language could account for the choices that the writers had made,
without requiring abandonment of the notion that these writers had conformed to their (probable) primings. In this chapter,[1] I want to test the lexical priming theory further by addressing directly the issue of the relation of
lexis and grammar.

According to the claims I make in Hoey (2003, 2005), and which I reiterated in the previous chapter, grammars exist as a product of our primings.
Each of us, presumably to different extents and with different outcomes
and different degrees of regularity, constructs a grammar – leaky, inconsistent, incomplete – out of the primings we have for the sounds, words,
phrases and so on that we encounter. This grammar, or perhaps one should
say these grammars, may in turn be used to regulate and remark on our
linguistic choices. Sinclair (1991 *et seq.*) argued that every word has its own
collocational and colligational patterns and that grammar is a system fallen
back onto when the collocational and other patterns failed. In my terms,
even that grammatical system is a product of the patterns, so that the language user in such circumstances merely draws on the patterning at a
higher level of abstraction. Such a formulation has the virtue of strengthen-
ing Sinclair's original insight and explaining where the fall-back grammar
comes from.

It is, however, all very well to claim that grammar is an output from our
primings and quite another matter to demonstrate it. Much of the most
important work that has been done on the patterning of our lexis (e.g.
Stubbs 1995, 1996) has been done on what we might intuitively regard as
'interesting' words, such as *make, cause* and *yield,* words that might reasonably be supposed to have distinctive patterns of use. My own accounts of
consequence, reason, immunity and *(a)round* in Hoey (2005) fall into the same
category. But if lexical priming, or any other corpus-driven theory of language, is to account for creativity in the Chomskyan sense, i.e. if it is to
account for the phenomena that theoretical grammars have traditionally

sought to explain, then it must look carefully at words whose use would appear to be entirely driven by real-world consideration and at the same time strictly limited by grammatical considerations. A case in point would seem to be the numeral system.

1 The numeral system in grammars

I do not want to linger long over the way numerals are handled in descriptive grammars, still less do I want to engage with theoretical perspectives on numerals (a preliminary engagement with grammatical theory can be found in Hoey, 2005, forthcoming), though both of these would be appropriate undertakings. A short list of observations on numeral from non-corpus-driven sources seems appropriate. Bloor and Bloor (1995: 21–2) comment, from a systemic-functional perspective:

> Numerals were also frequently classed as adjectives in traditional grammars, but ... their grammatical role is sufficiently dissimilar to justify classing them separately. In fact, in some instances – certainly not all – numerals are more like determiners than like adjectives. On some occasions ... [they] seem rather to resemble nouns. In fact, numerals are a rather anomalous set and are perhaps best treated as a class of their own.

Thompson (1996: 182–3) notes, again from a systemic-functional perspective:

> Overlapping with Deictics to a large extent is the category of Numeratives. These specify the number or quantity of the Thing, either in exact terms ('three', 'twenty') or inexact terms ('many', 'much'); or they specify order ('first', 'fifth'). Halliday (1994: 183) places these in a separate slot after Deictics ... but it is also possible to see numeratives as a different type of non-specific Deictic, since they can precede Post-Deictics (e.g. 'ten more years') and cannot follow non-specific Deictics.

As the above quotation suggests, Halliday (1994: 185) allocates them their own category:

Deictic	Deictic$_2$	Numerative	Epithet	Classifier	Thing
determiner	adjective	numeral	adjective	noun or adjective	noun

Martin (2004: 59), on the other hand, alludes to the possibility of labelling them adjectives.

Probably Leech (1992: 77) is right in saying that 'numerals have a small grammar of their own, within the larger grammar of the English'.

Given that they do not fit neatly into ready-made grammatical descriptions and at the same time might be expected to be independent of co-textual constraints, numerals seem to be a suitable area for investigation of the relationship of lexical priming and grammar.

This chapter accordingly seeks to test my claims about lexis and grammar by examining the numeral system. In the first place, I look at whether it is indeed the case, as one might intuit, that numerals are not primed for collocations, colligations and semantic associations in the way that words like *yield* and *reason* are. For this purpose, I examine a specific numeral – the number *sixty* – examining corpus data derived from *Guardian* corpus A (see page 10 for a full description), with a view to determining what kinds of way, if any, the word might characteristically be primed for a typical adult language user.

As a second stage, I then examine a corpus of sentences drawn from books written for very young children (ages 2–6) to see whether such data would plausibly result in the children being primed for number grammar. Obviously, these data are only indicative of the kind of exposure a child might have to the number words. It is unlikely that any child has been exposed to all and only the books I accessed and to no others; it is still less likely that any child who was so exposed would have heard no other uses of the numerals in talk with family and friends, and even if somewhere a child could be found who had had just the exposure that the data set represents, his or her experience would be altered by the likelihood that some of the books represented would be read to him/her more than once, thereby weighting the occurrence of individual instances differently. As always, the corpus can only suggest indirectly how we get primed and what we get primed for.

2 An examination of the number *sixty*

There were 294 instances of *sixty* (as opposed to *60*, which will be briefly looked at separately) in my data. I examined these in terms of each of the types of priming discussed in the previous chapter; as noted there, most of the types of priming are compatible or even identical with descriptive categories typically used without reference to priming, and it is to be hoped therefore that the description will still have value for those uninterested in the argument about grammar as a product of priming.

2.1 What collocations, if any, are we typically primed to associate sixty with?

One might imagine that there was not much to say about the lexical patterns of the word *sixty*. I begin by looking at the collocations, restricting attention solely to the place immediately following the word. On the basis of 294 concordance examples, the collocations of *sixty* are as follows, in descending order of frequency:

per cent	93
years	59
miles	11
people	6
minutes	5

It will be seen that the data point to certain typical collocational primings for most speakers. It is not the case, as we might have idly predicted, that *sixty* will accompany almost anything. Of course it can; the point is that routinely it does not.

2.2 Are we primed to associate sixty with other meanings in the environment?

If then we now examine sets of **semantically associated words** that occur to the immediate right of *sixty*, we find that *miles, minutes* and *years* are part of a larger pattern (Table 2.1). The figures include certain features that cannot be identified automatically such as anaphora and ellipsis of nominal head (e.g. *Sixty were injured* where *sixty* refers back to *people* in the previous sentence).

It is perhaps of interest that the collocation with *per cent* and the semantic association with TIME[2] account for over half of all instances of *sixty*; it is also worth noting that only 12 per cent of instances have none of the semantic associations or collocations listed. It will of course be such structures that we will need to return to later in the chapter.

Table 2.1 Semantic/lexical associations with *sixty*

Semantic association	Number of instances (out of 294)	% of instances of *sixty*
per cent	93	32
units of measurement of time	69	23
people	45	15
age (no noun is used)	25	9
units of measurement of distance	19	6
units of currency	8	3
none of these	35	12

2.3 Are we primed to associate sixty with any pragmatic functions?

As I note in Hoey (2005), another important association that *sixty* seems likely to have for most speakers is that of being marked for vagueness. It is accompanied in 19 per cent of the instances in my data by some marker of precision or, more normally, imprecision. These markers are grammatically protean in their structure. Here is a large (though not comprehensive) sample:

> about sixty
> over sixty
> around sixty
> more than sixty
> an average of sixty
> some sixty

almost sixty
nearly sixty
fifty to sixty
between fifty and sixty
fifty or sixty
sixty-odd
up to sixty
sixty-some
maybe sixty
getting on for sixty
no less than sixty
sixty or more
a good sixty
sixty plus
sixty or so

The percentage of examples with some marker is already fairly high at 19 per cent. It is a great deal higher if we eliminate all instances of the phrase *sixty per cent*, which are only marked in *Guardian* corpus A for (im)precision in two cases. With that combination eliminated, 27 per cent of instances of *sixty* are so marked.

2.4 Are we primed to associate sixty with any grammatical categories?

It is possible to discuss collocation without reference to any categories imposed on the data, apart from those implied by word boundaries and the assumption of underlying sameness despite intonational and typographical differences. It is even possible to discuss semantic and pragmatic associations without drawing upon preconceived categories, though the ghost of circularity raises itself for the first time here. It is however very difficult to talk about colligation without making use of existing grammatical terminology. Yet such terminology is the product of pre-corpus investigations, and it is the relationship between the speaker's individual grammar and their colligational primings that is under investigation; Hunston and Francis (2000) make use of an extremely simple grammatical terminology for analogous reasons. Despite this, I am going to simplify my discussion here by using grammatical terms that are widely accepted but which do not derive from the study in question (or any other corpus study). I shall be more cautious when examining the data derived from books written for young children.

One of the most fundamental primings is the priming a word has for grammatical category. The point here is that words are not nouns, verbs or whatever, they are typically primed for use as nouns, verbs etc. So *English* is primed for me to function as a noun in conjunction with *the* (*the English are a patient people*) and as an adjective (*English football*), though I could override my primings to utter something along the lines of *We have singularly failed to English the Scots*. The discussion of numerals in section 2 suggested that the characteristic primings of *sixty* may not fit neatly in with the usual grammatical categories. We can however note the following. First, 53 per cent occur in a position immediately prior to a noun, i.e. in a position compatible with categorization as determiner, adjective or numerative. In instances, also, such as *was well over sixty*, there would appear to be particular evidence in support for adjectival priming, though *over* is not associated with adjectives. A few cases occur on their own where what was being counted was derivable from the prior text (e.g. *Sixty surrendered during the day*); traditionally, ellipsis would be invoked. A few other cases occurred in structures such as *Sixty of England's best players*, where the question of the grammatical category of *sixty* is rendered uninteresting by the specificity of the structure. Thirty-two per cent occur in the structure *sixty per cent*, as we have seen, which might be seen as priming for noun category, but again this would be to impose a categorization on the data that would, I suspect, have limited psychological justification.

2.5 Are we primed to expect sixty *to participate in any grammatical structures or functions?*

The semantic and pragmatic associations and collocations listed in sections 2.1 and 2.2 have their colligational correlates. Consider Table 2.2:

Table 2.2 The grammatical associations of some collocations and a semantic association of *sixty*

Lexical or semantic association	Major grammatical associations	grammatical association as % of total of items
per cent	Subject	99% of instances of *per cent*
years	Adjunct	88% of instances of *years*
age (no noun is used)	Complement or Adjunct	56% of *sixty* used to measure age

The point here is that not only does *sixty* have a close lexical/semantic association with the items or semantic sets named but these associations bring with them colligational implications. If you choose to use *sixty* with *per cent*, there is only a low chance that you will not use the expression in subject position in the clause; in other words, the following example is the norm:

1. Sixty per cent of firms were more profitable in 1992.

   If on the other hand you choose to refer to *sixty years* you are highly likely to use the words as part of an adjunct in the clause, e.g.:

2. Sixty years ago, A J P Taylor began writing book reviews for the *Guardian*.

3. For almost sixty years, America had been a democracy on a constant war footing.

If you use *sixty* to refer to age, you are quite likely to use it in a complement[3] or an adjunct.

4. She is almost sixty.
5. Life begins at sixty.

I take it that the grammatical positions here noted are an effect of the choice of the lexical/semantic associations of *sixty* and not a direct effect of the choice of *sixty* itself. Even so it is of some interest that collocation and grammatical choice go closely hand in hand.

2.6 Are we primed to associate sixty *with any (position in any) textual organization?*

Over two-thirds of the cases of *sixty* in my data occur as the first lexical item of the sentence; most of these are in fact the very first word, lexical or grammatical. This is evidence of a strong colligational priming. In other words, *sixty* is overwhelmingly in Theme position even when it provides new information (as it does quite often). (Theme is here used to mean everything up to and including the first ideational element of the sentence – see Halliday 1994.) This also means that when *sixty* is part of an adjunct, that adjunct is characteristically fronted. The exact figures are that 209 instances of *sixty* (71 per cent) occur as first word of their sentence; a further 12 occur within the first group of the sentence or as the first lexical item of their clause.

What might be the explanation for this? One obvious one is that writers do not like to use figures at the beginning of a sentence. Where a writer might have a choice between letters or figures elsewhere, here this choice is denied her/him. But there is no traditional wisdom to suggest that writers dislike writing numerals in letters within a sentence (unless those numerals are large); indeed a standard practice (not followed in this chapter) is to put all two-figure numerals into their word form. So the proportion is still surprising. A second reason is that the great majority of corpus A is, as noted in the previous chapter, made up of *Guardian* newspaper text. Bell (1991) notes the importance of facticity in news text – little factual details such as numerals and names that convince a reader that this is 'real' news. Presumably placement in initial position emphasizes that facticity. But again this is only a partial explanation. It will account well for cases of *sixty per cent* but it provides no good explanation for the initial position of *sixty years ago* and similar expressions.

I suggest that the best explanation is that *sixty* is associated with the provision of background information. The basic textual questions that readers need answered as they seek to relate a text to their own experience are *when* and *where*. We have seen that almost a quarter of instances of *sixty* are used to orient the reader with regard to time, and we have seen that just under a tenth are associated with place. Place and time are associated with the provision of setting in Episodes in Longacre's system of narrative analysis (Darnton 1987, 1998; Longacre 1989); they provide background information allowing the reader to relate what is about to be said to what they already know and characteristically do so in fronted phrases/clauses at the beginning of Episodes. Indeed a classic episode boundary marker is *one day* . . .

Priming for sentence-initial position does not exhaust the textual colligations of *sixty* for which we would appear to be primed. As noted in Hoey (2005), there is also a strong tendency for *sixty* to occur in initial position in a text. Of all instances of *sixty* in my data (14 per cent of all sentence-initial instances), 10 per cent (29) are the first word in the text in which they appear, the first word being defined as either the first word of the title, subtitle or first full sentence. Just over a third of these (10) are in combination with *years*. Given that *sixty* is not an especially common word, these figures are very striking.

A reasonable objection at this point would be that the text-initial statistic might well be a direct, and therefore uninteresting, product of the very high preponderance of instances of *sixty* in sentence-initial position, especially since the texts of which my corpus is made up are likely to be short for the most part, given their newspaper provenance. We saw above, after all, that 71 per cent of all our instances of *sixty* were sentence-initial. In a corpus of shortish texts it is quite feasible that a word might appear frequently in text-initial position if it is put into sentence-initial position often enough. The logic of this position can be spelt out as follows: if the texts in which sentence-initial *sixty* appears are on average ten sentences long, then there must be a one-in-ten chance of sentence-initial *sixty* being text-initial, without there being any need for any further explanation.

To test whether this was in fact the case, I counted all the sentences in every text where *sixty* was the first word, and found that these texts were on average 20 sentences long. It follows, then, that there must be a one-in-twenty chance of sentence-initial *sixty* occurring at the beginning of a text just on the basis of random distribution. However, as I noted in passing above, 14 per cent of all cases of sentence-initial *sixty* are also text-initial – in other words, one in seven. What this means is that *sixty* is occurring at the beginning of texts three times as often as it should do on the basis of random distribution.

These figures are even more striking if we exclude instances of *sixty per cent*, for, once again, *sixty per cent* behaves differently from other collocations involving *sixty*: only three out of 91 instances of *Sixty per cent* in sentence-initial position are also text-initial. If we therefore remove these, we have 26 text-initial instances of *sixty* occurring out of 118 sentence-initial instances, which in turn means that nearly a quarter of all sentence-initial instances are also text-initial. That would suggest that *sixty* is occurring as first word of the text in which it appears about five times more often than would be predictable on the basis of random distribution.

Let us review what has been claimed about the characteristic primings associated with the numeral *sixty*. The following seem to be the main conclusions:

1. We are strongly primed to collocate it with *per cent* and *years*, and less strongly with *people, miles* and *minutes.*
2. Its collocations with *years* and *miles* are clues that we are likely to be primed to associate *sixty* with MEASUREMENT OF TIME and MEASUREMENT OF DISTANCE.
3. We are primed to associate *sixty* with some expression of im/precision.
4. We are primed to use *sixty* as a pre-modifier with some adjectival characteristics.
5. Depending on the noun it modifies, or the function it is serving if there is no noun, the colligations it appears in vary: characteristically, it is primed for the typical speaker to occur as part of subject with *per cent*, as part of adjunct with *years*, and as part of adjunct or complement when it refers to age.
6. In *Guardian* newspaper text, it is highly likely to be part of the Theme of its clause.
7. In *Guardian* newspaper text, it is more likely to be the first word of a text than one could have predicted on the basis of random distribution.

These observations suggest that even a word as terminally uninteresting as *sixty*, drawn from a category of words for which it might have been posited that they were driven by grammatical and real-world considerations, shows that it responds to description in terms of its collocations, colligations, semantic associations, pragmatic associations and textual colligations. It also suggests that there are no uninteresting words.

3 Comparisons with other numerals and other ways of representing numerals

Before we can conclude this part of the chapter, however, there are three important questions we need to ask of *sixty* or else we will not know the true significance of what we have found:

1. Are the features we have identified for *sixty* also true for the numerical form *60*?
2. Are the features we have identified for *sixty* also true for other numerals such as *sixty-three* or *sixty-seven*?
3. Are the features we have identified for *sixty* also true for other round numbers such as *forty*?

The answer to the first of these questions will tell us whether variations in our way of representing the word are associated with variations in its distribution, the answer to the second will tell us whether the roundness of the number affects its distribution, and the answer to the third will tell us whether the properties we have identified apply equally to other round numbers. With this in mind I looked in detail at 300 examples each of *60* and *sixty*; and 205 examples of the run of numerals from *sixty-one* to *sixty-nine* (that being the number that corpus A could supply).

3.1 How does sixty compare with 60?

Before looking at my randomly selected 300 instances of *60*, I looked at the overall collocational patterns for the word, using all 12,968 concordance lines generated by corpus A. These can be only taken as rough and ready because the full concordance included many items that would be eliminated from a more carefully constructed concordance (e.g. *60,567*; *3.60*; *60 million*; *page 60* – where this referred to the pages of the *Guardian*; and birthday lists). We must consequently be cautious about interpreting the figures in Table 2.3, which reports these collocations. The raw collocational figures hide polysemous use; they also do not reflect the variety of ways in which semantic association may be lexically realized. As an example of the first, note that *years* is occasionally used as a signal of semantic association with AGE, as in:

    6. 1.6 million were over 60 years of age.

Table 2.3 Immediate collocates of *60* in corpus A

60 per cent 2,268 (17%)	£60 1,532 (12%)	60 years 607 (5%)	aged 60 241 (2%)	60 people 165 (1%)	more than 60 476 (4%)
		60 days 138 (1%)	*age of 60* 128 (1%)		*about 60* 371 (3%)
		60 minutes 123 (1%)			*over 60* 282 (2%)
		60 seconds 53 (0.4%)			*some 60* 156 (1%)
		60 hours 52 (0.4%)			*nearly 60* 135 (1%)
					around 60 132 (1%)
		Total: 8%	**Total**: 3%		*almost 60* 98 (0.8%)
					at least 60 92 (0.7%)
					between 60 and . . . 88 (0.7%)
					others: 176 (1%) **Total**: 15%

where *years* is serving a slightly different function from normal. As an example of the second, the most common structure for referring to someone's age does not use the word at all:

7.   The equality lobby favoured giving both sexes a full pension at 60.

Despite these problems the collocational figures are reasonably revealing. Table 2.3 lists them in rough groups; numbers refer to instances immediately before or after the word and do not include instances occurring elsewhere in the concordance line.

Allowing for their limitations as data, when the raw collocations reported here for *60* are compared with the raw collocations found for *sixty*, certain similarities and differences immediately reveal themselves. While the percentages may not be reliable, the proportions of occurrence are more likely to be safe to use. So for *sixty* there are approximately 1.5 times as many instances of *per cent* as of *years*, reflecting a considerable importance for *years* in the collocational profile of *sixty*. For *60* on the other hand, *per cent* occurs over three times as often, despite an absolute drop in the percentage of instances of *per cent*. *Years*, then, is not as important a collocate of *60* as it is of *sixty*. The word *pounds* (usually represented as £) has however become an important collocation. This did not appear in the statistics for *sixty*, occurring just once, but it occurs 12 per cent of the time with *60*. (The word *age* has also become visible as a collocate.) Whatever the status of the actual percentages, they suggest a difference in use between the two words. (Note that I do not refer to them as different representations of the same word.)

We turn now to a more refined analysis, undertaken on 300 randomly selected concordance lines of *60* that were pruned of all extraneous matter and of all instances in non-sentential contexts such as lists and sports results. This concordance was analysed manually for collocations, colligations, semantic and pragmatic association and textual colligation. The results are presented in Table 2.4. As will be seen, there are similarities between the profiles of *sixty* and *60* – it would appear likely that for most of us they share the same semantic associations and collocates to a considerable degree – but they are not as striking as the differences.

First, notice the complementary distribution of the collocate *years* and the semantic association of AGE between the two words. If you want to refer to *years* you are almost three times as likely to choose *sixty* as *60*; if on the other hand you are writing about age, you are more than twice as likely to use *60* as *sixty*. Secondly, *60* is somewhat less likely than *sixty* to be used with *per cent* and correspondingly more likely to modify a non-collocating noun. One might infer from this that *60* is more commonly used as the exact figure, but the figures for imprecision and its opposite suggest otherwise; without *per cent*, *60*'s association with imprecision is slightly less than *sixty*'s, but with *per cent* it is actually marked for imprecision more often. Thirdly, the proportion of cases modifying people has halved. Finally, over a quarter of all cases of *60* are <u>not</u> associated with any of the semantic associations or

Table 2.4 A comparison of *sixty* and *60*

	sixty (294 instances)	*60* (300 instances)
Collocation or semantic association with:		
(1) *per cent*	32% (93)	21% (62)
(2) *years*	20% (59)	7% (22)
(3) AGE	9% (25)	19% (56)
(4) MEASUREMENT OF DISTANCE	6% (19)	7% (22)
(5) PEOPLE	15% (45)	7% (21)
(6) MEASUREMENT OF TIME (excluding *years*)	3% (10)	5% (15)
(7) CURRENCY	3% (8)	6% (19)
(8) **none of the above**	12% (35)	28% (83)
IMPRECISION **Pragmatic association with**		
(a) **including instances with** *per cent*	19% (57)	26% (78)
(b) **excluding instances with** *per cent*	30% (61 out of 202)	24% (56 out of 238)
Word appears in first position in:		
(1) **sentence**	71% (209)	4% (13)
excluding instances with *per cent*	58% (117 out of 201)	4% (9 out of 238)
(2) **text**	10% (29)	0.3% (1)
as proportion of sentence-initial instances	14%	8%
excluding instances with *per cent*	22% (26 out of 118)	11% (1 out of 9)

collocations we have been examining, as opposed to slightly under an eighth of instances of *sixty*.

The most striking difference between *sixty* and *60* perhaps lies in the tiny proportion of the latter that begin a sentence – and by beginning a sentence, I mean being the first lexical item in the sentence, not necessarily the very first word. *60* is rarely used to begin a text in the unlikely circumstance of its beginning a sentence (it only begins the one you are reading because it is a lexical datum). The only case occurring in my concordance is a short text – eight sentences long – and falls therefore well within the realms of chance. The evidence therefore suggests that we do not typically associate *60* with text-initial position, at least when we read the *Guardian*.

3.2 How does sixty *compare with* sixty-one, sixty-two, *etc.?*

We have seen that *sixty* and *60* differ somewhat in respect of collocations, semantic associations, colligations and thematic/textual position. How does *sixty* compare with *sixty-one, sixty-two* and so on? Interestingly, in a corpus of nigh on a hundred million words, there were only 205 instances of all nine words put together (after larger numerals had been excluded such as *sixty-seven thousand*, which were felt to complicate the picture). Analysed in a similar way to the data for *60*, these 205 lines produced the results set out in Table 2.5.

In respect of collocations and semantic association, there is little similarity between the data for *sixty* and those for *sixty-one*, etc. The latter occur half the time in conjunction with *per cent* (in marked contrast to both *sixty* and *60*), but they have only weak associations with most of the other collocations/colligations/semantic sets associated with *sixty*. It may seem unsurprising, perhaps, that there are very few instances of imprecision, but that is because we accept without hesitation the special role of *sixty/60* as a numerical landmark that allows us to make guesses as to number or specify a range of numbers. In fact, though, to the mathematician, 60 is as precise a numeral as 61, and the digit zero has no special status over the other

Table 2.5 A comparison of *sixty* and *sixty-x*.

	sixty (294 instances)	*sixty-one* etc. (205 instances)
Collocation or semantic association with:		
(1) *per cent*	32% (93)	50% (102)
(2) *years*	20% (59)	4% (9)
(3) AGE	9% (25)	4% (9)
(4) MEASUREMENT OF DISTANCE	6% (19)	1% (2)
(5) PEOPLE	15% (45)	17% (35)
(6) MEASUREMENT OF TIME (excluding *years*)	3% (10)	1% (3)
(7) CURRENCY	3% (8)	3% (6)
(8) none of the above	12% (35)	19% (39)
IMPRECISION **Pragmatic association with**		
(a) including instances with *per cent*	21% (63)	3% (7)
(b) excluding instances with *per cent*	30% (61 out of 202)	3% (7)
Word appears in first position in:		
(1) sentence	71% (209)	86% (177)
excluding instances with *per cent*	58% (117 out of 201)	73% (75 out of 103)
(2) text	10% (29)	7% (15)
as proportion of sentence-initial instances	14%	10%
excluding instances with *per cent*	22% (26 out of 118)	14% (14 out of 103)

digits when in combination with other numerals. The apparent obviousness of the special status of round numbers is, I suspect, an instance of the phenomenon Stubbs describes and challenges when he notes:

> There may be the illusion that they [lists of collocates] could have been provided, after a bit of thought, by intuition alone. But this is indeed an illusion. Intuition certainly cannot provide reliable facts about frequency and typicality. And whilst a native speaker may be able to provide some examples of collocates (which may or may not be accurate), only a corpus can provide thorough documentation.
>
> (Stubbs 1995: 250)

The drop in hesitation markers may have been in retrospect predictable but the figures above show hardly more instances of collocation with *years*, which even in retrospect seems less self-evident. Of course the argument of this paper would be that each of these numerals might itself be primed for most speakers to have a different collocational, colligational, semantic and pragmatic profile, but that will have to wait for investigation at another time.

Important points of similarity and difference lie in the area of Theme/ text position. As with *sixty*, *sixty-one* etc. are closely tied to first position in the sentence; indeed an even higher proportion are sentence-initial than was the case for *sixty*. We can hypothesize therefore that we are primed to expect numerals written as words to occur within the Themes of their clauses/ sentences, despite the newness of the information that they are characteristically carrying. This would then be an instance of a quasi-grammatical generalization derived from more specific primings. Interestingly, though, the similarity between *sixty* and *sixty-one* etc. in this respect does not extend to the text-initial position. A lower proportion of the latter appear in first position in the text and, much more importantly, the texts that *sixty-one* etc. do begin are characteristically *very* short. Of the 15 text-initial examples in my data, two were unavailable for more detailed inspection;[4] of the remainder, eight had four or fewer sentences, and six of these comprised just one sentence. Compare this with the average of 20 sentences length for texts beginning with *sixty*; only three of the 27 instances I was able to inspect were as short as four sentences long and only one of these was a single-sentence text. We must conclude therefore that *sixty-one* etc. have a strong association with Theme but no association with any special text position.

3.3 *How does* sixty *compare with* forty?

Finally, we need to look at how *sixty* compares with other round numbers. One might predict that here at least the words are best treated as a class. The results of comparing the numerals, however, as reflected in Table 2.6, are slightly surprising.

There are some similarities between *forty* and *sixty* with regard to collocation, colligation and semantic and pragmatic association. In both cases we would seem to be primed to associate them with CURRENCY and PEOPLE, and

Table 2.6 A comparison of *sixty* and *forty*

	sixty (294 instances)	*forty* (546 instances)
Collocation or semantic association with:		
(1) *per cent*	32% (93)	15% (80)
(2) *years*	20% (59)	34% (185)
(3) AGE	9% (25)	12% (66)
(4) MEASUREMENT OF DISTANCE	6% (19)	2% (9)
(5) PEOPLE	15% (45)	14% (74)
(6) MEASUREMENT OF TIME (excluding *years*)	3% (10)	6% (34)
(7) CURRENCY	3% (8)	3% (15)
(8) none of the above	12% (35)	15% (83)
Pragmatic association with IMPRECISION		
(a) including instances with *per cent*	21% (63)	15% (83)
(b) excluding instances with *per cent*	30% (61 out of 202)	18% (83 out of 66)
Word appears in first position in:		
(1) sentence	71% (209)	68% (369)
excluding instances with *per cent*	58% (117 out of 201)	62% (289 out of 466)
(2) text	10% (29)	11% (62)
as proportion of sentence-initial instances	14%	17%
excluding instances with *per cent*	22% (26 out of 117)	20% (57 out of 289)

[handwritten marginalia: "Half line", "More", "double", "Inversely", "always this caveat."]

with roughly the same strength of priming; equally worthy of note, the same proportion of each set of data combines with none of the identified collocates and participates in none of the semantic associations. Significantly, *sixty* and *forty* also have similar patterns of behaviour with regard to their being thematized and being text-initial. But there are perhaps more differences than one might have expected. These deserve a moment's attention.

Perhaps the first thing to note is that in corpus A, *forty* counts things nearly twice as often as *sixty* (and *forty-one* etc. are also used twice as often as *sixty-one* etc.). Next, one notes that the proportion of instances of *forty* used with *per cent* is half that of *sixty* and that, despite the much larger number of instances of *forty* overall, this marks an absolute as well as a relative drop. The reason for this, I tentatively suggest, may be that *sixty per cent* represents a clear majority and is therefore inherently more newsworthy than *forty per cent.* It must again be remembered that corpus A is largely made up of *Guardian* newspapers and that all the conclusions reached in this paper are conclusions about our probable primings for words in newspaper text.

The second discrepancy to note is the doubling of measurements of time in conjunction with *forty*. This is because sixty seconds is a minute and sixty minutes an hour. Although references to both do occur in the corpus for *sixty*, there are naturally more references to *forty seconds* and *forty minutes* for which no other obvious linguistic expression exists.

The third large discrepancy is the marked increase in the number of instances of collocation with *years*. At first sight this is hard to explain. It might however be relevant that the phrase *sixty years on* occurs just six times in the *sixty* concordance but occurs 40 times in the *forty* concordance. Why should this be? A possible explanation may lie in the special use that *X years on* has textually. It marks a textual contrast between two states separated by time (a textual semantic association). To report such a contrast one characteristically has to have recall of the earlier state. Of the 40 instances, 34 allowed inspection of the larger textual context, and of these exactly half (17) directly contrast someone's personal experience of the past and the present, with a further three arguably doing the same. Whereas one only has to be in one's late 50s to have memories that might be contrasted with life 'forty years on', one has on the other hand to be nearly 80 to have memories of adult life that could be contrasted with another state 'sixty years on'. There are clearly more people in the former class than the latter.

The small increase in percentage in the salience of the semantic association with AGE might be accounted for in terms of the 'threshold of middle-age' significance ascribed to the age of 40, but I am unable to find any explanation for the drop in percentage and absolute numbers of instances of association with MEASUREMENT OF DISTANCE.

With regard to association with (IM)PRECISION, there is once again a discrepancy and here surprise might be tinged with concern about the reliability of the figures. After all, *sixty* and *forty* are both round numbers; it would not be unreasonable to expect them to be equally likely to need modifying or qualifying. However there is a possible explanation. This is that it is reasonable to suppose that accuracy in counting or estimation will improve the lower the number to be counted or estimated. Logically, therefore, we should expect the lower numeral words to need fewer markers of imprecision or precision. In support of this explanation, I would note that seven of the markers for *forty* are in fact markers of precision, as opposed to just two for *sixty*. (In passing, we might note that something similar would help explain the raw difference in the total number of instances of the two words and of the related *sixty-one/forty-one* etc.: smaller numbers are easier to count; above a certain level one may not want to be bothered.) This explanation could be tested by checking whether there is a steady rise in the number of approximation markers as round numbers rise and also whether there is a steady decline in the numbers of attested examples in a corpus of constant size.

A minor factor in the discrepancy – and one that again points to the possibility that text organization may also affect the way the proportions compare – is that *forty years on*, already noted as signalling contrast and as contributing to the discrepancy in the proportion of cases of the two words collocating with *years*, is never attested in corpus A with a marker of either precision or imprecision.

3.4 Conclusions from these analyses and comparisons

What my findings for *sixty* seem to show is that *sixty* is indeed primed for many if not most speakers, in newspaper text at any rate, to be expected with a unique combination of collocations, colligations and semantic associations, though separately these characteristics are shared by other numerals and by the same numeral represented as numerals rather than letters. This therefore in turn seems to show that lexical priming can reflect sensibly upon even items that might at first sight be expected to be exempt from the idiom principle and be driven in their use by real-world and grammatical considerations. The issue now has to be considered of whether the data young children are exposed to could plausibly result in their being primed for the grammar of numerals.

4 Are children primed for the grammar of numerals?

It is patently absurd to make any claims about the way children acquire language without reference to evidence of the things they say (or, in the later stages, write). The following sections are not intended as investigation of language acquisition, but of the inherent plausibility of claims about language acquisition that centre on lexical priming. The best outcome that could be expected of such investigation is that the data permit the possibility that children may be primed in particular ways and that these primings would be a reasonable basis for certain grammatical inferences.

The corpus I used to investigate these possibilities was built from a stock of 29 books written for children aged between 2 and 6, which my wife gave me in her capacity as Director of the Bolton Literacy Trust. To avoid copyright problems, I read each book carefully and kept in my corpus only those sentences that contained a numeral. Because I was interested in what a child would be primed for as a result of being read to, I did not distinguish between numerals written as words or as figures. (The vast majority were in word form, as it happened.) The books varied greatly. Some were collections of nursery rhymes, some were retellings of popular stories (e.g. Winnie the Pooh, Aladdin), some were 'action books', one was a Tweenies annual. All were suitable for being read to a young child.

As I noted above, these books represent no one child's experience of being read to, nor does the corpus take account of the likelihood that certain texts might be repeatedly read to the child (nor of the possibility that parts might be skipped in reading) but they can point to the possible primings that a child that was exposed to such books might acquire.

4.1 Sequence and the semantic set of NUMBER

Perhaps if my children were much younger or if I were a grandfather, I would not have been surprised by the first strong collocation that came out of the data. Quite simply, any child encountering these books would be primed to associate any number with its place in the sequence. The word *two,* for instance, collocates with *one, three, four, five, six* and *seven.* In a set of 77 concordance lines for *two,* 19 (25 per cent) are straight sequences, e.g.

Build a house with five bricks, One, two, three, four, five

A further instance gives the sequence in reverse:

'Three, two, one, GO!' shouted Fizz.

So one of the first effects of exposure to such text would be that the numbers would be seen to collocate with each other and since the speech action of counting would presumably be accompanied by actions of touching images of items, the child would be licensed to assume that they formed a semantic set.

The child is not dependent on the presence of such sequences, likely though they are to occur in the talk as well as the texts that the child experiences. Independently, ample data are provided for the establishment of the semantic set of NUMBER. These take the form, amongst others, of repetitive rhymes in which only the numeral changes. Consider, for example, the following concordance selections:

Concordance 2.1 Part of the concordance for *duck** in the children's writing corpus

```
1    day. Five Little Ducks. Five little ducks went swimming one
2     hammers this fine day. Five  Little Ducks. Five little ducks
3   ck, quack," And all the five  little ducks came back. [All from
4    uack, quack," But only four little ducks came back. Four
5   little ducks came back. Four little ducks went swimming one
6    quack, quack," But only one little duck came back. One little
7     little duck came back. One little duck went swimming one
8   ittle ducks came back. Three little ducks went swimming one
9    ack, quack," But only three little ducks came back. Three
10   little ducks came back. Two little ducks went swimming one
11   quack, quack," But only two little ducks came back. Two
```

The words *duck* and *little* in the text which generated the lines in this concordance temporarily collocate with each other. More importantly they allow a semantic association with NUMBER to be created in the child's mind. Similar data are the following:

Concordance 2.2 The concordance for *monkey** in the children's writing corpus

```
1     Clap, Clap Hands] Five Little Monkeys Five little monkeys jumping
2     ve Little Monkeys Five little monkeys jumping on the bed, One fell
3     and the doctor said, "No more monkeys jumping on the bed!"
```

```
 4  jumping on the bed!" Four little monkeys jumping on the bed, One fell
 5      and the doctor said "No more monkeys jumping on the bed!" Three
 6  ing on the bed!" Three little monkeys jumping on the bed, One fell
 7      and the doctor said, "No more monkeys jumping on the bed!" Two
 8  jumping on the bed!" Two little monkeys jumping on the bed, One fell
 9      and the doctor said, "No more monkeys jumping on the bed!" One
10  jumping on the bed!" One little monkey jumping on the bed, One fell
11      and the doctor said, "No more monkeys jumping on the bed!" Two
```

Again, the words *monkey* and *little* collocate at least for the duration of the text and again they apparently prime the child to see *one, two, three, four, five,* etc. not just syntagmatically as collocates but paradigmatically as members of a semantic set. There is indeed strong evidence in my data for believing that for a young child *little* is quickly primed to collocate firstly with *one, two, three,* etc. and then, I would argue, with the semantic set NUMBER. Consider the following data as evidence:

Concordance 2.3 Selected lines from concordance for *little* in children's writing corpus

```
 1       y fly. [Clap, Clap Hands] Five Little Monkeys Five little monkeys
 2     ands] Five Little Monkeys Five little monkeys jumping on the bed,
 3       k. [Hickory Dickory Dock] Five Little Soldiers Five little soldiers
 4    quack, quack," And all the five little ducks came back. [All from
 5    e hammers, this fine day. Five Little Ducks Five little ducks went
 6     ne day. Five Little Ducks Five little ducks went swimming one day,
 7     Dock] Five Little Soldiers Five little soldiers standing in a row,
 8     re Happy and You Know It] Five Little Peas Five little peas in a
 9  You Know It] Five Little Peas Five little peas in a pea-pod pressed One
10    e out? [Shapes and Sizes] Five Little Men in a Flying Saucer Five
11    le Men in a Flying Saucer Five little men in a flying saucer flew
12    , quack, quack," But only four little ducks came back. Four little
13  four little ducks came back. Four little ducks went swimming one day,
14    day. So one man flew away. Four little men in a flying saucer flew
15  monkeys jumping on the bed!" Four little monkeys jumping on the bed,
16    day. So one man flew away. One little man in a flying saucer flew
17   monkeys jumping on the bed!" One little monkey jumping on the bed,
18    , quack, quack," But only one little duck came back. One little
19    one little duck came back. One little duck went swimming one day,
20  little babies met in a lane. Ten Little Fingers I have ten little
21    schoolboys met in a lane. Two little babies met in a lane. Ten
22    men bow down to the king, Ten little men dance all day, Ten little
23    amed Peter One named Paul. Ten Little Men Ten little men standing
24    named Paul. Ten Little Men Ten little men standing straight, Ten
25  Ten little men open the gate, Ten little men all in a ring, Ten little
26  Ten little men all in a ring, Ten little men bow down to the king, Ten
27    tle men standing straight, Ten little men open the gate, Ten little
28    little men dance all day, Ten little men hide away. Peter Works
29    quack, quack," But only three little ducks came back. Three little
30  day. So one man flew away. Three little men in a flying saucer flew
31    little ducks came back. Three little ducks went swimming one day,
32    ys jumping on the bed!" Three little monkeys jumping on the bed,
33  day. So one man flew away. Two little men in a flying saucer flew
34  tall policemen met in a lane. Two little schoolboys met in a lane. Two
35    d!" Two Little Dicky Birds Two little dicky birds Sitting on a
36    little ducks came back. Two little ducks went swimming one day,
37    k, quack, quack," But only two little ducks came back. Two little
38    schoolboys met in a lane. Two little babies met in a lane. Ten
```

```
39    nkeys jumping on the bed!" Two little monkeys jumping on the bed,
40    nkeys jumping on the bed!" Two Little Dicky Birds Two little dicky
```

There are forty instances of *little* occurring with NUMBER out of a total of 253 lines for the numerals *one, two, three, four, five, six, seven, eight, nine, ten, eleven* and *twenty*, which represents almost 16 per cent of the NUMBER data. Straight comparisons cannot be made with other kinds of writing, as my children's book corpus only contains instances of *little* in close association with one or more of the numerals. I am therefore unable to calculate the proportion of instances of *little* that are so associated. But in adult text as represented by corpus A, *little* has a low occurrence with NUMBER, there being only 13 examples of the association in a sample of 2,820 lines. So it would seem that this is a priming that will be later weakened to the point of unimportance; at this stage, though, it may well serve the function of reinforcing the integrity of the NUMBER set.

4.2 *What does a child learn to associate with NUMBER?*

Once the number set has been established in the child's mind, the issue arises of what it is then primed to occur with. The data for *four* are typical:

Concordance 2.4 Concordance for *four* in children's writing corpus

```
1      rye;       Four and twenty blackbirds, Baked in a pie.
2      crown      four blue shoes on horse's feet five wobbly
3     'BANG!'     fFour fat sausages frying in a pan, All of a sudden
4      three      four five one two three four five six one two
5   two three     four five one two three four five six one two
6   two three     four five one two three four five six one two
7   two three     four five six one two three four five six seven
8   two three     four five six seven eight one two three four
9   two three     four five six seven eight nine one two three
10     three,     four, five Now I raise them up so high, Make my
11     three,     four, five! [The Beehive] The clock struck one,
12   three . . . four . . . five . . . SIX FEET LONG!" said Nasan. "And be
13   three . . . four . . . five . . . six feet long" and "one . . . two . . . three
14   three . . . four . . . five . . . six feet long", and "one . . . two . . . three
15   three . . . four . . . five . . . six . . . seven . . . eight . . . nine . . . TEN HANDS
16     with       four hammers, four hammers, four hammers, Peter
17  hammers,      four hammers, four hammers, Peter works with four
18  hammers,      four hammers, Peter works with four hammers, this
19     with       four hammers, this fine day. Peter works with
20    Which       four hats should we choose? This is one of the
21   Do all       four! [If You're Happy and You Know It] Five Little
22    ears,       four legs and a tail on the yellow card, using the
23    bed!"       Four little monkeys jumping on the bed, One fell off
24    only        four little ducks came back. Four little ducks went
25    ack.        four little ducks went swimming one day, Over the
26    away.       Four little men in a flying saucer flew round the
27    three       four one two three four five one two three four
28     for        four places? [accompanied by picture]. Four small
29     to         four players. [Tweenies BBC Annual 2004] One warm
30   cture].      Four small squares of cake make one big square. Can
31   through      four strawberries, but he was still hungry. On Friday
32  chooses       four things to wear as a costume. Then, each player
```

What grammar might a child infer from the primings s/he received from data such as these? Looking at the data set for all the numerals in my data except *one*, a number of semantic sets seem to be associated with NUMBER in my data. Table 2.7 represents sets that a child might recognize as a result of encounters with the data in my corpus of writing for children. Of these, the COMPONENT category seems the most fragile, and I would not want to place too much weight upon it. It is probable, given the human qualities of many of the animals in the data – they speak, wear clothes, solve problems, etc. – that the PEOPLE and ANIMATE sets are not separate in the child's mind for the purposes of their relation with NUMBER.

So the child is primed to recognize NUMBER as having a semantic association with other semantic sets. Impressionistically it would appear as if the majority of data associated with UNITS OF MEASUREMENT is targeted at a slightly older age group. It may therefore be that the PEOPLE/ANIMATE category/ies comes first. The process might well be for one child a progression from PEOPLE/ANIMATE to part of the same (BODY PARTS) to other solid objects (FOOD). For another, it might be a move from a general semantic set of VISIBLE BOUNDED OBJECTS to UNITS OF MEASUREMENT. Not only are the data that each child receives unique but so must, at least in principle, be the primings. The challenge to each initial priming that new, non-compliant data provide must presumably be met in different ways in each child.

Whether or not this is the case, the child is certainly being primed by such data for several important colligations. In the first place, the semantic association of each numeral (and subsequently of the semantic set of NUMBER) with the PEOPLE/ANIMATE sets is accompanied by a regular (but not quite invariable) grammatical patterning. There is a strong colligation for NUMBER to take a position immediately before a member of the PEOPLE/ANIMATE sets listed or immediately before a describing word that is itself before such a member; in other words, numerals come

Table 2.7 Semantic sets associated with NUMBER in the children's writing corpus

What is counted	246
UNITS OF MEASUREMENT	41 – *Older children.*
PEOPLE	31
ANIMATE (other than people)	31
UTENSILS	20
FOOD	19
BODY PARTS	17
COMPONENTS	17
none of these	70

before a noun or before an adjective/noun combination. From the data in my children's writing corpus for the PEOPLE/ANIMATE sets, the child could begin to construct a tentative grammar of the nominal group along the lines just mentioned.

Encounters with data that do not conform to the semantic sets (e.g. lines 20 and 32 in the concordance for *four* above) will simultaneously result in the beginning of a new priming (for CLOTHING in this case) and in the reinforcement and prioritization of the positional/colligational priming. At the same time, encounters with data that do not conform to the colligation pattern just described will usually reinforce one of the existing semantic associations but may form the kernel of a new colligation. The following two instances reinforce the priming for BODY PARTS and ANIMATE respectively but provide data for the beginning of a new priming for numerals:

Well, naturally when I said six feet I meant **six of my** feet, not yours.

I like animals. Here I am with **two of my** favourites.

Sometimes the establishment of a new semantic association will be accompanied by a new potential colligation. Look, for example, at the full form of lines 13 and 15 from the data set for *four* given above:

13 'And be sure to make it six feet long and three feet wide.' 'One . . . two . . . three . . . four . . . five . . . six feet long' and 'one . . . two . . . three feet wide.'

15 sure to choose a chestnut mare, ten hands high,' said Nasan. 'One . . . two . . . three . . . four . . . five . . . six . . . seven . . . eight . . . nine . . . TEN HANDS HIGH.' 'I said ten hands high . . .

From such data a child may not only (begin to) be primed to associate numerals with UNIT OF MEASUREMENT but may be primed for the pattern NUMBER + UNIT OF MEASUREMENT + SCALE (or simply NUMBER + UNIT OF MEASUREMENT + *high*, NUMBER + UNIT OF MEASUREMENT + *wide*, NUMBER + UNIT OF MEASUREMENT + *tall*, NUMBER + UNIT OF MEASUREMENT + *thick*, etc).

The data are likely to result in a further, and rather different, priming. The presence of /z/ at the end of *blackbirds, shoes, hammers, legs*, etc. is the more noticeable from its absence from equivalent data for *one*, which is, it will be remembered, regularly set up in strictly parallel structures with the other numerals. There is therefore a positive priming for NUMBER and /z/ and a negative priming for *one* that it does not occur with /z/. The same argument follows for /ɪz/ and /s/.

I have been arguing that the data young children are exposed to in the course of being read to, both in the forms of traditional rhymes and tales and of modern publications, could plausibly result in their being primed for the grammar of numerals. Whether they actually are so primed is a matter for separate investigation. The evidence for all the numerals from *two* onwards suggests that subconsciously (or in several of the recent publications, quite possibly consciously) such literature is designed to facilitate swift and effective priming.

I mentioned above the negative priming for *one*, but it may have been noticed that my discussion has not made specific mention of any examples using *one*. I have in fact deliberately left *one* to last because the data are fuller and more complex and need separate discussion. There are in my small corpus 179 instances of *one*. Many of the uses are identical to those already discussed. So *one* participates in number sequences (*one, two, three* ...) and is found in association with PEOPLE, ANIMATE, BODY PARTS, etc. Sometimes the data suggest a particular function in establishing these semantic associations, e.g. the following for association with BODY PARTS. (There are nine further lines on the same pattern.)

> We'll all be merry and bright. One finger, one thumb, one arm, one leg, one nod of the head, keep moving, One finger, one ...

However, *one* occurs in a number of patterns not shared by other numerals. The following are some of the data that fall outside the regularities so far identified:

a checked one	[four cases of *a* DESCRIPTION *one*]
the stripy one,	[three cases of *the* DESCRIPTION *one*]
one another	
this one	
One by one,	[three such cases, all sentence-initial]
one day,	[17 cases, eight sentence-initial]
one end of the concertina	
One evening,	
One fell off	[five cases]
unless one fell ... when it would be ... easy.	
One for the master	[four cases of *one for* PERSON]
One grew, two grew and so did all the rest.	
one hundred eggs	
down the middle of each one.	
one more time.	
One named Peter	[two cases of *one named* NAME]
one of these	
one of my fine horses	
one of the Tweenies' favourite dressing-up games,	
one of my finest horses	
one of the Six Pine Trees,	[two cases]
one of their stockings.	
one of the Fiercer Animals	
the other one	
the odd one out	[three cases].
except one.	
The clock struck one,	

a number from one to six, for example three.
One warm August night,
One was stripy   [three cases of *one was* DESCRIPTION]
All of a sudden one went 'BANG!'   [four cases]
the last but one
one with rings around it called Saturn.

I have in places in this list kept separate what others would put together, but my intention was to list the patterns for which a child might be primed. A number of important patterns are, in many cases, repeatedly present; where the pattern is present only once, it will be dependent on whether the book is read a number of times (or, of course, on the talk the child hears from other sources) whether the child gets primed for them. Patterns which the child might be primed for include *the* + DESCRIPTION + *one, odd one out, one day/morning* [often sentence-initial], *from one to six, one . . . called, the other one, one of the, one by one, the last but one, one another, one* (= I, you, etc.), *one* (referring to a category just mentioned), and *except one*. In some cases, these patterns will in due course present themselves with other numerals (*from two to six, the other two, two of the, two by two, the last but two*), though the child is unlikely to find itself needing to generalize in such a way for a while to come. In other cases, the connection with the remaining number system may never be strong. How many adults connect episode-boundary *one day* with the counting of period of time? The point here is that the data for *one* already point to the messiness and patchiness of the grammar that the child may be creating. The data are indeed sufficient to allow a child to begin the process of grammar-creation, built out of the colligations that are repeatedly offered in the books they are read, but the very same data contain such complexities that some of the primings may remain isolated and outside the key generalizations. In other words, the priming that underlies and explains the existence of the idiom principle is occurring at the same time as the priming that is giving rise to the apparent regularities of a grammar.

Conclusions

In this and the previous chapter I have tried to put my claims about lexical priming to two stern tests. The first was to see whether a lexical priming theory could account for the unexpected choices made by literary writers, in short whether it could provide the basis for a description of linguistic creativity. A negative answer to this question would have meant that it had failed to meet one of the key criteria for a satisfactory theory of language. However, I believe the analyses in the previous chapter amount to a positive answer. There is clearly more to do. In particular, it needs to be investigated whether 'creative' sentences constructed on external principles (e.g. each word beginning with a successive letter of the alphabet, each word – apart from the first – beginning with the letter that ended the previous one) can also be accounted for.

The second test was to see whether my claim about the processes of priming, and in particular the claim that a person's grammar is built out of his or her primings, was supported by the kinds of data available for the priming of children, the focus of my investigation centring on the number system. No confident conclusions can be drawn from any investigation that relies on the written word, since at least some children will access the number system through the oral mode only, but again preliminary results suggest that it is quite possible that children might be primed by the stories and rhymes they are read in such a way that they would construct a provisional and leaky grammar of number for themselves. Further work will of course be necessary to see whether what we know about caretaker–child exchanges are similarly supportive.

There are many other tests that lexical priming will need to be put through before it will be safe to assume that it offers a valid account of corpus-derived phenomena, but at least these chapters suggest that it is worthy of undergoing such further tests.

Notes

1. Parts of this chapter appeared originally on a CD-ROM festschrift for John Sinclair and were subsequently published in *Pesquisas em Discurso Pedagógico* 3.1 (2004). I am grateful to the editors for permission to reproduce them here.
2. Capitals are used here and in the previous chapter to indicate a semantic association.
3. I follow Sinclair (1971) in distinguishing Complement from Object. Thus, here, Complement refers to the clause function that follows (characteristically) a stative verb (e.g. *You are the difficult one*).
4. For some reason, WordSmith could not retrieve the full text from which these lines came. The lines themselves, however, made it clear that they were indeed text-initial, in that (part of) a title in capitals was present in the line.

References

Bell, A. (1991) *The Language of News Media*. Oxford: Blackwell.

Bloor, T. and Bloor, M. (1995) *The Functional Analysis of English: A Hallidayan Approach*. London: Arnold.

Darnton, A. (1987) *Episodes in the Development of Narrative Awareness in Children*. Unpublished MLitt. thesis, University of Birmingham.

—— (1998) *The Way through the Woods: New Directions in Narrative Analysis*. Unpublished PhD thesis, University of Liverpool.

Halliday, M. A. K. (1994) *An Introduction to Functional Grammar* (2nd ed.). London: Edward Arnold.

Hoey, M. (2003) 'Why grammar is beyond belief', in J.-P. van Noppen, C. Den Tandt and I. Tudor (eds), *Beyond: New Perspectives in Language, Literature and ELT*. Thematic Issue. *Belgian Journal of English Language and Literatures*, New Series 1. Ghent, Belgium: Academia Press, pp. 183–96.

—— (2005) *Lexical Priming: A New Theory of Words and Language*. London: Routledge.

—— (forthcoming) 'Corpus-driven approaches to grammar: a search for common ground' to appear in U. Römer (ed.), *Exploring the Lexis–Grammar Interface*. Proceedings of a conference held in Hanover, 5–8 October 2006.

Hunston, S. and Francis, G. (2000) *Pattern Grammar. A Corpus-driven Approach to the Lexical Grammar of English*. Amsterdam: John Benjamins.

Leech, G. (1992) *Introducing English Grammar*. London: Penguin.

Longacre, R. E. (1989) *Joseph: A Story of Divine Providence. A Text Theoretical and Textlinguistic Analysis of Genesis 37 and 39–48*. Winona Lake: Eisenbrauns.

Martin, J. R. (2004) 'Grammatical structure: What do we mean?' in C. Coffin, A. Hewings and K. O'Halloran (eds), *Applying English Grammar. Functional and Corpus Approaches*. London: Arnold, pp. 57–76.

Sinclair, J. M. (1971) *A Course in Spoken English: Grammar*. London: OUP.

—— (1991) *Corpus, Concordance, Collocation*. Oxford: OUP.

—— (2004) *Trust the Text: Language, Corpus and Discourse*. London: Routledge.

Stubbs, M. (1995) 'Corpus evidence for norms of lexical collocation', in G. Cook and B. Seidelhofer (eds), *Principle and Practice in Applied Linguistics: Papers in Honour of Henry Widdowson*. Oxford: OUP.

—— (1996) *Text and Corpus Analysis*. Oxford: Basil Blackwell.

Thompson, G. (1996) *Introducing Functional Grammar*. London: Arnold.

3 *Parole*-linguistics and the diachronic dimension of the discourse

Wolfgang Teubert

Introduction

In this chapter, I want to discuss the notion of the discourse as a core concept of corpus linguistics. Once we accept that the object of corpus linguistics is to make sense of what is said in the discourse, we move away from the psychological or mental perspective of linguistics which is underlying the paradigm of cognitive linguistics. Corpus linguistics, I suggest, should instead subscribe to a sociological perspective. Discourse is part of our society. It is essential for society. A group of people in which we would not find some form of verbal exchange of content between its members could hardly be called a society.

In section 1, I explore the relationship between language and society, as I see it today. Section 2 argues that the remit of linguistics is confined to recorded, i.e. normally written, language. In section 3, I discuss my concept of meaning. For me, the meaning of a text or a text segment is everything that has been said or is being said about it. This is the position of social constructionism. Section 4 compares my concept of the discourse to that of Michel Foucault. For him a discourse is an ontological reality, something that really exists out there. This is the view I challenge. Section 5 introduces the diachronic dimension of the discourse. For whatever we say, we say it in response to something that has been said before. In section 6, I explore the relationship between diachronic corpus linguistics and hermeneutics, the discipline of text interpretation as it was developed over the last centuries on the Continent.

The last section discusses the contribution linguistics can make to the interpretation of texts. The discourse is democratic, and it is up to all its members to participate in the negotiation of meaning. Linguists have no privileged status. Everyone has the same right to accept, discuss, modify or reject the constructions of reality that they are confronted with in the discourse. There is no conceptualization that could make a claim to being true. Only a relativistic perspective can be the basis of a pluralistic, democratic society.

1 Society presupposes language, and language presupposes society

With Niklas Luhmann (Luhmann 1998), we can understand society as a structure of and for the interactions between people, human beings with autonomous minds, with a sense of self-awareness and intentionality. This implies that the people themselves and their consciousness are not a part of the society as defined here. The self-awareness, the intentionality, the first-person experiences, the intentions of any one of the members of the society, including this member's understanding of what the others say, is outside of the society. This is not the usual understanding of what society is. Many sociologists would disagree. Max Weber, for instance, saw society as the aggregate of the intentionalities of its members (Weber 1972: 1). The problem is, however, that the intentionality of a person is not directly accessible. From the outside we can observe people's behaviour. But how this behaviour is connected to a person's beliefs, attitudes and intentions is a matter of interpretation. Because one person's thoughts are not accessible to another person, they cannot be part of the interactions between the members. Only the (verbal) testimony people give of their state of mind is accessible. The place where (verbalized) content is shared and exchanged is the discourse. It is this exchange of content that assigns meaning to all interactions between the members of a society. To exclude the members of society from a structural analysis of society is, at least at first glance, a startling thing to do. What do we gain from saying that society is what is left of a (large) group of people after you have taken away their intentionalities? I think to talk of society only makes sense if what goes on in a (large) group of people is more than the aggregate of these intentionalities. This is why Niklas Luhmann is proposing 'a radically antihumanistic, a radically antiregionalistic and a radically constructionist concept of society' (Luhmann 1998: 35). For the difference between what is happening in a (large) group of people and the part of it that can be reduced to the intentionalities of the persons making up this (large) group is the sense that this group makes of itself, the way this group interprets itself as a group, and the interactions as having a meaning. The difference is therefore the discourse of this group. Therefore it is the ways in which the interactions occurring in that group are discussed, commented and negotiated in the texts contributed by the members of such a discourse community that construct the society as an object of this discourse. This is why society presupposes language.

Interaction unless interpreted is meaningless. We always have to be told what it is about. If we are celebrating a baptism, it needs to be said that this is what we are doing. Therefore only what members of the society contribute to the discourse constitutes society. What is being exchanged is not the first-person experience or an intention itself but only its verbalization. It is the (written or spoken) testimony of first-person experiences and intentions. The discourse of a society, more specifically, of a discourse community consists of the texts which its members have been and still are contributing to it. The structure of a society, to the extent to which it can be interpreted (which means to the extent it is symbolic), manifests itself in the discourse, in the entirety of all the verbal utterances of this discourse community. Social practices are, in my view, only part of the social structure in so far as they are symbolic, as they are talked about in texts and thus can be interpreted. A social practice that is not talked about cannot be part of a discursively constructed reality. This is my main criticism of the programme of critical discourse analysis as it has been formulated by, among others, Norman Fairclough (Fairclough 2003) and Ruth Wodak (Wodak 1988). Their agenda juxtaposes the discourse and social practices which are considered to be external to the discourse.

Only people organize themselves as a society. In order to do that they have to rely on language. For only language makes it possible to conceptualize behaviour as a social practice. Baptisms, weddings, birthday celebrations, excursions, all collaboration, the division of labour, anti-war rallies, religious services are social constructs, and therefore they need a verbal expression to be understood. Without a word for work there would not be the social construct 'work', nor would there be, without the words, constructs such as 'property' or 'justice' or even 'society'. For only human beings can be aware (and reflect the fact) that they are members of society. They can only be aware of it because society is something people talk about.

Human society can only exist where there is language. Yet it is also true that to learn to use language we need human society. We learn language because we want to communicate with other members of our discourse community, because we want to exchange and share content. But we cannot learn it by ourselves. Children who grow up in isolation, outside of society, do not learn to speak. Therefore they cannot develop an autonomous mind. Without becoming part of a society, we would remain dumb, incapable of speech.

2 Empirical linguistics deals only with recorded language

The discipline of linguistics presupposes written or otherwise recorded language, language archived in whatever form, language that is available for analysis. Spoken language, language that already fades in the instant of its production cannot be subjected to analysis. Even when we investigate speech, we have to rely on recordings and transcripts. Empirical sciences need empirical data. Any discipline, including linguistics, presupposes a community, a community of experts. They have to discuss the data they are confronted with, with the aim of agreeing on an interpretation of this data. Therefore it is their discourse which turns linguists into members of the linguistic community. Unless they have data they can discuss, there will not be a dialogue. Without a dialogue, there will not be a community of experts. Yet spoken language, unless recorded, does not provide the linguistic community with data. To the extent that linguistics views itself as an empirical science, it has to deal with the artefacts that are produced in the discourse at large, that is with real language data. This is why we have to accept that without writing or other recording techniques there would not be linguistics, at least not a discipline that could call itself empirical.

There are, of course, still many linguists insisting that spoken language is the primordial form of language. Historically they are right, of course. There was spoken language before writing. Therefore many linguists have claimed that it is, first of all, spoken language which should be the remit of linguistics. It was de Saussure who contended time and again that he was dealing with spoken language and nothing else. Roy Harris, however, has argued, in my eyes convincingly, that 'Saussurean linguistics is essentially the linguistics of "typographic man"' (Harris 1987: 51). Because it is impossible to analyse the spoken language of an oral society without transcribing it, it has to be turned into written (or otherwise) recorded language. A transcript, however, is never equivalent to the speech event itself. We lose the immediacy of the situational setting, the embeddedness in the lifeworld, the intonation, the facial expressions and the gestures, the acts of deixis and of ostentation. Even if we manage to capture these aspects in some restricted way, we are still bound to focus our inquiry on the meaning of the uttered texts, not, as the hearers of an informal conversation would do, on the speaker's intentions. We analyse such a text as if it were dissociated from its context, even if we add all the situational data and treat them as signs that have a meaning. By treating texts (and accompanying data) as symbolic representations and not as someone's intentions we have already moved from speech to written (or otherwise recorded) language.

How texts are meant by their speakers, how they are being understood by their hearers, is not accessible to us. I can never fully express what a particular text, for instance my favourite poem, means to me. I have, somehow, converted it into a first-person experience, and no textual testimony will ever give full justice to this experience. That does not mean it is not possible, in a dialogic interaction, to negotiate its meaning. How I personally understand a text can be quite independent (and different) from what we can agree upon as its meaning. The intentionalities of speaker and hearer will always remain elusive. Any attempt to integrate them into a model of the mind would necessarily lead to an infinite regress. This has been shown, independently of each other, by John Searle and Daniel Dennett. For we would have to accept a homunculus (Searle 1992) or a central meaner (Dennett 1991) who would have to make sense of the representations inside our minds, and then another homunculus/central meaner on top of them, and so on (Dennett 1991: 264 ff.; Searle 1992: 212 ff.). There must be other ways to accommodate meaning.

In the framework of Luhmann's social theory, we must take the discourse to be systematically dissociated from the speaker's and hearer's consciousness. For him, 'society is a system that is closed in terms of communication. It generates communication through communication' (Luhmann 1998: 95). Of course, 'all communication [i.e. the discourse] is structurally linked to consciousness' (Luhmann 1998: 103). But it is only language that 'enables a structural link between systems of consciousness and systems of communication' (Luhmann 1998: 108).

In spoken language situations speaker, hearer, situational setting and social structure are inexorably intertwined. In the case of unrecorded spoken language it would be impossible to dissociate what is being said from the situation in which it is said. It would be impossible to exclude the speaker from the analysis. But in the case of written language it is the meaning of the text, not the speaker's intention that counts. For its inter-pretation, the text is disconnected from its speaker. The author's intentions are irrelevant for the meaning of a text. This is why, in my view, corpus linguistics should exclude the speaker and his or her intentions from its scope. Paul Ricoeur has said this a long time ago:

> Inscription becomes synonymous with the semantic autonomy of the text, which results from the disconnection of the mental intention of the author from the verbal meaning of the text, of what the author meant and what the text means. What the text means now matters more than what the author meant when he wrote it.
>
> (Ricoeur 1976: 29)

As John B. Thompson interprets Ricoeur's approach to hermeneutics, the exclusion of the author's presumed intentions from the interpretation of a text does not imply the reader's suspension of 'any judgement concern-ing the referential dimension of the text, treating the latter as a wholly worldless and self-enclosed entity'. Rather, the reader is asked to 'seek to unfold the non-ostensive references of the text' (Ricoeur 1981: 14). Yet as I see it, these cannot be references to some discourse-external reality (as in spoken language) but to other texts of the discourse, namely those texts to which the text in question is a response. The two modes are, it seems to me, incompatible, and they also signify the key difference between spoken and written language. When someone tells me there are five apples on a tree, the Gricean maxims suggest that the speaker's intentions are to make a statement that he or she considers true, referring to a reality out there. When I find a written text telling me that there are five apples on a tree, my interpretative task is to find out which role this text has in the discourse in which it occurs, i.e. to which texts it can be seen as a response, and to reconstruct its meaning from that analysis. For written language, the issue is meaning, not truth.

It makes little sense to talk about a discourse of unrecorded spoken language, because the utterances of such a discourse are not accessible for an investigation of meaning. The division between spoken and written is not absolute, though. I can, in spoken as well as in written language, report something someone else has said. But in the British judicial system, such evidence would be inadmissible as hearsay. If the utterance I report is not available as a text of the discourse, independently of my report, then what I say cannot be established as true or false. Court proceedings are conducted orally, because truth, not meaning is at stake. Spoken and written language are two different things.

Roy Harris proposes a programme of 'integrational linguistics'. To understand the creative process that language is we have to view it as a part of human interaction that is based on the cotemporality of the world outside of a speaker, a world that includes my audience, their non-linguistic behaviour, the situational setting in which an interaction takes place, and his or her memories, knowledge of the world and powers of reasoning. This might well be a programme that can deal with (recorded) spoken language, as long as all these other data are available for analysis. Such an approach might help to explain the 'all-pervasive – and perhaps only authentic – characteristic of the individual's involvement in language' and 'would provide an account of linguistic experience' (Harris 1987: 164). Would it, really? How can I ever be sure that what I have described is somebody's linguistic experience, given the inaccessibility of any kind of first-person experience?

Three conclusions can be drawn. One is that we should refrain from endeavouring to describe people's linguistic experiences. The other is that, as long as it is impossible to record all the other data that are inexorably part of oral interactions, including memories, knowledge of the world and reasoning powers, any integrational approach, as attractive as it seems, will have to be severely limited. The third is that oral interaction, spoken language, cannot be dealt with by the kind of linguistics we have today. Let us take the key example for dealing with the pragmatics component of linguistics, as found right at the beginning of Jenny Thomas' introduction to pragmatics *Meaning and Interaction* (Thomas 1995: 1): 'It's hot in here.'

Conventional linguistic wisdom has it that if the speaker of this utterance is a person of authority in a room with windows shut in which the air had become hot and sticky, and if the audience consists of people in awe of the speaker, then the speaker probably intends with his utterance that one of the hearers opens the window. The intentions of the speaker can be gleaned by a perusal of the segment of reality in reach of this group of people (hot air, windows closed, no air conditioning), by memories of situations comparable to the one given, and by appropriate inferences on part of the hearers. Often, when we talk about pragmatics, we talk about situations like these in which apparently the speaker's intentions are not clearly expressed but hidden behind a rather inconspicuous remark. To reveal the 'true' meaning it would take an integrational approach. Or would it?

Instead of carrying out an integrational analysis of the utterance and the situation in which it occurs, we can try to query the discourse for the meaning of this utterance. For the speaker did not come up with his or her utterance on a *tabula rasa*. He or she was making a contribution to a discourse which had been going on for thousands of years, in plenty of languages all over the globe. What he or she said has to be interpreted on the foil of this discourse. The utterance has been made countless times before. Google, on 27 November 2006, finds 58,800 occurrences of 'It's hot in here'. If we add to our query the words *window* and *open*, we still find 10,800 hits. That tells us that in 20 per cent of all cases when someone says *it's hot in here*, there is also talk about opening a window. There is even a webpage (www.openthewindow.blogspot.com/) which is named 'open the window . . . because it's hot in here'. Typical are text segments like this one 'It's hot in here. It's unbearably stuffy. Please open the window!', found on this webpage: www.jewishworldreview.com/hillel/goldberg_2004_03_25.php3.

The example shows that once we restrict the investigation of meaning to written discourses there is an alternative to a pragmatic or integrational approach. The (written) discourse can tell us all we need to know about the possible implications of a simple sentence such as *It's hot in here*. The discourse opens an escape route from the realization that it is, at least for the linguist, impossible to determine all the relevant conditions, such as communicational setting, memory, analogy, comparability, the ways in which we reason and draw inferences. For it is the discourse that has taught us the relevance of all these conditions. I do not wish to imply that it is impossible to intuitively open the window when someone complains about the temperature of a room, without ever having encountered this connection in the discourse before. But that would be beginner's luck. It is the discourse that tells us what a discourse community accepts as rational behaviour, not so much in abstract terms but in an infinity of examples. It is these examples that we find in the discourse which inform our conceptualization of rational behaviour, not the other way around. Most of this discourse that is responsible for our priming (see Michael Hoey's chapters in this book) will consist of spoken language, and therefore it will be lost for linguistic investigations. But fortunately the discourse of recorded (written) texts is so vast that it amply makes up for this loss. In the end, it is always the discourse where we, as linguists, can find out what texts, or segments of texts mean.

When it comes to making sense of written language we can even more easily do without the discourse-external reality. The external reality and the reality constructed in the discourse are only related to each other through our first-person experiences. This link is more visible in oral communication. The apple that is talked about may be the apple we see hanging from a tree. What is being said is embedded in a situational setting, and deixis and ostentation help us to relate what we hear to our sensory perceptions and experiences. But what we see also depends on what has been said. How do we know that angels have wings? Is it because we have seen them in paintings, stained-glass windows and sculptures with their wings? But how then did the first artists who painted angels know that they had to paint them with wings? They were led to assume that they must have wings, just as other beings able to fly are equipped with them. It is Daniel 9:21 where we find the textual source telling us that angels indeed can fly:

> While I was still speaking in prayer, the man Gabriel, whom I saw in the vision at first, approached me in swift flight about the time of the evening offering.

All conceptualizations of the visible (or audible or tangible) world are textual. We could not tell an apple from a pear if the difference of the two concepts had not, at some stage, been explained to us. There are cultures who lack the concept of winged angels, and there are languages like Italian which force us to distinguish between *blu, azzurro* and *celeste*. For people whose native language is English, *blu, azzurro* and *celeste* are all *blue*. For Italians, they are different concepts. But there is apparently also a Mayan language which does not distinguish between blue and green (Levinson 1997: 22). It is not because Italians and these Mayan people live in a different reality. All there is to it is that they are part of different discourse communities. For by and large, we experience only what is already conceptualized in the discourse. Nobody would ever dream of falling in love if they had not heard that this is commonly done and that it is largely fun. The reality that we can turn into our own personal experience is a reality that has been constructed socially, a reality that has been conceptualized in the discourse. We can easily participate in the discourse even if we have never seen an apple or a painting of a winged angel, if we ourselves do not take part in baptisms or cannot remember having been in love. Language dissociated from deixis and ostentation poses no problem for us. We do not need to see angels to be fascinated by them. It is quite enough if we have read about them. We understand stories about angels because what we are told ties in with innumerable other snippets we have been told before. Angels are constructs of the English and other related discourses. Whether there is a discourse-external reality in which we would find winged angels is of no importance.

The discourse, the recorded or written discourse in particular, is the manifestation of language. But what is language? Does it help to look at the discourse-external reality to find out what language is? I do not think so. 'Language' is an abstraction, a reification, a hypostasation, of ideas devoid of a visual image. Language is less 'real' than facial expressions or gestures. Yet we do not have a word for communication by gestures. It was only with the invention of writing, the invention of material signs, that language became a discourse object, something that became a topic one could talk about. Language is, like the discourse object 'angel', a construct, an object that has been constructed in and through the (mostly) texts that have been contributed to the discourse. In oral societies with little or no contact to literate societies it is a social practice that people are mostly unaware of. In an oral society, people do not talk about language. The anthropologist Jack Goody believes that most oral societies do not even have a word for what we call a word (Goody 1987: 274). But what about the people who interpret what a member of another tribe says in their own language? Surely they must have a concept of what (a) language is? I do not believe that this must necessarily be the case. Children growing up bilingually will have no problem in choosing the appropriate language without being aware that what they are doing is switching from one language into another. They are expressing their intentions, unaware that they are using (a) language. In

oral societies people believe that what is being said are the speaker's intentions. This is what hearers are interested in. Speaking and hearing is
simultaneous, as Harris says 'cotemporary'. The discourse-external reality is
within sight of what is said. The discourse of oral societies deals with concrete things. There is little venture into abstraction. People are just not
interested in reflections on how things are connected on a metaphysical
level. For them, such thoughts would make no sense. As it would be impossible to preserve the fruits of such reflections for future use, every effort
spent on them would prove ill-spent. IQ tests, as we know them, would be
totally inapplicable to people living in oral societies. Even simple syllogisms
are beyond comprehension (Luria 1976: 102 ff.). Apparently not even the
confrontation with other discourse communities, with people speaking a
different language, leads to an awareness of language. Rather these out-
siders are described as barbarians, i.e. as people who just babble, or as mute
people (e.g. the Czech expressions for 'German': *Němec* and for 'mute':
němý), or as foreigners (English *Welsh*, German *welsch*), that is a people
outside of our community. Oral societies do not know schools, philosophy
or linguistics.

In an oral society the thought that language is symbolic, a system of signs,
is inconceivable. A sign always is something material, something that has
form in addition to having content. Spoken language is a transient phenomenon; it seems immaterial. The idea that an utterance can have a
meaning independently of the speaker's intentions is unimaginable in an
oral society. To understand language as a symbolic system presupposes lit-
erality. Metaphors cannot be recognized as such, because here a word or a
phrase stands for some other word or phrase. As long as meaning is only
thought of as the speaker's intentions, a concept of metaphor cannot exist.

Deixis is the sustenance of spoken language. Whatever the speaker wants
to say must be applicable to a concrete situation, must be amalgamated into
a first-person experience by the hearer, and must be available as an item to
be remembered. Discourse objects which cannot be turned into a lifeworld
experience (for instance, the existence of angels) must have the form of a
myth, must be unreal, ahistorical, but iterable. That these stories can always
be told in the same way is only possible if they make sense to the narrator, if
he or she can tie them to their first-person experiences. A society without
writing has a collective memory only in a limited way. Instead of history as
a discourse object, always connected to the idea of change and development, there is only the presence of the eternal same, linked with the regular recurrence of lunar phases, of the seasons, of years and generations.
Instead of history we find timeless myths. The discourse of an oral society
has a diachronic dimension only to the extent that something that has been
said becomes a re-usable formulaic expression. Under normal circumstances, however, it will be impossible to compare something said just now
to what has been said days, months or years ago.

Once a society becomes literate, the immediacy of speech becomes back-
grounded. Writing is, unlike speech, not an event in which the hearer/

reader takes part. Normally, the reader is not present in the act of writing. For the readers, what is said is not any more embedded in a situational setting shared with the writer, and intonation, gestures and facial expressions have become inaccessible. The link of what is said with some discourse-external reality, tenuous as it always was, has now fully been lost. Without deixis, without ostentation, language ceases to refer to the world outside and can be only understood in relationship to what else is said in the discourse. It becomes auto-referential. The discourse, the entirety of all that has been exchanged, in form of verbal utterances, between the members of a discourse community, constructs a reality of its own. What is being said or written now refers to texts that have been written before, by the same writer or by someone else. Thus a dissociation is created which is absent from speech, and which can only be overcome by the reader in a conscious act of appropriation (Ricoeur 1981: 143). If I want to understand what is written I have to actively convert it into first-person experiences, by supplying, from memory and through analogy, applicable and comparable situations. Every abstraction I find in the text will increase my distance from experience. The more literate a society is, the more abstraction we find. Instead of narration we find increasingly contemplation and argumentation, until in the end we become unable to supply or generate first-person experiences relating to what we have read. Philosophical and theological texts are good examples. They alienate the reader from their concrete lifeworld. Instead, such a discourse generates its own objects, constructs such as family, childhood, religion, school, nation, depression, beauty, property, work and language. Even to the extent these discourse objects become reified as social institutions, these institutions remain discursive constructs and draw their meaning only from the discourse (Berger and Luckmann 1980; a contrary view is offered by Searle 1995). The discourse is self-referential. What any discourse object means is the result of a dialogue, of negotiations inside the discourse. It is only after we have accepted these discourse constructs that we begin to believe that we can observe them in the discourse-external reality. What constitutes a family, for instance, has little to do with a discourse-external reality. It is a social construct, and it is far from universal. Even where it exists, the concept of a family has undergone and is undergoing constant change, and it tends to mean different things in different cultures.

Once the members of the discourse community have learned the concept, or discourse object 'family', they will understand it and be able to apply it whenever they encounter it; and as long as they use it, in their contributions to the discourse, in ways similar to those in which it has been normally used, they will be understood. The kind of first-person experience the encounter with the concept 'family' evokes for someone is something we cannot know. The testimony people might give us of their private understanding of 'family' can never be a full mirror of what they feel. Qualia cannot be communicated.

Linguists have to rely on real language data; they have nothing but the discourse, understood as the communication, past and present, between the members of the discourse community. In my view, any new text entered into the discourse should not be viewed as an intentional act of creation. Rather, it should be explained as a recombination or permutation of text segments already found in previous texts, plus, possibly, some new text segments (neologisms). This view presupposes, though, that we have to explore the diachronic dimension of a discourse. Indeed, by disregarding the intentionalities of the members of the discourse community, we can take the view that the discourse is an autopoietic system, a system that reproduces itself by continually generating new texts. Thus the discourse keeps changing its state. However, not all new texts cause a change. Only those to whom subsequent texts refer do. Many of the texts that have entered the discourse never leave any trace in subsequent texts. Many articles in newspapers (or in academic journals) are never mentioned again. But a speech by the Pope, however select its audience may be, can have wide repercussions. Such texts contribute to the discursive construction of reality. What they contribute are, from a formal perspective, the traces they leave in subsequent texts: quotes, similar text segments, comments, modifications, even rejections.

The discourse is language as a concrete object. It is, in the sense of Ferdinand de Saussure, *la parole*. While *la langue*, the language system, remains, of necessity, an object of speculation, it is only the discourse that can be empirically analysed. Thus the prime object of corpus linguistics is, in my view, *la parole*. This sets it apart from most of the paradigms that have dominated the discipline of linguistics in the twentieth century, structural linguistics on both sides of the Atlantic, generative transformational grammar with all its revisions, and cognitive linguistics.

3 Meaning is in the discourse

Ferdinand de Saussure has taught us that the linguistic symbol, for de Saussure normally the word, for me any text or text segment that can be analysed as a unit of meaning, can be viewed under two aspects: form and meaning. These two aspects are inseparable. A form can only be a sign if it has a meaning. There is no content unless it is represented. This is what makes thoughts so elusive. Only when they have been expressed they become tangible. We can also look at it the other way around. Only what has a form and a meaning can function as a text or a text segment. A text or text segment has a meaning. So what are we actually looking for if we ask for the meaning of a text? A text means what it means. When we ask for its meaning, we are not looking for such a tautology, but for something more. What we are expecting as a response is something else: an explication, a summary, a paraphrase. Let us take the text segment *weapons of mass destruction*. It is a linguistic sign, and we can look at it from the perspectives of form and of meaning. It means what it means. But not all members of our discourse community may feel sure they know what it means. If they ask us for its meaning, they want to have some kind of explanation, maybe even a definition of the kind we would find in a dictionary.

In traditional lexicographic theory, a dictionary definition consists of two parts. The first part is the *genus proximum*, what is called the hyponym in modern lexicology, and the *differentia specifica*, i.e. what is specific to this particular concept and separates it from its co-hyponyms. The structuralist concept of meaning is rather similar. The meaning of the word is what makes it different from all other words. A possible dictionary definition is: 'Weapons of mass destruction are nuclear, biological, or chemical weapons with a capacity to inflict death and destruction on a massive scale.' Does such a definition give us the full meaning of the lexical item? Is this what we are looking for if we ask for an explanation of the concept of 'weapons of mass destruction'? Again, I think, we have to distinguish *langue*-linguistics from *parole*-linguistics. A dictionary definition should ideally be a generalization of the meaning of a given lexical item. It should describe the lexical item as a type, as a common denominator of all the different occurrences, the tokens, which it represents. It should be compatible with all (or most of the) occurrences of the item in the discourse. But such a definition does not capture what a particular occurrence of this lexical item means. Every occurrence makes its own contribution to the whole meaning. We have to analyse it therefore not just as a token of a generalized type, but also as a unique event, differing from all other occurrences. It is up to *parole*-linguistics to find out what this particular contribution is. I have to analyse it as a part of an ongoing negotiation of the meaning of the discourse object 'weapons of mass destruction'.

Discourse objects are social constructs, independently of the issue whether such an object exists in the discourse-external reality. A discourse object is constituted by all that has been said about it. This means we have to give up the traditional distinction between lexical meaning (what I find in the dictionary entry) and encyclopedic meaning (what I would find in an encyclopedia). From the perspective of corpus linguistics, all that has been said about this discourse object contributes towards its meaning (Teubert 2001). Innumerable texts have talked about weapons of mass destruction. Some of these things have been said time and again. There are, in Google, 275,000 hits for *Iraqi weapons of mass destruction*, but only 178 hits for *American weapons of mass destruction*. Of course, nothing can keep me from talking about American weapons of mass destruction. However, my chances of being referred to in subsequent texts seem to be much smaller than if I had talked about Iraqi weapons of mass destruction. Thus for the meaning of this discourse object the connection with Iraq seems to be more relevant than the one with America. There are, as Google shows, many other things that can be said about this discourse object. Among the first ten hits we find:

Iraq's **weapons of mass destruction are** in breach of international law

weapons of mass destruction are overrated as a threat to America

Iraq's **weapons of mass destruction are** controlled by a murderous tyrant

weapons of mass destruction are fundamentally different from other threats to peace

'weapons of mass destruction' are to George W. Bush what fairies were to Peter Pan

weapons of mass destruction are either nuclear, biological, or chemical weapons

weapons of mass destruction are especially abhorrent to the conscience of humanity

weapons of mass destruction are a threat to our national security

what we refer to as **'weapons of mass destruction' are** actually not very destructive

All these statements can be taken as paraphrases that tell us something about the discourse object. The question is not whether they are true, i.e. whether they correspond to what we find in a discourse-external reality. The question is how *weapons of mass destruction* are being discussed.

To repeat it yet again, from a corpus linguistics perspective, meaning has nothing to do with reference to the discourse-external reality, and it also is less part of the language system than of *parole*, of the discourse. As soon as we accept this idea, the distinction between lexical meaning and encyclopedic meaning vanishes. When I explain what *weapons of mass destruction* are I have also defined the lexical item *weapons of mass destruction*. This is what distinguishes natural languages from all other codes or formal languages, like programming languages or the calculus of mathematics or of logic. Natural languages are self-referential. We use the English language to talk about the English language. But we need a language to explain what mathematical operations mean. The meaning of mathematical and logical symbols cannot be explained in the calculus of mathematics or logic. But when we want to explain the meaning of an English lexical item we use the English language. Paraphrasing lexical items is tantamount to explaining discourse objects. Such paraphrases do not belong to some 'metalanguage'; they are part of language itself. Only the pedantry of the nineteenth century makes us want to use quotation marks, inverted commas and italics in vain attempts to separate object language from meta-language as in two of the examples quoted above.

'The word water means,' Hilary Putnam kept saying, while he still thought of himself as a metaphysical realist, 'what water really is.' For the Hilary Putnam of 'The Meaning of Meaning' (1975), meaning was reference. This is the common stance of analytic philosophy. But we might ask ourselves how many of the discourse objects we constantly mention and talk about in our contributions to the discourse really have their equivalents in the discourse-external reality. American structural linguistics had come to the same conclusion a generation earlier. In his book *Language*, Leonard Bloomfield identifies the meaning of a word with the scientific concept of the 'real' object for which it stands:

> We can define the meaning of a speech-form accurately when this meaning has to do with some matter of which we possess scientific knowledge. We can define the names of minerals, for example, in terms of chemistry and mineralogy, as when we say that the ordinary meaning of the English word *salt* is 'sodium chloride (NaCl)', and we can define the names of plants or animals by means of the technical terms of botany or zoology, but we have no precise way of defining *love* or *hate*, which concern situations that have not been accurately classified – and these latter are in the great majority.
>
> (Bloomfield 1933: 139)

To the remit of which science belong the concepts of love and hate? They are discourse constructs as much as the angels I have discussed above. Having read Odell Shepard's book *The Lore of the Unicorn* (1993), I am sure I know a lot more about unicorns than about rhinos, even though unicorns seem to be less real than the other species. It is true that we can see rhinos in the zoo, or perhaps even in Africa, and that there is no zoo featuring unicorns. Unicorns and Iraqi weapons of mass destruction are discourse objects, and most would agree that they do not refer to any discourse-external reality. But at least tigers are real, are they not? We can inspect them in zoos and in Asia, perhaps even in Africa. Yet a lot of what we know about tigers we have not learnt from inspection. For instance the discourse tells us that they are bold. What endears a tiger, but not a hyena, to us? Is it what we can observe in the safari park? Or is it something we have heard about them? Apart from a visual image, there is hardly anything we would gather from inspecting tigers that we would not find in the discourse.

What linguistic signs, words, lexical items, more or less fixed expressions, text segments or even full texts mean is what we can learn about them in the discourse. This is the way we learn about the meaning of new discourse objects. We know what *globalization* means because mass media keep us constantly informed. A Google query on 13 July 2006 brings up approximately 135,000 hits for *globalisation/globalization means*, among the first 20 of them these examples:

globalization means diversity

business-driven **globalization means** uprooting old ways of life and threatening livelihoods and cultures

globalization means people, information, and money can travel further and faster than ever before

Globalization Means Oil and War

globalization means 'borders don't matter anymore'

true **globalisation means** businesses decide how to run their businesses with less heed to national borders than in the past loosely defined, **globalisation means** that the world is becoming compressed into "a single space"

Globalisation Means Opportunities

Globalisation means that events elsewhere have a direct impact at home

GLOBALISATION MEANS JOB LOSSES FOR UNIONISED LABOUR

Everything said about a discourse object becomes part of its meaning once it is taken into account. For if it is taken into account this means that it will have left a trace in a subsequent text. But if this is what I call, from a corpus linguistics perspective, meaning, then the full meaning of a discourse object is always provisional. Every new occurrence of *globalisation* will add something to its meaning, either by repeating what has been said or by actually saying something new.

Meaning is what has been said about a lexical item, a more or less fixed expression, or any text segment that has been talked about. Meaning, seen in this way, is in the discourse. We can retrieve it by looking at the paraphrases, the things people say about discourse objects. This is what I call interpretation. If we attempt an interpretation of a lexical item such as *globalisation*, we aim at a condensation of the meaning. No interpretation is ever complete. It never can be more than an approximation. Nobody in their sane mind would actually scan through the 135,000 citations Google comes up with for *globalisation/globalization means*. The verb form *means* is, of course, only one of a sheer endless list of devices signalling a paraphrase. It does not render more than the tip of the iceberg. Google lists around 2.4 million occurrences for *globalisation/globalization is*. Not all paraphrase devices are obvious. In many cases we will not find a signal that tells 'Here is a paraphrase.' In the end, it is up to the researcher to interpret any citation of a unit of meaning as a paraphrase. Thus the sentence (also found on the internet):

> it is both **false** and futile to pretend that alternatives to **globalisation** do not exist

informs us that globalization is perhaps not as unavoidable as global warming. It is, the discourse tells us, a contingent state of the world, and alternatives exist. What I want to show is that no interpretation can possibly be complete. Interpretation is not the same as understanding. Understanding is the individual mental appropriation of a lexical item, a text segment or a text. It implies the generation of a corresponding first-person experience, something to which other people cannot have access. Interpretation, on the other hand, is a social, a dialogic activity, in the Bakhtinian sense. It is the production of a text that will be submitted to the discourse. When I attempt to interpret a lexical item, I want others to agree with me. It would be stupid to put forward an interpretation that I know would be unacceptable to my peer group. This makes an interpretation something different from someone's individual understanding. The rules, the laws, the mechanisms, the procedures invoked to bring about an interpretation are not outside of the discourse. They may be invoked by a subsequent text claiming my interpretation is flawed because it violated a rule. As such, one interpretation is as good as another. Once my interpretation is submitted to the discourse, it becomes a text like all the other texts of the discourse; it will become a paraphrase. If subsequent interpretations of the lexical item in question will refer to it more than to other paraphrases, it will have been successful. If no other text ever refers to it (or if it is rejected), something went wrong. This is what *parole*-linguistics can investigate, but not how such an interpretation is produced by a mental mechanism. The language system is conceived of as something fixed and rule-governed. But when it comes to meaning, there seem to be few rules determining what can be said and what not. The language system, in form of a dictionary definition, tells us that a tiger is a 'very large solitary cat with a yellow-brown coat striped with black'. The discourse, however, is full of surprises. While Google knows 1.3 million citations for the co-occurrence of *tigers* and *stripes*, such as:

> No one knows exactly why **tigers** are striped, but scientists think that the **stripes** act as camouflage.

we also find an impressive number of 255 hits for *tigers* combined with *without stripes*, such as:

> The existence of black **tigers without stripes** has been reported, but has never been substantiated by specimens or photographs. White **tigers without stripes** also exist but are much rarer. These **tigers** are not albinos as they do not have pink eyes.

> The only wild report to be documented was of a '**tiger without stripes**' at Similpal **Tiger** Reserve.

The possible existence of tigers without stripes is perhaps not an important aspect of the meaning of the discourse object 'tiger'. But it shows us how limiting and limited the structuralist view of lexical meaning is. What can the language system tell us about the meanings of words or phrases, once we look at occurrences as unique events?

Meaning is accessible only to the extent that the discourse is recorded and archived. What has been said but subsequently lost without leaving traces is forever lost. Nobody has access to even the archived part of a discourse. Therefore the object of our study is hardly ever the full discourse, the complete compilation of all the texts that fulfil the parameters that we have set up. What we normally work with is a corpus which we claim to be a cross-section, a sample, a balanced representation of the discourse. It contains the texts that could be assembled within the restrictions of a given research project. Such a limitation is not without problems. By having to rely on a limited set of texts rather than on all the texts fulfilling our criteria, we lose a possibly critical amount of intertextual links. A parallel study, using the same discourse parameters but as its corpus a different selection of texts, may end up with strikingly different results. However, in rare cases it is possible to define the discourse in such a way that we actually can compile all the texts in our corpus, so that discourse and corpus are co-extensive. For my exemplification of diachronic corpus linguistics in Chapter 4 I have chosen such an example.

The unavoidable shortcomings of working with corpora are similar to our individual situations as members of a discourse community. Each of us has only their own limited perspective of the meaning of a lexical item. If different perspectives clash, we have to compare our data basis in a dialogic interaction. I have to accept the evidence of my dialogue partners, and they have to accept mine. Then we can negotiate an interpretation acceptable to all of us. It is important to bear in mind, though, that such an agreement is always provisional, due to the diachronic dimension of the discourse. The interpretation we reach today concerning the meaning of the discourse objects 'weapons of mass destruction', 'globalization' or 'tigers' becomes part of the discourse itself. Subsequent texts may refer to it, accepting, modifying or rejecting it. Every paraphrase can engender a new paraphrase. Meanings are never stable.

4 What is the discourse?

There are few linguistic terms used for a wider variety of concepts than the rather ubiquitous label 'discourse'. For some linguists, discourse refers only to spoken communication. For critical discourse analysts, discourse is not an archive of texts but a practice. In this section, I want to explain what discourse means for my way of looking at language. My usage of this term is indebted and, in some ways, related to the way Michel Foucault uses it. How, then, does my concept of discourse differ from his? For me, the discourse is the entirety of all the utterances of a discourse community. But what is the discourse community? In its widest sense, it is the community of all those who have contributed and are contributing, through their utterances, to the global discourse, ever since mankind began contributing utterances to the discourse. This is the global discourse community, and the discourse that they have been producing I call the discourse at large. Most of this discourse has vanished. What has been spoken, and was not recorded (or remembered and later written down) has disappeared as soon as it was uttered. Probably most of what has been written has disappeared as well. Tons of papyrus scrolls have been lost forever. The contents of the library of Alexandria has been used as heating fuel, as Luciano Canfora believes (Canfora 1991). Day after day people commit sheaves of paper to their waste-paper basket. But even the tiny fraction of what is left is by far too large for perusal. It is literally impossible to collect all the texts that have been written, or otherwise recorded, on the day Queen Victoria was crowned. Nobody would waste the time and the money to collect all these texts from archives, libraries, attics, or wherever people store texts all over the world. The complete surviving discourse is much too amorphous and gigantic that it could be made the object of analysis.

As this discourse, the discourse at large, is beyond our reach, we will have to accept that we will never be able to grasp the full meaning of any discourse object. This might be one of the reasons why many linguists have come to prefer the language system to *la parole*. But to substitute some equally elusive abstraction, or, as cognitive linguists suggest, inaccessible mental concepts, for real language data, is not a convincing answer to our problem. The conceptual representation of a lexical item people find or generate in their minds (if only it were accessible) could tell us about their private understanding, it would not tell us about its meaning, as I see it, for meaning is a social, not a psychological, construct. The meanings of lexical items are in the discourse. But this discourse at large is as boundless as the heaven above us. How, then, can we find a solution to the meaning problem?

I think we have to accept that we have to break down the discourse at large into smaller, more manageable lumps. These lumps do not exist as such. Linguists do not discover them. They invent them. The discourses we are investigating are not natural entities but linguistic (or sociological) constructs. Instead of one global discourse, there is a virtual infinity of them. For each research question, a researcher is at liberty to define the discourse from which she or he expects to extract the answer. This is not a solution that all linguists would embrace. To accept that a discourse we are analysing is an arbitrary, contingent and artificial construct would invalidate, for many researchers, the whole concept. How reliable would results be obtained from a collection of texts reflecting the subjectivity of the compiler?

For Michel Foucault, such a solution was out of the question. Foucault, however, did not see himself as a linguist. The paradigms of linguistics he was aware of were structuralism as inspired by de Saussure and Chomskyan linguistics as advertised by Claude Lévi-Strauss, it was the linguistics of the language system. Even though he purposefully disregarded the linguistic form of his discourses, he saw them as real objects, objects comparable to the artefacts digged up by archaeologists. But for Foucault, a discourse is more, it is also a formation formed according to principles. Whether a given text belongs to a given discourse depends on its being covered by the rules underlying this discourse. In his view, there has to be a set of research-independent regularities that pertain to what he calls a discursive formation, and not the arbitrary decisions of the researcher that makes a discourse a discourse:

> If I succeed in showing, as I shall do shortly, that the law of such a series [a group of acts of formulations is precisely what I have called so far a *discursive formation*, if I succeed in showing that this discursive formation really is the principle of dispersion and redistribution, not of formulations, not of propositions, but of statements (in the sense in which I used this word) the term discourse can be defined as the group of statements that belong to a single system of formation.
>
> (Foucault 1972: 107, emphasis in the original)

This is repeated some pages later: 'Now, what has been described as discursive formations are, strictly speaking, groups of statements' (Foucault 1972: 115). What binds these groups of statements together had already been explained. It is a law. In order to find out what binds the statements of nineteenth-century doctors together, 'we must first discover the law operating behind all these diverse statements' (Foucault 1972: 50). The identity of the discourse is established by a law, by regularities, by a set of rules operating in the texts belonging to a given discourse. This is a theme repeated countless times in the *Archaeology of Knowledge*. Another example is: '[The] "discursive practice" . . . is a body of anonymous, historical rules, always determined in the time and the space that have defined a given period, and for a given social, economic, geographical, or linguistic area, the conditions of operation of the enunciative function' (Foucault 1972: 117). The final goal of the discourse researcher is to write the archaeology of a given discourse. 'Archaeology . . . is to uncover the regularity of a discursive practice' (Foucault 1972: 144).

For Foucault, the discourse therefore is not a theoretical construct but a real-world entity whose identity rests on laws, rules and regularities. The question he does not address in a straightforward way is the nature of these principles. Are they, as the word *law* would imply, comparable to the immutable laws of nature, such as the famous second law of thermodynamics? Are they rules instituted by social convention, be it explicit or implicit? Are they maxims each member of a discourse society has to follow out of a moral obligation? 'The rules of the formation [of a text]', he says, operate not only in the mind or consciousness of individuals, but in the discourse itself; they operate . . . 'on all individuals who undertake to speak in this discursive field' (Foucault 1972: 63). For me, this sentence is more an obfuscation than a clarification.

Foucault was writing at a time in which, in his terminology a 'discourse rupture' took place. In French intellectual circles, particularly in the *Tel Quel* grouping, the former fascination with structuralism was increasingly clashing with the rediscovered charms of hermeneutics and the kick-off of post-structuralism. For reasons for which we perhaps have to search in Foucault's biography, he was vitally attracted to the concept of order in the chaos of reality, to the quest for some Archimedean point which would distinguish necessity from contingency. He was repelled equally by de Saussurean structuralist and by Chomskyan mentalist linguistics which, in his view, could contribute nothing to the interpretation of past discourses. Therefore he insists that his discursive formations are not analysable by linguistic methods. Yet he also insists on retaining the structuralist obsession with the concept of a language system, only that for him it is the discourse, rather than the language, which he hypostasizes as a system. While the whole point of his enterprise is to use discourses for the interpretation of the thought archives of the past, he does not establish them as emanations of *la parole*, but of a system based on rules. Hermeneutics, however, the art of interpretation, deals with the text, or the text segment, as a unique occurrence, as something that has been said in a certain way even though it could have been said differently. Thus Foucault's approach leads him, in the end, into a cul-de-sac. He is, in all his writing, unable to give us a clear example of what the laws, rules and regularities are that establish the identity of a discursive formation.

Of course it is true that the aim is to establish, in our endeavour to interpret what has been and is being said, discourses that serve this purpose. If I want to find out what can be said and what not in contemporary British applied linguistics, my corpus should contain texts from this field. Some texts (for instance those published in the journal *Applied Linguistics*) will be more relevant than others (e.g. essays written by undergraduate students). While it is unproblematic to find out what all these texts talk about, it is much more challenging to say what they cannot be about. Is there a deeper reason why we cannot find, in *Applied Linguistics*, texts extolling the virtues of corpus linguistics? Are corpus linguistics and applied linguistics logically incompatible? Have the editors decreed that corpus linguistics can have no relevant place in applied linguistics? Are the articles submitted by corpus linguists regularly inferior to those submitted by applied linguists? What tells me whether a statement such as 'Corpus linguistics is the very core of applied linguistics' is a violation of a law, a rule or a regularity? If, however, I were to find such a statement in a text of my applied linguistics corpus, is my corpus then not a true reflection of the applied linguistics discourse? Perhaps not every text published in *Applied Linguistics* belongs to the discourse of applied linguistics? Or have we misread the rules that govern this discourse? How can we be sure about the laws, rules and regularities of discursive formations? Hermeneutics is about interpreting texts, about interpreting what has been said, about *la parole*. Laws and rules are about language systems, about what can be said and what not. The two perspectives are irreconcilable.

A discourse that can be made the object of a linguistic (or a sociological) investigation is a construct. It is up to the researcher to delimit and define the discourse(s), i.e. the collection of texts in which they investigate certain phenomena. The peer community, i.e. the community to which the researcher belongs (i.e. language studies people), must be made aware of the parameters that define a given discourse. Such parameters are, for instance, a language, an area, a time slice, a genre, a domain, the availability of a text in printed or electronic form, the number of copies published, audience data or the occurrence of (or saturation with) certain keywords (Teubert 2005). Such a discourse might consist of all the texts written in English, dealing with arranged and forced marriages, published in British national quality newspapers in the year 2006, addressing a Middle England audience and containing at least two occurrences of *human rights, Muslim/ Islam(ic/ist)* and *violation.* Being a construct, a discourse does not exist in isolation. Many other texts talk and have talked about arranged and forced marriages, legal texts, cultural history texts, anthropological texts, religious texts and even novels, texts which can be compiled into other discourses.

Investigating one discourse, therefore, does not mean interpreting it by comparing it to social reality itself but by comparing it to all relevant texts outside of the defined discourse. This task is, of, course, impossible. What is it that makes a text relevant? How should we find all these texts? The discourse at large is outside of our methodological grasp. Any such selection will have to be arbitrary. Thus there are two reasons for the limitations of the methodology of corpus linguistics in the framework of hermeneutics. One is the arbitrariness of the discourse that I define. The other is the inexhaustibility of the discourse at large. Any interpretation of a discourse object such as 'arranged/forced marriage' is therefore, of necessity, limited and provisional.

Many years ago, Dietrich Busse and I claimed that the texts belonging to a given discourse have to deal with the object, topic, epistemic complex or concept of the study, are semantically related and share a set of statements, communicative situations, functions and purposes (Busse and Teubert 1994: 14). Today, I would be more reluctant. All these conditions are themselves constructs. It is the researcher who in the end decides whether two texts are semantically linked or share a certain function. The researchers have to negotiate with the members of their discourse community that the discourses they construct are, if arbitrary, at least useful.

5 From the synchronic to the diachronic dimension of the discourse

What we describe as the language system, as *la langue*, is a set of regularities which we have obtained by generalizing individual cases on the basis of those features which are common to all of them. When we generalize, we are not interested in how one occurrence of a linguistic phenomenon had an effect on subsequent occurrences. All occurrences have equal weight in our data pool. This is the synchronic dimension of corpus linguistics. It is the perspective we have to choose if we want to infer the language system from empirical data. This is why Ferdinand de Saussure favoured synchronic over diachronic linguistics. He was not interested in the contingencies of *la parole*. The possibility to use statistical significance for detecting what John Sinclair calls 'regular expressions' has, for a long time, been the main fascination of corpus linguistics (Krishnamurthy 2004). In the meantime, the available methodology for frequency analysis has become rather sophisticated. An impressive toolbox of computer programs is at our disposal. While the generalization of our findings and the systematization of our linguistic knowledge will always be a key task of linguistics, and of corpus linguistics in particular, the synchronic perspective by itself cannot cover fully the phenomenon of meaning. Just as the language system and *la parole* complement each other, synchronic linguistics by itself will never reveal the full picture. It needs to be balanced by the analysis of the diachronic dimension of the discourse (Teubert 2005).

The texts which make up a discourse are not entered into it simultaneously. Whenever a new text is being contributed, we have to understand it as a reaction to something that has been said before, and as a request to comment on it subsequently. In the text *Marxism and the Philosophy of Language*, which claims Valentin Voloshinov as its author but was probably conceived by Mikhail Bakhtin, we find these sentences:

> [T]he monologic utterance is, after all, already an abstraction. . . . Any utterance – the finished, written utterance not excepted – makes response to something and is calculated to be responded to in turn. It is but a link in a continuous chain of speech performances.
>
> (quoted in Holquist 2002: 59)

Each new text repeats to a considerable extent things that have already been said. Text segments, collocations, complex and simple lexical items which were already in use, are being re-combined, permuted, embedded in new contexts and paraphrased in new ways. A new text repeats, accepts, comments, modifies, reinterprets or rejects what is contained in previous texts. That makes it a unique occurrence, something that in some aspects differs from all previous and subsequent occurrences.

Therefore it makes sense to look at the discourse as a sequence of textual contributions. Earlier texts leave their traces in subsequent texts, and later texts refer to previous texts, sometimes explicitly, but more often implicitly. It is the phenomenon of intertextuality that provides the links between the texts. The word and the concept of *intertextuality* is relatively recent. It is attributed to Julia Kristeva, who introduces it in her exegesis of Bakhtin's terms 'dialogue' and 'ambivalence': '[A]ny text is constructed as a mosaic of quotations; any text is the absorption and transformation of another. The notion of *intertextuality* replaces that of *intersubjectivity*' (Kristeva 1986: 39, Kristeva's emphasis). What Kristeva is describing here is the mental process that, in the perception of intertextual links, engenders a communication between the author and the reader. Since the introduction of the new term, it has been used in different ways. 'Intertextuality, as a concept, has a history of different articulations which reflect the distinct historical situations out of which it has emerged' (Allen 2000: 58). As I have no knowledge of intertextuality as a mental phenomenon, I exclude the psychological reading of intertextuality. To some extent, intertextuality is directly observable. Explicit quotations and obvious cases of plagiarism are good examples. But largely it is something that is proposed and argued in the interpretation of a text segment. If I believe that something I find in a text is a trace of a previous text it needs to be negotiated with the peer group to whom the interpretation is addressed. It can be endorsed by some and rejected by others. Intertextuality is, like the concept of the discourse, arbitrary and in the eye of the beholder; it is not an objective parameter.

We can obtain a clearer view of intertextuality if we investigate paraphrases. If someone says what a lexical item means, or if they explain this discourse object (which is, as I have argued above, the same thing) they normally do this on the background of what has already been said about it in other contributions to the discourse. As a *parole*-linguist, I am not

interested why they do this or how they do this; all I can say is that these
links become obvious in an analysis of the discourse in question. While
similarity with earlier occurrences can indicate intertextuality, contradiction can do the same. However, to argue the case for the existence of a
covert link (and to exclude random phenomena), we have to look for more
common features of those texts from which we have taken our citations.
Thus we can assume that when we compare the texts we find on the web
page of British Euro-sceptics they are somehow related to each other and to
those texts in particular which became foundational for the movement,
texts such as Margaret Thatcher's famous speech she gave in Bruges on
20 September 1988. There she said, among other things:

> Europe will be stronger precisely because it has France as France, Spain as Spain,
> Britain as Britain, each with its own customs, traditions and identity. It would be
> folly to try to fit them into some sort of *identikit European* personality.
>   (www.brugesgroup.com/about/index.live, my emphasis)

The collocation *identikit European* apparently did not exist before this
speech. It is rather unusual, and statistically it would be quite improbable
(though not impossible) that it had been invented a second time. Google
(on 18 April 2006) cites 86 occurrences for the collocation (and another
57,000 hits for texts in which both words co-occur). Many of the occurrences are explicit quotations from the speech text; but others use it in new
contexts, sometimes as a kind of Euro-scepticism label, sometimes, too, to
criticize Euro-scepticism, and often to add an ironical twist to a statement.
Here are a few examples:

> Who is trying to create some sort of **Identikit European** personality,
> who are your real targets in that speech?

> Gone were Cardiff's decaying docks, replaced by **identikit European**-
> style waterfront developments.

> There is no '**identikit**' model for structural reform of **European**
> economies.

> The **identikit** of **European** recession is completed by the impoverish-
> ment of families while the remaining cast reads like an **identikit** of
> **European** cinema.

By adding a few more words from the Bruges speech, namely *traditions*,
customs and *identity*, we find an increasing portion of eurosceptic texts:

> Our **identity** as a nation is migrating to the **European** Union and we are
> left empty as a result. . . . its own **customs**, **traditions** and **identity**.

> I would see it as a net loss actually in the **European tradition**, . . . in a
> sort of **identikit** way, in order to try and create a pseudo-**European**
> **identity**, . . .

> superiority and the desire to protect **traditions** are just as easily held by
> those on the . . .

reducing British **identity** to 'some sort of **identikit European** . . .

After all the crowing about the superiority of the **European** social model in the . . .

undermine age old **traditions** and even the intrinsic **identity** of a nation . . .

embrace oral **traditions**, **customs**, languages, . . . We might also stray into the **European** debate as it affects how we feel about losing our **identity**

This shows that intertextuality, defined here as the recurrence of selected keywords, is a useful parameter, in addition to those of time, genre, domain etc., to define discourses. Intertextuality can also be used to gauge the relevance of texts within a discourse. Relevance in this sense is a discourse-internal feature that tells us whether one text is more important than another. It is related to the issue of power as it is frequently discussed in critical discourse analysis studies. A given text within a discourse is more relevant than another if it leaves more traces in subsequent texts. Of course, except in the case of explicit references, it is hard to prove that the recurrence of selected keywords implies that there is such a link. But, as said above, the question whether the author of a text was indeed influenced by the earlier text, whether he is aware of it or not, is outside of our scope. Intertextuality, as I use this concept, only testifies similarities between texts which are not, or not likely, coincidental. In this sense, intertextuality is certainly more crucial than indicators such as the circulation of a text or its audience size which have been used to gauge its relevance. Tabloid texts have a notoriously high circulation, but they are rarely quoted and quickly forgotten. Margaret Thatcher's Bruges speech had a rather small audience. But its impact on the British eurosceptic discourse of today is immense.

6 Hermeneutics and the diachronic dimension of the discourse

The diachronic dimension of a discourse comes into play when we want to find out what a text, a text segment or a lexical item meant in a specific context, at a given time. The meaning of a lexical item is, as I have defined it above, everything that has been said about it up to the moment when the text in which it occurs was entered into the discourse. This definition takes account of all the intertextual links that connect a given occurrence with previous citations. More specifically, it is the entirety of explicit and implicit paraphrases of the lexical equivalent, equivalent with the explanations and description of the discourse object represented by this item. This definition implies that it does not matter whether the members of the discourse community are aware of its meaning. Indeed, due to the limitations in accessing all the relevant data, the full meaning can never be ascertained. This is a definition of meaning that takes refuge neither to mental representations nor to the real world. Meaning, as understood here, is in the discourse and nowhere else. The meaning of a lexical item can be interpreted. Such an interpretation will become another text of the discourse, and it will have an impact on the meaning of the item in question. Interpretations are aimed to generate agreement and thus to leave traces in subsequent texts. They are addressed at an audience of the same or another discourse community in the expectation that they will provoke a reaction. Interpretations therefore are dialogic. An interpretation is always an interpretation for others (Teubert 2003).

Interpreting a text, a text segment or a lexical item is different from understanding it. As I said above, my private understanding of a poem, the way I appropriate it is an experience that is loaded with qualia and cannot be fully communicated. I will never be able to describe to someone else what it means for me. Only by giving verbal testimony of this experience, can I perform a first step from understanding towards interpreting. Understanding is an individual mental act. Understanding does not require verbalization. An interpretation is always expressed verbally. It is a collective activity in that it involves other members of the discourse community as (at least imagined) recipients.

Hermeneutics has its origins in the Reformation. By rejecting the role of tradition in the Catholic Church, the Reformers accepted only the Bible as the authentic word of God. Its meaning, however, was far from obvious. Close reading was seen as a necessity for all Christians. Yet the goal was more than anyone's individual appropriation of the text. It was the attempt to reach an understanding that was shared by all members of the community. Therefore the art of reading the Bible had to be developed into a methodology, the discipline of exegesis. Later, in the eighteenth century, this discipline was taken over by the philologists who wanted to make sense of the multitude of ancient texts then discovered. It was then that hermeneutics replaced, as a label, what had been called (and is still called in theological studies) exegesis. Hermeneutics, in so far it is concerned with language, is concerned with writing. Wilhelm Dilthey explicitly states that it is about the 'interpretation of written testimonies of human life' (quoted in Mueller-Vollmer 1986: 27). This is hardly surprising. Written texts (with few exceptions) do not provide us with the option of asking their author about their intentions. In the words of Paul Ricoeur, 'writing renders the text autonomous with respect to the intention of the author ... The relation between writing and reading is no longer a particular case of the relation between speaking and hearing' (Ricoeur 1981: 139). In the eighteenth and nineteenth centuries, however, under the impact of invention of man as an autonomous, unique person and the ensuing psychologization of human relations, writing was understood as a gateway to the author's inner self. Immanuel Kant apparently was the first to demand that the goal of hermeneutic analysis should be 'to understand the author better than he had understood himself' (quoted in Hermanns 2002: 139). This was taken up famously by Friedrich Schleiermacher who defined the hermeneutic task as 'to understand an utterance first as well and then better than its author' (quoted in Frank 1977: 94) and finally by the philologist August Boeckh: 'The interpreter consequently understands the author better than the author understands himself' (Mueller-Vollmer 1986: 138).

Hermeneutics today, however, is less concerned with the authors' minds than with the meaning of a text, a text segment or a lexical item. For its interpretation, it does not matter whether the book quoted above, *Marxism and the Philosophy of Language*, was indeed written by Volshinov or by Bakhtin. Both Michel Foucault and Roland Barthes have marginalized the role of the author. Likewise, Paul Ricoeur, referring to Hans-Georg Gadamer's *Truth and Method*, states that writing 'renders the text autonomous with respect to the intention of the author' (Ricoeur 1981: 139), and claims: 'What the text signifies no longer coincides with what the author meant' (Ricoeur 1981: 91).

Yet how does hermeneutics work? If we want to know what any old text, say Plato's *Republic*, or any text segment, any key lexical item in it, means, it is not sufficient to read it on the horizon of our contemporary conceptualization. Rather, we have to interpret it in the context of other texts from roughly the same period, texts to which the *Republic* is a reaction, and texts which referred to it. But this is not enough. We also have to make ourselves aware of to what extent our reading of the text is indebted to what has taken place since. We have to realize how subsequent texts have influenced our perception. There is no straightforward way to regain the freshness of the experience that Plato's work had in its time. The only way to approximate the original meaning is by making ourselves conscious of the traces Plato's text has left ever since. We find these traces in the form of explicit or implicit quotes, comments and many fully fledged interpretations called commentaries. Yet we also have to take into account all the ideas that were invented later and form an integral part of our ways to think about society. Can we imagine a time when the concept of equality or of human rights was not yet available? To take an example from the history of music, it is impossible to pretend we could hear Bach today as his music would have sounded to his contemporaries. The revolution he brought about has been relativized and marginalized by the music of, say, Mendelssohn and Mahler.

Let us look at a concrete example. In the very first sentence of the *Republic* we encounter the Greek verb προσευχομαι. It still exists in Modern Greek and is usually translated into English as *to pray*. But what might προσευχομαι have meant in Plato's days? What we call praying today is some special kind of a very personal, bilateral though asymmetric communication with God. Was this also true for Plato's times? Or were prayers then the verbal equivalence to the sacrifices that people offered to their gods? Then it would rather be a unilateral piece of communication. The deity would not be expected to respond, even if the sacrifice was intended to generate goodwill on her or his part. Plato's text in itself does not provide the answer. It takes up, without comment or paraphrase, what was then generally understood as the concept of προσευχομαι. Yet this concept was a result of negotiations among the general ancient Greek discourse community. There is an abundance of classical Greek texts dealing with it. Experts have scanned them time and again in order to come up with interpretations of the old concept. The many translations we find of this book take these interpretations into account. We find these equivalents of προσευχομαι, among other phrases: *make my prayers, offer up my prayers, offer up prayer, say a prayer, pray, pay my devotions, pay my devoirs, worship*. All of them can be read as paraphrases which try to bridge the abyss between what προσευχομαι was then and what praying is today. We cannot come up with an interpretation of the ancient Greek word without, at the same time, interpreting also the present-day concept of 'praying'. To come to terms with what praying means today we have to scrutinize layer after layer of what has been added, subtracted, metamorphosed since classical Greek times. This is the key message of Hans-Georg Gadamer: 'The horizon of the present cannot be formed without the past ... Understanding is always the process of fusing of these supposedly different horizons' (Gadamer 1965: 289, my translation). Whatever we do, we cannot read προσευχομαι as Plato's contemporaries would have read it. Our 'horizon' was not available to them, and we cannot liberate ourselves from it. The famous hermeneutic circle is better described as an infinite spiral that will approximate the meaning of something that has been said before only in an asymptotic fashion.

The hermeneutic approach to meaning, as I have sketched it here, forsakes all hope for meaning as something stable or systematic. There is no universal, timeless, language-independent set of concepts, innate in our minds or carved into the granite of some metaphysical semantic ontology. Hermeneutics is not about *la langue*, it is about *la parole*. It looks at meaning not in the synchronic, but in the diachronic dimension. In this perspective, meaning is never final, it is always provisional. Each new occurrence of a lexical item in a text, each new reference to a text, adds something to its meaning. This may let *parole*-linguistics look less satisfactory than *langue*-linguistics. But if our social reality is a construct of the discourse it is only *parole*-linguistics that allows us to access it.

7 The linguist is not an expert for meaning

Neither linguists nor lexicographers are experts for meaning. They can prepare the evidence: the corpus containing the texts selected from the discourse in question; they can apply the methodology of corpus linguistics and extract the relevant data. But they are not experts who could tell us exactly what the meaning of *love* and *hate* is. They can show how lexical items are used and paraphrased. They can present possible intertextual links based on surface similarities between texts. But we must give up the idea that there is a 'true' or 'correct' interpretation of a lexical item, a text segment or a text, and that there are specialists on whom we can rely. The meaning of a lexical item is present in the discourse, and we can find it in the negotiations between the members of a discourse community. There may be disagreement, and there may be discord. Pluralism is the hallmark of any democratic society. Only a totalitarian regime would like to enforce a uniform language use. Each member of a discourse community has the inalienable right to paraphrase the word *globalization*, to describe and explain the discourse object 'globalization' as they like it. If he or she cannot convince his fellow members and therefore remains alone in their interpretation, then this new paraphrase will leave no traces in subsequent texts. Therefore it is in the interest of each of us to use lexical items in such a way that others find it wise to refer to these usages.

The negotiation of meaning never comes to an end. If we look closely we find that much of what is said, in private or public, is about making other people accept our point of view. Lexical items are always changing their meaning. Fifty years ago, no one would have dreamt of calling *abortion* the murder of unborn babies. There was no discourse object 'murder of unborn babies'. Today it is becoming increasingly ubiquitous. But we, as members of the discourse community, do not have to agree. Our contributions to the discourse can have an impact on our social reality. For this reality is socially constructed. There is nothing out there that makes us equate *embryo* with *unborn baby*, nor is there anything that keeps us from doing it.

The discourse is, in principle, a democratic system. Everybody has, in principle, the inalienable right to contribute to it. Everybody has, in principle, the right to be heard. Whether *globalization* means 'oil and war', or whether it means 'opportunities' is not a matter of truth but of persuasion. That we tend to think differently is the almost innate conviction that language is, or should be a mirror of a reality that would also be there if there were no language. For oral societies this is largely true. They would recognize a weapon of mass destruction if they saw one. No one, except perhaps their shamans, would dare to talk about discourse objects that one cannot see, smell or touch. Oral language is situated in gestures, facial expressions, deixis and ostentation. It takes a literate society to ponder over the meaning of Plato's *Republic*.

In the oral society, reality indeed can exercise some kind of control over what is said. If the 274th hunt for unicorns returns back to the cave unsuccessfully, it will have an impact on the community's beliefs and attitudes. But what about angels? What about Iraqi weapons of mass destruction? It is not reality, but the homogeneity of the discourse that makes these discourse objects real. The more homogeneous it is the easier it is to create the illusion of a reality that is but a mirror of the discourse. Today it is the media whose role it is to homogenize the discourse. The more power they have over us the more we tend to accept as real what they want to make us believe.

In our modern literate global society a democratic discourse could be seen as a danger. When what is described is outside of what we can see or hear or smell, how should we know if we should accept it? Without the power that media have over us the pluralism of a democratic discourse would be boundless. Jürgen Habermas believes that a society can only be called democratic if it enables a symmetric dialogue between its members that would enable agreement based on the rationality of argumentation. In his view, it is the distortions brought about by power in the social sphere and by the traumata of our psyche that prevent us from being reasonable. But would a sanitized discourse community that has abolished power and undergone psychotherapy be the solution? This was the question behind the famous debate between criticism of ideology, as proposed by Habermas, and the hermeneutics of Hans-Georg Gadamer. For Gadamer, it is the discourse which tells us what is rational. In a pluralistic discourse, there can be no method to decide which of the versions of rationality is 'true' (*Hermeneutik* 1971). What is reason? In his infamous Regensburg speech of 12 September 2006, Joseph Ratzinger (Pope Benedict XVI) maintained that reason is always in harmony with the Christian dogma. Is it then the Catholic Church that determines what is reasonable? Is pluralism possible in such a situation? Is the existence of multiple contradictory interpretations of our social reality a danger for our discursively constructed society, or is it the condition for it?

Apart from the narrow confines of our lifeworld, the discourse-external reality is and will remain inaccessible for us. Everything we are confronted with is the realities which we find in the discourse. The only way to come up with our own point of view is by comparing these realities. To facilitate such a comparison is, as I see it, the prime task of *parole*-linguistics. This brand of linguistics may be less concerned with the regularities of co-occurrence or system-immanent oppositions than with the meaning of what has been and is being said in the discourse at large. This is a kind of linguistics founded on hermeneutics, a kind of linguistics that is interested more in the diachronic than in the synchronic dimension of the discourse.

Acknowledgements

I would like to thank Anna Čermáková and Michaela Mahlberg for their valuable comments on an earlier draft.

References

Allen, G. (2000) *Intertextuality.* London: Routledge.
Berger, P. L. and Luckmann, T. (1980) *Die gesellschaftliche Konstruktion der Wirklichkeit.* Frankfurt am Main: Fischer.
Bloomfield, L. (1933) *Language.* New York: Henry Holt and Co.
Busse, D. and Teubert, W. (1994) 'Ist der Diskurs ein sprachwissenschaftliches Objekt? Zur Methodenfrage der historischen Semantik', in D. Busse, F. Hermanns and W. Teubert (eds), *Begriffsgeschichte und Diskursgeschichte.* Opladen: Wetdeutscher Verlag.
Canfora, L. (1991) *The Vanished Library.* London: Vintage.
Dennett, D. C. (1991) *Consciousness Explained.* Harmondsworth: Penguin.

Fairclough, N. (2003) *Analysing Discourse: Textual Analysis for Social Research.* London: Routledge.

Foucault, M. (1972) *The Archaeology of Knowledge.* London: Tavistock.

Frank, M. (ed.) (1977) *F. D. E. Schleiermacher, Hermeneutik und Kritik.* Frankfurt am Main: Suhrkamp.

Gadamer, H.-G. (1965) *Wahrheit und Methode* (2nd edn). Tübingen: J. C. B. Mohr.

Goody, J. (1987) *The Interface Between the Written and the Oral.* Cambridge: Cambridge University Press.

Harris, R. (1987) *The Language Machine.* Ithaca: Cornell University Press.

Hermanns, F. (2002) 'Linguistische Hermeneutik', in A. Linke, H. Ortner and P. R. Portmann-Tselikas (eds), *Sprache und mehr: Ansichten einer Linguistik der sprachlichen Praxis.* Tübingen: Niemeyer, pp. 125–63.

Hermeneutik und Ideologiekritik (1971) Mit Beiträgen von Karl-Otto Apel, Claus v. Bormann, Rüdiger Bubner, Hans-Georg Gadamer, Hans Joachim Giegel, Jürgen Habermas. Frankfurt am Main: Suhrkamp.

Holquist, M. (2002) *Dialogism.* London: Routledge.

Krishnamurthy, R. (ed.) (2004) Sinclair, J., Jones, S. and Daley, R., *English Collocation Studies. The OSTI report.* London: Continuum.

Kristeva, J. (1986) *The Kristeva-Reader,* ed. by T. Moi. Oxford: Blackwell.

Levinson, S. C. (1997) 'From Outer to Inner Space: Linguistic Categories and Non-Linguistic Thinking', in E. Pedersen and J. Nuyts (eds), *Language and Conceptualization.* Cambridge: Cambridge University Press, pp. 13–45.

Luhmann, N. (1998) *Die Gesellschaft der Gesellschaft.* Frankfurt am Main: Suhrkamp.

Luria, A. R. (1976) *Cognitive Development: Its Cultural and Social Foundations,* ed. by M. Cole. Cambridge, Mass.: Harvard University Press.

Mueller-Vollmer, K. (ed.) (1986) *The Hermeneutics Reader.* Oxford: Blackwell.

Putnam, H. (1975) 'The Meaning of Meaning', in K. Gunderson (ed.), *Language, Mind and Knowledge.* Minneapolis: The University of Minnesota Press.

Ricoeur, P. (1976) *Interpretation Theory: Discourse and the Surplus of Meaning.* Fort Worth, Texas: The Texas Christian University Press.

—— (1981) *Hermeneutics and the Human Sciences,* ed. and translated by J. B. T. Thompson. Cambridge: Cambridge University Press.

Searle, J. R. (1992) *The Rediscovery of Mind.* Cambridge, Mass.: MIT Press.

—— (1995) *The Construction of Social Reality.* New York: The Free Press.

Shepard, O. (1930, reprint 1993) *The Lore of the Unicorn.* New York: Dover Publications.

Teubert, W. (2001) 'Corpus Linguistics and Lexicography'. *International Journal of Corpus Linguistics,* special issue, 125–54.

—— (2003) 'Writing, hermeneutics and corpus linguistics'. *Logos and Language,* 4, 2: 1–17.

—— (2005) 'My version of corpus linguistics'. *International Journal of Corpus Linguistics,* 10, 1: 1–13.

Thomas, J. (1995) *Meaning in Interaction.* London: Longman.

Watzlawick, P. (1977) *How Real Is Real?* New York: Vintage Books.

Weber, M. (1972) *Wirtschaft und Gesellschaft* (5th edn). Tübingen: J. C. B. Mohr.

Wodak, R. (1988) *Language, Power and Ideology: Studies in Political Discourse.* Amsterdam: John Benjamins.

4   *Natural* and *human rights, work* and *property* in the discourse of Catholic social doctrine

Wolfgang Teubert

Introduction

In this chapter, I present a case study that applies diachronic corpus linguistics to two interesting keywords of our social organization, namely *work* and *property* in their relationship to the concepts of 'natural law' and 'human rights'. This study is an example of the workings of what I have called, in my previous chapter, *parole*-linguistics. My aim is to show that corpus linguistics can not only help us to become aware of the regularities of our language use, but that it is also an adequate approach to observe the construction of social reality in a given discourse at a given time.

Corpus linguistics presupposes not only corpora, but also a methodology to extract relevant data. Corpora are principled collections of texts in electronic form, and the methodology employs computer programs, to detect and extract data. Over the last 40 years, when much corpus work was concerned with lexicography and collocation, the most used tool, apart from statistical programs, has been the concordancer. It embeds the lexical item under investigation, the node, in its context, usually consisting of one line. Concordances are often sufficient when the aim is to come up with generalizations, to find out what is common to a large number of citations. But when we are interested in what distinguishes one citation from another, or when we look for possible links connecting the expression in question to occurrences in previous and subsequent texts, concordance lines rarely provide all the information we need. Diachronic corpus linguistics, as I have tried to develop it in my previous chapter, is less interested in generalizations, less in what is common to a large number of occurrences. Rather, it aims at investigating the change that socially constructed discourse objects undergo over time. This change can be observed if we look at citations as unique events which respond to what has been said previously, and which leave traces in subsequent texts. For this purpose, we normally need a wider context, often several contiguous sentences and sometimes even a whole paragraph. For diachronic corpus linguistics, a concordance constitutes only a first step. It allows us to select those citations which suggest change, and to discard the rest as they are more or less repetitions.

With one exception, I therefore refrain from presenting concordance lines. The exception is concordances of the key words *ownership* and *property*, as they occur in the encyclicals *Laborem exercens* and *Centesimus annus*. These concordances illustrate well my contention that for diachronic linguistics they can give us no more than candidate citations from which we must then choose the relevant ones. Diachronic linguistics has to go a longer way to demonstrate semantic change. More than may be the case for synchronic corpus linguistics, the findings of diachronic corpus linguistics are in need of interpretation. This means giving up the claim to empirical objectivity. While the computational analysis of real language data can claim a 'scientific' status, an interpretation is always contingent. Other researchers might select other citations and interpret the data differently. In the end, interpretation has to be dialogic activity. It is the discourse community of the researcher, his or her peer group whose task it is to negotiate an interpretation that can be shared.

Diachronic corpus linguistics makes sense only if we look at language from a social constructionist perspective. Concepts such as 'work' and 'property' are social constructs, not entities of a discourse-external reality. As such, they are under constant renegotiation by the texts contributed to a given discourse. Diachronic corpus linguistics differs from comparable approaches, e.g. the history of ideas, *Geistesgechichte*, or the history of mentalities, in that it takes the concept of the discourse seriously. All there is to know about human artefacts, be they concrete such as works of art, or be they abstract such as the concepts 'work' and 'property', is what is said about them in the discourse at large. For the purpose of analysis, we have to construct a manageable discourse reflecting our research interests, while being aware that the texts inside our discourse are not only linked to each other, but have links with a multitude of texts outside. For diachronic corpus linguistics, the concepts are analysable only as objects of a discourse. While any specific discourse itself is constructed by the researcher and needs the assent of his or her peer group to be considered relevant, it is only in a discourse where we can find social reality.

Work and property were not always seen as related concepts. It was John Locke who, in his *Second Treatment on Government*, first legitimized property through work. Ever since the relationship between these two concepts has become a political issue. When in the nineteenth century labour movements began to call for a more equitable society and Karl Marx and Friedrich Engel formulated, in the *Communist Manifesto*, their assault on the ruling bourgeois class, the Christian Churches on the Continent offered themselves as the trustworthy mediators between the interests of capital owners and the working class. While the Protestant Church developed a rather comprehensive programme for resolving the conflict between work and property, its influence remained limited to academic circles, due to its lack of a powerful organizational structure at the grassroots level, and a to more pervasive lack of interest among its followers in its religious and social teachings.

The Catholic Church, however, traditionally encompasses the lives of its followers in a more comprehensive way. In particular, it realized early the importance of addressing the working class outside of the strictly religious sphere in a number of ways, through nurseries, schools, youth and sport centres and local workmen's clubs. On the national level, it set up, in competition with secular trade unions, its own workers' associations, supporting workers' demands to be treated in accordance with their needs, and at the same time banned all Catholics from joining the existing secular unions (see Pfürtner and Heierle 1980: 56).

Simultaneously, the Church offered their services also to the factory owners by negotiating with them an agenda that would uphold the inviolability of private property, the moral obligation of hard work, as far as the workforce was concerned, and the sinfulness of industrial action. Up to the 1880s these activities were carried out more on a national than a European level, in countries like Italy, to a limited extent also in secular France, and prominently in Austria and Germany. Then, with the first social encyclical *Rerum Novarum*, issued in 1891, the Vatican assumed the global responsibility for the Catholic social doctrine, spread over the more Catholic parts of Europe, Latin America and even the United States. Since then, encyclicals and other comparable texts have been published from time to time in order to adapt the social doctrine to changing demands of time while protesting its overall continuity.

The social encyclicals were highly influential on the European discourse on property and work. They had a strong impact in non-Catholic countries, as well, including Great Britain and the United States. This set of texts provides a good example of a discourse that is constituted by parameters including time (1891 to 1991), domain (social doctrine), origin (the Pope representing the Vatican), and genre (encyclicals plus some comparable texts). It is held together by numerous intertextual references, providing a high level of discursive coherence. An important parameter missing is that of language. The encyclicals and other texts of this discourse are texts with several authors writing in several languages. Only in the process of final compilation would one language be chosen. This would often be French and German, for the early texts of our discourse, and generally Italian later on. The Latin versions usually arrived quite late even though, strictly speaking, they are the authoritative ones. In this chapter I will refer only to the English versions, even though a comparison of the various versions can be a fruitful exercise in itself.

The discourse I am working on consists, as said above, primarily of the 'social encyclicals'. But as Catholic social doctrine is also discussed in some other documents (including some other encyclicals), I have included these texts, as well. During the Second World War, there are some important wireless addresses by Pope Pius XII which are customarily referred to in this connection (e.g. in the collection *Texte zur katholischen Soziallehre* (1992)).

It goes without saying that Catholic social doctrine in particular, and the relationship between work and property as seen by the Catholic Church, has been the topic of innumerable other texts, some of which have left their traces in my discourse, while the texts of this discourse have been referred to, explicitly or implicitly, in many other texts. But I have to leave these texts outside of my discourse. The reason why I have confined this study to such a limited discourse is that it makes it possible to actually compile a corpus of all texts that belong to a given discourse, so that in this case the corpus is co-extensive with the discourse I have constructed. Normally, corpora tend to contain only a sample of a discourse. Of course, this chapter can only investigate a limited number of intertextual references. But my goal is to show that these links can be assumed, and that we can use them to explore the development of concepts (or, as I like to call them, discourse objects) such as 'work' and 'property' over a longer period of time. In section 5, I will look at a few texts outside of my discourse, showing some of the traces the Catholic natural law discourse leaves in the wider public discourse and demonstrating that intertextuality always transcends the confinement of a discourse.

My claim is that we can understand what is said today better if we are aware of the previous texts to which it is a reaction. For whenever we say something, we never start at point zero. Something always has been said before, has become part of the discourse at large, and we have to take a stance in relation to it. What has been said about a given discourse object is hardly ever homogeneous or monolithic. A broad range of opinions has been voiced over the discourse object 'work'. Members of the discourse community can accept some of them, may want to comment on certain ones, or to amend or modify them while rejecting others. A healthy discourse is always pluralistic and keeps negotiating meaning without ever coming to a close. Any discourse has, of necessity, a diachronic dimension. It is the opposition of what is said now to what has been said before that lets us fully realize the meaning of a given discourse object. This is what I want to exemplify in this diachronic analysis of a discourse.

1 The discourse of the Catholic social doctrine

The first text of my discourse of Catholic social doctrine is the encyclical *Rerum novarum*, published over 100 years ago, in 1891, written or at least authorized by Pope Leo XIII. The discourse has continued since then. After 100 years, in 1991, the encyclical *Centesimus annus* by Pope John Paul II was published. Since then, no social encyclical has been issued.

Catholic social doctrine has always presented itself as progressive, aimed at the betterment of the conditions of the working class and professing an impartial balance between worker and employer interests. In 1966, Pope Paul VI described the achievement of the Catholic social doctrine as follows: 'The church has inspired and still is inspiring today a legislation which opposes egoism and protects the weak, the modest, and the disinherited' (Address at the 75-year anniversary of *Rerum novarum*, § 4).

For the sake of embedding my discourse in a wider context, I divide it up into seven phases corresponding to what is conveniently thought of as external 'facts', even though these phases are only accessible through other texts of the discourse at large. My divisions do not lay claim to any objectivity. Their sole purpose is to point to the wider context in which these texts have to be seen.

Phase (1) Leo XIII: Capitalism is put under pressure by the pre-revolutionary atmosphere among the working class; the Catholic Church is isolated due to the loss of the Italian Papal States, the French laicist movement, and an anti-Catholic mood throughout Europe.
Text: Leo XIII, (encyclical) *Rerum novarum* (1891)

Phase (2) Pius XI: The Church is affected by fascist thought; the Pope pleads for a traditional corporational state.
Text: Pius XI, (encyclical) *Quadragesimo anno* (1931)

Phase (3) Pius XII: Influenced by the end of the war and the threat of left wing and popular front regimes in many Western European countries; the Pope makes concessions towards the working classes that are quickly withdrawn again.
Texts: Pius XII, (wireless addresses) Epiphany address (1941), Christmas address (1944), ACLI address (1945)

Phase (4) John XXIII: Pope John XXIII introduces the Third World problematic; he replaces natural law with human rights, yet keeping up the status quo in all other respects. He also upholds the condemnation of communism.
Texts: Johannes XXIII, (encyclical) *Mater et magistra* (1961), (encyclical) *Pacem in terris* (1963), (pastoral constitution) *Gaudium et spes* (1965)

Phase (5) Paul VI: Pope Paul VI is surprisingly progressive with respect to the question of property and the concept of a welfare state and he increasingly opens up the doctrine to emancipatory ideas. His anticommunist attitude is restrained.
Texts: Paul VI, *75th Anniversary address on the occasion of the 75th anniversary of the Italian corporation «Esso Italia»* (1966), (encyclical) *Populorum progressio* (1967), *International Labor Organization address* (1969), (encyclical) *Octogesima adveniens* (1971); Synod of bishops (Vaticanum II), *De justitia in mundo* (1971)

Phase (6) John Paul II: Pope John Paul II gradually returns to traditional positions. For him, the concept of welfare for everyone bears the danger of materialism.
Texts: John Paul II, (encyclical) *Laborem exercens* (1981), (encyclical) *Sollicitudo rei socialis* (1987)

Phase (7) John Paul II: After the breakdown of socialism, Pope John Paul II renews the alliance of Church and Capital and sees the main danger for society in pluralism which he equates with a lack of orientation in basic values.

Text: Johannes Paul II, (encyclical) *Centesimus annus* (1991)

2 The discourse objects 'property', 'work', 'natural law' and 'human rights'

The discourse objects 'property' and 'work' are the two foci of this study. Yet in order to understand the role they play in the Catholic social doctrine, we have to look at two more concepts which stand in a complementary relationship towards each other, namely 'natural law' (also sometimes referred to as 'natural rights') and 'human rights'. They are important for our analysis since one of the key arguments has been and still is whether property and/or work can claim a natural law or a human rights status. This question has been discussed continually over these 100 years, and the answer can have a grave social impact. For instance, if the inviolability of private property is a natural law, then all the property expropriated by East German laws has to be given back to its original owners after the German unification. But what about the expropriation of Irish freeholders after the invasion of the Cromwellian army? Are some expropriations lawful and others not? And who determines whether the inviolability of private property is also a human right?

We therefore have to investigate our texts in order to determine whether the transition from the natural law argumentation to the human rights argumentation had an influence on the construction and re-construction of the two discourse objects. It was only in the 1960s that, in the discourse analysed here, the natural law argument, which had been central for the Catholic Church, was replaced by the concept of human rights. The early social encyclicals still based the dogma of the inviolability of property on natural law. In *Centesimus Annus*, however, it is referred to as a human right. Therefore we have to familiarize ourselves with these concepts.

Work is strongly related to property, inside and outside of our discourse. In the view held by the Catholic social doctrine since the nineteenth century (borrowed largely from John Locke, without ever revealing its source), it is primarily work that creates property. Property is seen as the result of work and it is legitimated thereby. This dogma, however, has to lead to an argumentative inconsistency if we consider that many people working really hard, farmhands in former times, or modern industrial workers, usually do not acquire any property worth speaking of with the exception of a few staple possessions.

The accentuation of the work–property relationship has changed considerably over the years in the social encyclicals. This is partly due to a functional shift of the keyword *work*. Whereas work was considered an inalienable duty based on natural law up to the middle of the twentieth century, it began to be discussed, after the Second World War, as a possible item within the human rights canon. But the Church never required the state to implement this right, as it had done in the case of property.

The analysis presented here is based on the hermeneutical approach described in my previous chapter. As explained there and elsewhere (Teubert 2001, 2004), I work under the assumption that the discourse we are analysing here is a self-referential system. It can be viewed as a system in which lexical items are paraphrased, or, to say it differently, in which discourse objects are described and explained, regardless of their existence or non-existence outside the discourse. This self-referentiality of a given discourse as a research construct is only a methodical claim that does not deny that intertextuality as such transcends the boundary of any discourse we construct and is fully realized only in the discourse at large, the entirety of all the texts entered into it by all members of mankind. The discourse as a research object and the discourse at large both have a diachronic dimension. Even such closed discourses as the one I am analysing here can be interpreted fully only *post festum*. Therefore the negotiation of meaning is a never-ending process. Meaning is always provisional. Each new interpretation of the meaning of a lexical item adds to its meaning. Each new paraphrase has an impact. Phrases like *it is right/wrong that . . .; naturally . . .; this means that . . .; it used to be like . . .; you cannot say that . . .*, etc. abound in any discourse. There are numerous ways, often quite inconspicuous and implicit, to propose a change of meaning.

There is a good example demonstrating the workings of paraphrases in encyclical *Mater et magistra* (1971). There we read, in § 109: 'The right of private ownership of goods, including productive goods, has permanent validity.' The insertion *including. . .* indicates such a subliminal paraphrase. For it maintains, what is denied by others, that 'productive goods' have to be considered as any other kind of property, that one can own a factory as one can own an umbrella. The difference between the two is that in a factory the labour of the workers produces new property for the owner. My possession of an umbrella, however, does not make me richer.

In *Quadragesimo anno* (1931), we read in § 52: 'That ownership is originally acquired both by occupancy of a thing not owned by any one and by labor . . ., the tradition of all ages as well as the teaching of Our Predecessor Leo clearly testifies.' Since things belonging to no one do not exist any more, property today can only be created through work. Why then does the worker, hard as he may ever work, acquire no property? It is because the owner of the means of production reaps in the fruits of the labour. The authors of the encyclicals were by no means blind to the special role of 'productive goods'. The value created by the factory worker belongs, in the teaching of the Church, only to the owner of the factory. The worker is only entitled to a wage that keeps him and his immediate family alive. But does this not violate the principle that property is acquired by work only? *Quadragesimo anno* solves this dilemma as follows:

> [H]owever, only that labour which a man performs in his own name and by virtue of which a new form or increase has been given to a thing grants him title to these fruits.
>
> (§ 52)

The word *however* indicates that this statement is certainly controversial and that it is more an assertion than an obvious truth.

In this aspect as well, the Catholic Church takes on the paradigm developed by John Locke about the property-acquiring quality of work and, similar to John Locke, it virtually puts itself into the service of the propertied classes, whether aristocratic landowners or the modern masters of the industrial world. The traditional, pre-Lockean, paradigm had based property on *occupatio rei nullius*, the acquisition of things not owned, and aristocracy had based its property rights on this. Until John Locke's time, the dogma that work and property contradict each other was widely accepted. The political power in England rested with the aristocracy and the gentry who made it a point not to have to work for their income. In John Locke's time, the growing new bourgeoisie demanded their share in policy-making. With Locke's revolutionary thesis that it is work and nothing else which leads to the acquisition of property, the rising bourgeoisie acquired a right to participate in power. The obstinacy with which the Catholic social doctrine tries to avoid each reference to John Locke and to give the impression of an unbroken continuation of Thomistic teaching is remarkable. This is particularly true for the distinction between work in one's own name and work in the name of someone else, as it was invented by Locke and then became common ground in all the social encyclicals. In Locke's words, 'a free man makes himself a servant to another, by selling him for a certain time, the service he undertakes to do, in exchange for the wage he receives' (Locke 1982: 50 (§ 85)). Even if the servant carried out his work on the common of the village in which he and his master lived, he could not become the owner of the product of his work, for in Locke's understanding the 'common' was common property not of all the inhabitants but only of the landowners of that village: 'Thus the grass my horse has bit; the turfs my servant has cut; and the ore I have digged in any place, where I have a right to them in common with others, become my *property* without the assignation or the consent of any body. The labour that was mine, removing them out of that common state they were in hath *fixed my ('recte') property* in them' (Locke 1982: 19 (§ 28); emphasis in the original). For a more comprehensive treatment, see Brocker (1992: 218 ff. and *passim*).

Thus there are two types of property, property that the owner uses himself, e.g. an umbrella, and the other type of property: large estates and other productive goods like factories or ships where the owner employs workers to create property for himself. Is it the stance of Catholic social doctrine that these two types have to be treated alike?

3 Approaching meaning through scenarios

One way of approaching the meaning of lexical items is by investigating which role they play in our social and verbal interactions. In the context of which other discourse objects/lexical items do they occur and what is their relationship with them? Such an investigation will reveal the scenarios in which the discourse objects may be encountered. Frame semantics, as developed over the past 20 years or so by Charles Fillmore (e.g. Fillmore 1982), is the most comprehensive elucidation of this approach.

The key question in this context is: How do we find and ascertain the relevance of such scenarios? My position is that we have to find evidence for them in the discourse. It is not enough to claim that these scenarios are part of our social reality, and then to query the discourse for possible examples. This would be a top-down approach that assumes that there pre-exists a conceptual system of frames or scenarios more or less regardless of whether we find evidence for them in the discourse or not. Such an approach would be *langue*-linguistics, and I am not quite sure whether Fillmore would not want to regard frame semantics as a part of the language system. *Parole*-linguistics uses only the bottom-up approach. Social reality is constructed only in the discourse, and only what we find in the discourse can then be categorized into semantic frames, or scenarios. Thus these scenarios do not make any claim to reality; they are nothing but constructs whose only right to existence is their acceptance by the other members of a given discourse community.

It is exactly this sense that I want the scenarios which I present here to be understood. I claim that all I say here can be substantiated by discourse-internal accounts (though not within the narrow confines of the discourse of Catholic social doctrine as I have defined it above). In principle, for each scenario (in our case, 'property', 'work' and 'natural law'/'human rights') a special discourse would have to be constructed. This discourse will inform us about the key concepts of each scenario and the relationships obtaining between these concepts. In a second step, we must assure that the scenario is relevant beyond the narrow confines of the discourse we have taken as its basis. For instance, very few contributions (outside of a specialist discourse) discuss today the natural law issue. Very few people are aware that there is such a scenario. But in the discussions about the future of Cuba, the issue is very real. Should the expropriations over the past 40 years be reversed once Castro's regime comes to an end because the positive law (i.e. the legislation issued after Castro's takeover that was the basis for the expropriation) can have no effect on the inviolability of private property? This would be the position of the natural law advocates. Or are legislators justified to pass laws that allow expropriation under certain statutory conditions? This would be the position of those who claim that there is no natural law above the *volonté générale*. Thus even if the lexical item in question is largely absent from the more public contemporary discussions, the scenario itself is still efficacious.

Unfortunately I was not able to put together the discourses that would have put my scenarios on a solid basis. I had to rely on what may be called common knowledge. It would certainly be a worthwhile undertaking to construct the discourses reflecting these topics which, each in its own way, are crucial to the human condition. This has to wait for some future time. However, some years ago I attempted to sketch the European history of the concept of 'work' (Teubert 1996).

3.1 Scenario 1: The meaning of property

The meaning of *property* that we are interested in in our investigation is paraphrased thus in the first edition of the OED (published in 1933):

> The condition of being owned by or belonging to some person or persons; hence the fact of owning a thing; the holding of something one's own; the right (*esp.* the exclusive right) to the possession, use, or disposal of anything (usually of a tangible material thing); ownership, proprietorship.

This definition is an attempt to profess ideological impartiality. Controversial aspects are excluded as far as possible. The question of the quality of law remains unresolved, that is, the focal question is whether property finds its legal basis in positive law or in a law removed from human legislation. The definition includes the concept of ownership of things that are not used personally such as means of production and rental real estate.

A fuller scenario of 'property' would spotlight additional aspects of meaning, including those (and predominantly those) aspects that are ideologically controversial:

The origin of property
- In archaic times, property results from the establishment of a (physical) relation between the owner and the object (as long as it is not owned by anyone else).
- In the *contrat social*, the community members agree to mutually recognize and respect every member's property relations.
- The formation of property: according to common understanding up to the seventeenth century, property is acquired through occupancy of things not owned (*possessio rei nullius*, incidentally the legal basis for the appropriation of Australia), since John Locke's *Second Treatise on Government* (1689), property is viewed to be generated through work.
- The legal basis of property: property is a natural law which is removed from legislation and jurisdiction of a society (above the range of human jurisdiction), property is a human right which, once it is declared, cannot be suspended, property is based on positive law and subject to legislation.

Limits/limitations of property
- Property is not absolute but is linked to a complex and dynamic network of claims against and responsibilities towards third persons (e.g. in pre-Roman Germanic feudal law).
- Property is inviolable and principally exempt from state interference.
- Property entails responsibility in a moral (e.g. Christian) but not in a legal sense.
- Different types of property: property in one's own use, property of means of production, property generated by the work of others, property not used at all (e.g. large estates of absent landowners, left uncultivated).

The temporal dimension of property

- Does property not in personal use diminish in value or decrease in legal status over time?
- Does property as a claim continue to exist in spite of lawfully regulated expropriation?
- Does property have to be passed on to the heirs *in toto*, or can the state exercise distributional justice by taxing inheritance?

3.2 Scenario 2: The meaning of work

The meaning of *work* we are interested in is paraphrased thus in the first edition of the OED (definitions I.2 and I.4):

> Something to be done or something to do; what a person (or thing) has or had to do; occupation, employment, business, task, function.

> Action involving effort or exertion directed to a definite end, esp. as a means of gaining one's livelihood; labour, toil; (one's) regular occupation or employment.

Instead of outlining the scenario laid down for the Western concept of work in Teubert (1996), I will present here a different methodological approach, namely spelling out the metaphors underlying the common usage of the word *work*. This is, of course, George Lakoff's approach, and in his book *Moral Politics* (1996), he analysed the concept of work in a way very suitable for our analysis (Lakoff 1996: 54). Lakoff sees two metaphors at work, the 'Work Reward' metaphor, embedded in the issue of moral order, and the 'Work Exchange' metaphor. Lakoff attributes these statements to the 'Work Reward' metaphor:

- The employer is a legitimate authority.
- The employee is subject to that authority.
- Work is obedience to the employer's commands.
- Pay is the reward the employee receives for obedience to the employer.

These are the statements Lakoff attributes to the 'Work Exchange' metaphor:

- Work is an object of value.
- The worker is the possessor of his work.
- The employer is the possessor of his money.
- Employment is the voluntary exchange of the worker's work for the employer's money.

Today, it seems, the 'Work Reward' metaphor has by and large become superseded by the 'Work Exchange' metaphor. Perhaps it is noteworthy that George Lakoff does not consider here the aspect of work as a generating force of property. Somehow it seems the discourse has primed us to accept that other people's property is, or should have been, accrued from work, but it has not primed us to demand that our own work deserves the full profit it brings about. Rather we content ourselves with the hope that work should be compensated by a (just) wage.

3.3 Scenario 3: The meaning of natural law and human rights

For *natural law*, we can extract the following definition from the first edition of the OED:

> Law based upon the innate moral feeling of mankind; instinctively felt to be right and fair, though not prescribed by any enactment or formal compact.

Probably most experts with different ideological backgrounds would accept this definition. The discourse object 'natural law' is rarely discussed these days, even though it still looms forcefully in the background. Today the lexical item *natural law* occurs, if at all, mostly in academic contexts where certain ideological movements search for philosophical foundations. Robert Nozick, an extremely influential philosophical adviser to Margaret Thatcher, advocates a doctrine of a minimal state which basically reduces the state's operations to the protection of private property, the only 'natural right' that he recognizes (Nozick 1974). Positive law, i.e. law set by legislative bodies, is principally rejected by him. Edward Younkins sums Nozick's philosophy up in these words:

> Nozick believes that his argument justifies the minimal state and that anything beyond the minimal state violates natural rights. He has argued that a minimal state could arise without violating anyone's rights.
>
> (www.quebecoislibre.org/020413–9.htm)

It was John Locke who first reclaimed the natural law philosophy from its theological foundation and placed it in a secular setting. For him, there were only three natural rights: life, liberty and property. These rights were defined as negative rights. It was up to the state to protect you from interference with them; but the state was not obliged to actively promulgate your rights, e.g. to medicate you when you were suffering from an illness. The state also was not to exercise a distributive justice which would have each citizen participate in the common weal. In the words of Francesco Fagiani (2004: 163):

> Locke maintains a *negative* and *formal* conception of justice: justice prohibits interference with others' liberty of appropriation. Alongside the justice is the *positive* and *conditional* obligation of charity which prescribes the transfer of some of one's own goods to others who need them in order to survive. But for Locke there are precise limits on the obligation of charity: the application of charity suspends the application of justice only when the immediate physical survival is at stake; in all other cases justice leaves no room for charity.

These issues are far from obsolete. While human rights are at the forefront of the political discourse, the natural law ideology exercises a surreptitious though powerful influence on decisions which affect all of us. As we shall see, both discourses, though, are closely connected by intertextual links.

Our scenario of 'natural law' tries to highlight ideological differences concerning the meaning of this lexical item.

The basis of natural law
- nature as an abstract creative power
- nature as an instinct, innate moral feeling
- nature as the absolute truth revealed in the holy scriptures
- universal reason

Schools of natural law
- Stoa (*ius naturalis/ius gentium/ius civile*)
- Scholasticism, especially Thomas Aquinas (*ius naturalis/ius gentium/ius civile*)
- Protestant school of enlightenment (Hugo Grotius and Samuel Pufendorf)
- John Locke for whom natural law and human rights are identical
- Natural law as the backbone of Catholic social doctrine

Consequences of justification via natural law
- natural law in its function as a non-negotiable argument
- natural law being subject to expert opinion (or revelation) only
- natural law existing independently of any form of proclamation

The nature of natural law
- natural law as a system of rights and obligations

For *human rights*, the Collins Cobuild English Language Dictionary supplies the following, very general definition: 'Human rights are basic rights which most nations agree that all people should have.' This definition is probably quite uncontroversial and would be accepted by most ideological backgrounds. Difficulties arise in connection with specific features. One of these features concerns the democratic status of human rights. It is the people themselves who have to agree on each right, and the human rights acquire their legal character by proclamation or declaration. Human rights are public, they are negotiable, and they are neither perennial nor necessarily global. They can be amended, modified and changed by democratic procedures.

This is what makes the human rights, as a concept of the age of reason and enlightenment, different from natural law. Even when John Locke liberated natural law from religious dogmatism and naturalized it in the province of reason, he made it very clear that the required kind of reason is far from universal. In a Latin essay, not published during his lifetime, he wrote: 'Not the majority of people should be consulted but those who are more rational and perceptive than others' (quoted in White 1987: 80). So while natural law is said to be self-evident to reason, theorists such as Locke 'impose a restriction on those who can see self-evidence', while effectively denying 'that everybody is entitled to have a voice in the matter' (White 1987: 81).

Human rights belong both to national and international law. They are subject to a democratic process. They must be declared to be applicable, declared by a democratically empowered body, or by a general referendum. That means we can redefine human rights, and we can add new rights to the list and disclaim older ones. We can redefine the right to private property, and we can introduce an enforceable right to work. Our scenario of 'human rights' attempts to address the controversial aspects of this concept.

The basis of human rights
- nature
- reason
- *la volonté générale*

Historical aspects
- fruit of enlightenment
- proclamation of human rights in connection with radical political changes
- rejected by the Catholic Church until at least 1945

Patterns of human rights reasoning
- What constitutes a particular human right is negotiable.
- All have to decide about the adequacy of a human right.
- Human rights exist unconditionally and are independent from duties or responsibilities.
- Some human rights are more moral guidelines than legally recoverable rights.
- Human rights are proclaimed (usually as constitutional rights).

The nature of human rights
- Human rights are not complemented by a system of 'human obligations'.

It is one of the fruits of enlightenment that the human rights are viewed as an endowment with which we are born. One does not have to earn them, for instance by good behaviour, and even by violating other people's human rights one does not lose them. Thus the famous United States Declaration of Independence states:

> We hold these truths to be self-evident: that all men are created equal, that they are endowed, by their Creator, with certain unalienable Rights, that among these are Life, Liberty, and the Pursuit of Happiness.

Ever since in the Catholic social doctrine the human rights argumentation has replaced the natural law argumentation, we can observe an attempt to change the meaning of this lexical item. The essential property of inalienability, the idea that these rights cannot, under any circumstances, be withdrawn, is replaced by making them conditional on people's compliance with their duties, obligations, or increasingly, their 'responsibilities'. Natural law, at least in its Catholic interpretation, had always been more about responsibilities than rights, particularly if it is the public at large which is addressed. Thus when the Catechism of the Catholic Church (www.scborromeo.org/ccc/p3s1c3a1.htm) discusses natural law, it quotes, in § 1954, Leo XIII's encyclical *Libertas praestantissimum*, which says:

> Foremost in this office comes the *natural law*, which is written and engraved in the mind of every man; and this is nothing but our reason, commanding us to do right and forbidding sin.
> (www.vatican.va/holy_father/leo_xiii/encyclicals/documents/hf_l-xiii_enc_20061888_libertas_en.html)

While today the lexical item *natural law* (or *natural rights*) is rather sparingly used by the Catholic Church, the substituted item *human rights* is interpreted in the natural law framework as an entitlement conditional on our proper behaviour. The constantly reiterated message is that there are no rights without responsibilities. Conservative politicians all over the world, including Britain, are enthralled by such an agenda:

> Tony Blair has recently indicated he wants to see whether new laws are needed to tackle the issue of courts using human rights laws to overrule the government. . . . During the 2005 general election campaign, former leader Michael Howard pledged he would revise or scrap the [1998 Human Rights Act, which incorporated the European Convention on Human Rights into UK law]. Mr Cameron made clear he was not proposing to withdraw from the convention. . . . He said: 'It . . . hasn't really protected our human rights. . . . Why not try and write our own British bill of rights and responsibilities, clearly and precisely into law, so we can have human rights with common sense?'
> (BBC News 25 June 2006)

What the Catholic Church did, was to adopt the existing expression *human rights*, and to assign to this expression the meaning of the lexical item *natural law/natural rights*. Thus the expression *human rights* became ambiguous. Now it became possible to stipulate the acceptance of the human rights framework as it evolved in the age of reason, while pushing the traditional natural law agenda. As I will show in the next section, this ambiguity was used to establish the Catholic Church as a prime protector of human rights, while never giving up its traditional views. It is not surprising that this ambiguity suited politicians, as well. It enabled them to protest a progressive stance while actually promoting conservative values.

4 The meaning of *property, work, natural law* **and** *human rights* **in the Catholic social discourse**

I turn now to the actual analysis of the keywords I have chosen on the basis of citations taken from the encyclicals. My findings make it advisable to examine the concepts of 'property', 'natural law' and 'human rights' together, whereas the concept of 'work' will be examined independently.

In this section, I present the more salient citations which speak for themselves when viewed on the background of the scenarios drawn above. Wherever necessary, brief comments will be added. With this presentation of citations and glosses, I will attempt to trace the semantic change over the last hundred years, change that affects the objects of the discourse as well as the lexical items representing them.

4.1 Property, natural law *and* human rights

Up until well into the 1960s, the Catholic social doctrine consistently referred to 'natural law' as revealed in the Holy Scriptures and the traditions of the Church whenever it was necessary to legitimize its system of precepts and interdictions, rights and duties transcendentally. This was its ideological response to the structurally similar claim of Marxism to act in accordance with the immutable course of history, determined by the secular 'law of nature'. 'Natural law' corresponds nicely to the 'law of nature'. They are both inviolable. The difference is that Marxism claims to be founded on science, while the Church invokes the authority of God. This natural law doctrine had been developed by medieval scholasticism, most prominently by Thomas Aquinas. Natural law, as it is seen there, is eternal, unalterable, and prior to any law established by society: it is not subject to human legislation. Imputing natural law means to make one's position unquestionable. In 1964, Josef Ratzinger, who later became the keeper of truth in the Vatican, before finally being promoted *Pontifex maximus,* still held more heretical views when he said that the reference to natural law also comprises 'ideological' elements, that is, 'trains of thought that only superficially have the character of natural law . . ., [but] that in reality stem from a historical social structure experienced as "natural" which therefore is inconspicuously declared as normative' (quoted in Pfürtner and Heierle 1980: 71). From an orthodox point of view, only the Church can claim to possess certain knowledge of the contents of natural law, as it is revealed in the Holy Scriptures and the tradition of the Church. This was a comfortable tool for Leo XIII. The encyclical *Rerum novarum* recognizes two natural rights, one of them being the coalition right and the other being the right to property. As for identifying the right to property as a natural right, Leo XIII explicitly refers to Thomas Aquinas. This reference in the wider context of the encyclical lets the reader assume that he is the authority for Leo's claim. The relevant sentence reads as follows: 'It's lawful,' says St Thomas Aquinas, 'for a man to hold private property, and it is also necessary for the carrying on of human existence' (*Rerum novarum* § 22). This is a intentional misquotation (which is repeated 40 times on Google [20 November 2006]). Property for Thomas Aquinas was not a *ius naturale*, as he explicitly states:

> Community of goods is said to be part of the natural law not because the natural law decrees that all things are to be possessed in common and nothing held privately, but because the distribution of property is not a matter of natural law but of human agreement which pertains to the positive law. Therefore private property is not against natural law but it has been added to natural law by the inventiveness of human reason.
>
> (The Summa of Theology Question 66, 2)

Property, for Thomas Aquinas, is subject to historical change and thus to human legislation. Expropriation and the community of goods, as it is practised in Cuba, for instance, is not a violation of natural law. But his is not Leo's view.

What does *Rerum novarum* concretely tell us about property?

> Every man has by nature the right to possess property as his own.
>
> (§ 6)

> The first and most fundamental principle, therefore, if one would undertake to alleviate the condition of the masses, must be the inviolability of private property.
>
> (§ 15)

But has not God promised the use of material goods to all mankind? *Rerum novarum* interprets this entitlement in a rather narrow way:

> The fact that God has given the earth for the use and enjoyment of the whole human race can in no way be a bar to the owning of private property. For God has granted the earth to mankind in general, not in the sense that all without distinction can deal with it as they like, but rather that no part of it was assigned to any one in particular, and that the limits of private possession have been left to be fixed by man's own industry, and by the laws of individual races. . . . Those who do not possess the soil contribute their labour; hence, it may truly be said that all human subsistence is derived either from labour on one's own land, or from some toil, some calling, which is paid for either in the produce of the land itself, or in that which is exchanged for what the land brings forth.
>
> (§ 8)

This shows how intricately property and labour are linked. Everyone can enjoy the material goods. Some may have to work for them, others may not. Property for Leo first of all serves one's own needs. Charity comes in much later:

> [N]o one is commanded to distribute to others that which is required for his own needs and those of his household; nor even to give away what is reasonably required to keep up becomingly his condition in life. But, when what necessity demands has been supplied, and one's standing fairly taken thought for, it becomes a duty to give to the indigent out of what remains over. . . . 'Of that which remaineth, give alms.' (Luke 11: 41) It is a duty, not of justice (save in extreme cases), but of Christian charity – a duty not enforced by human law.
>
> (§ 22)

It is interesting to see how closely Leo follows John Locke in what he has to say about charity, even though he attributes it to Thomas Aquinas. Locke would certainly have agreed with this statement in *Rerum novarum*, as well:

> The right to possess private property is derived from nature, not from man . . . The State would therefore be unjust and cruel if under the name of taxation it were to deprive the private owner of more than is fair.
>
> (§ 47)

The concept of property of Pius XI in *Quadragesimo anno* is the same as Leo's. We read:

> The natural right itself both of owning goods and of passing them on by inheritance ought always to remain intact and inviolate, since this indeed is a right that the state cannot take away.
>
> (§ 49)

But how then have the rich become rich? Definitely not through labour since it is held:

> That ownership is originally acquired both by occupancy of a thing not owned by any one and by labour, or, as is said, by specification, the tradition of all ages as well as the teaching of Our Predecessor Leo clearly testifies. [. . .] however, only that labour which a man performs in his own name and by virtue of which a new form or increase has been given to a thing grants him title to these fruits.
>
> (§ 52)

Again there is no reference to Locke; instead the *tradition of all ages* is invoked.

In the *Pentecost Address* of 1941, Pius XII, in view of the ongoing war, fought in the trenches by mostly unpropertied soldiers, departs from his predecessors in carefully chosen words and distinguishes, again with regard to natural law, between the usufruct of all men to the goods of this earth and private property. Thus he can both claim continuity in the doctrine and depart from it. Apparently he feels that something has to be offered to those who fight, something that makes it worth fighting for. Therefore in this specific situation, usufruct takes precedence over the academic question of ownership:

In fact every man has, as a rational natural being, in principle the right to use all the material goods of this earth, and this right can by no means be abolished, not even by other . . . rights.

(quoted in *Texte* 1992: 158, my translation)

Shortly after the war, Pius XII can even imagine 'a socialization of companies in such cases where it seems vital for the public welfare' (ACLI speech, quoted in *Texte* 1992: 157, my translation).

In *Pacem in terris* (1963), John XXIII brings about the transition from natural law to human rights. Since in the meantime the whole world had embraced the human rights concept and hardly anyone could remember the old natural law argumentation, the reference to human rights had become ubiquitous. There was hardly any state constitution or any international declaration that did not at least pay lip service to them. The universal declaration and recognition of human rights had been a consequence of the Second World War. Open resistance against such a powerful idea was deemed counterproductive by the Church. This is one of the very rare moments where this venerable institution, which derived so much of its strength from continuity, seemed to be forced to relinquish one of the pillars of its doctrinal system in order to be able to continue playing an important role in the public moral discourse. The task was to maintain continuity while professing to endorse the universally accepted morality of the human rights agenda. The solution was to subvert the existing construct of human rights by offering an alternative version of this discourse object, i.e. by dressing up natural law as human rights. Thus it became possible to send ambiguous messages to multiple addressees. The experts for theology and conservatively oriented ethics would understand that nothing but the terminology had changed, while the wider public was led to believe that the human rights sanctioned by the Catholic dogma were identical with the human rights of a democratic society.

Pacem in terris prepares this change in nomenclature cautiously by first drowning the natural law concept in a sea of obfuscation:

But the mischief is often caused by erroneous opinions. Many people think that the laws which govern man's relations with the State are the same as those which regulate the blind, elemental forces of the universe. But it is not so; the laws which govern men are quite different. The Father of the universe has inscribed them in man's nature, and that is where we must look for them; there and nowhere else.

(§ 6)

What is implied here is first an equation of (holy) natural law with (scientific) laws of nature, and then, in a second step, the opposition of these laws of nature with laws inscribed into the nature of man. Thus we are offered, as an intermediate concept, human nature. It is not unusual for this text type that this implication is something we can infer as what is probably meant, but that, if ever necessary, this entailment can be rejected as inaccurate. In the following paragraphs, the encyclical oscillates purposefully between natural law and man's rights. We find:

> But first we must speak of man's rights. Man has the right to live. He has the right to bodily integrity and to the means necessary for the proper development of life, particularly food, clothing, shelter, medical care, rest, and, finally, the necessary social services. In consequence, he has the right to be looked after in the event of ill health; disability stemming from his work; widowhood; old age; enforced unemployment; or whenever through no fault of his own he is deprived of the means of livelihood.
>
> (§ 11)

This is certainly going a step beyond *Rerum novarum* in which these conditions were to be amended by charity, a moral obligation, but not a duty enforced by natural law. It is noteworthy, though, that instead of the lexical item *human rights* we find *man's right*. The reason cannot be that the text is only referring to the male part of humankind, for widowhood, for instance, can affect men and women. A little further we read what almost amounts to a fair copy of the United Nations' *Universal Declaration of Human Rights*, only that these rights are referred to as *natural* rights, thus appropriating them to the old framework:

> Moreover, man has a natural right to be respected. He has a right . . . – within the limits of the moral order and the common good – to freedom of speech and publication, and to freedom to pursue whatever profession he may choose. He has the natural right to share in the benefits of culture, and hence to receive a good general education, and a technical or professional training consistent with the degree of educational development in his own country.
>
> (§ 12, 13)

One paragraph further down we find:

> Also among man's rights is that of being able to worship God in accordance with the right dictates of his own conscience, and to profess his religion both in private and in public.
>
> (§ 14)

Interesting is the phrase *right dictates of his own conscience* (in the Italian version: *il dettame della retta coscienza*), suggesting that this right is conditional on having the proper belief. *Pacem in terris* stops short of declaring the right to work, still calling work a *duty* rather than a *right*, but asserts, unsurprisingly, the right to private property. The rights mentioned here are rights according to *man's nature*, rather than *human rights*:

> A further consequence of man's personal dignity is his right to engage in economic activities suited to his degree of responsibility. The worker is likewise entitled to a wage that is determined in accordance with the precepts of justice. . . . 'Nature imposes work upon man as a duty, and

man has the corresponding natural right to demand that the work he does shall provide him with the means of livelihood for himself and his children. Such is nature's categorical imperative for the preservation of man.'

> (Pius XII's broadcast message, Pentecost, 1 June 1941,
> quoted *in Texte* 1992: 201)

The encyclical *Pacem in terris*, too, contains an explicit link between natural law and human rights:

> Every basic human right draws its authoritative force from the natural law, which confers it and attaches to it its respective duty. Hence, to claim one's rights and ignore one's duties, or only half fulfil them, is like building a house with one hand and tearing it down with the other.
> (§ 30)

This quotation is interesting for two reasons. It postulates natural law as the superior concept, and thus puts the Church's authority in charge also for the definition of human rights. For only the Catholic Church has the expertise to determine the true nature of the natural law. It also makes the granting of a human right conditional on fulfilling one's duty. Thus, it seems, little has changed, and continuity in the doctrine has been preserved, while paying lip service to the changing times. It is perhaps not so astounding that, eight years later, the Roman *Episcopal Synod* of 1971 *De iustitia in mundo* passes in silence over the *Universal Declaration of Human Rights* of the United Nations and tells the world: 'The encyclical "Pacem in terris" gave to us the Magna Charta of human rights' (§ 57). In recent relevant literature, too, it sometimes seems as if human rights had been invented by the Catholic Church. How elegantly official texts manage to fuse the democratic concept of human rights with the Catholic Church's own version of this discourse object can be seen in the *Intervention by the Holy See at the 58th Session of the General Assembly of the United Nations* (10 December 2003):

> My delegation is pleased to join the observance of the Fifty-fifth Anniversary of the promulgation and adoption of the Universal Declaration of Human Rights. This extraordinary development in the protection of fundamental human rights was based on the greatest traditions of the *jus gentium* – the Law of Nations – which is founded upon the objective moral order as discerned by right reason. The principle of right reason is at the core of the natural law which has inspired and continues to give vitality to the Universal Declaration. Eminent scholars have noted the inextricable connection between the natural law and the reality that all human rights and fundamental freedoms of the human person and of peoples are inalienable.

The past triads of hatred against the American and French declarations of human rights in 1776 and 1785 are nowadays submerged in a sea of ambiguity. After all, it is only as recent as 1832 that Gregory XVI called the freedom of conscience 'madness' and an 'epidemic error' in his encyclical *Mirari vos*. Continuity is preserved even in this aspect. For it takes 'the right reason' to discern 'the objective moral order'. Whoever does not accept the Catholic interpretation of human rights is clearly devoid of reason.

I now return to the concept of property that, pace *Pacem in terris*, has been transmogrified into a human right. But as such it has changed. There is now more emphasis on the responsibility that comes with property:

> Secondly, private ownership of property, including that of productive goods, is a natural right which the State cannot suppress. But it naturally entails a social obligation as well. It is a right which must be exercised not only for one's own personal benefit but also for the benefit of others.

(§ 19)

John XXIII repeatedly refers to his predecessor, though I was unable to establish the specific text. Whoever it was (probably Pius XII) stresses that everybody has the right to their share in the common weal which, in contradiction to *Rerum novarum*, and even to his own *Pacem in terris*, has precedence over the natural right to private property:

> Concerning the use of material goods, Our Predecessor declared that the right of every man to use these for his own sustenance is prior to every other economic right, even that of private property. The right to the private possession of material goods is admittedly a natural one; nevertheless, in the objective order established by God, the right to property cannot stand in the way of the axiomatic principle that 'the goods which were created by God for all men should flow to all alike, according to the principles of justice and charity'.

(§ 40)

How much this encyclical is in line with the progressive spirit of the 1960s also shows in this sentence:

> From this it follows that the economic prosperity of a nation is not so much its total assets in terms of wealth and property, as the equitable division and distribution of this wealth.

(§70)

For all its innovative drive, *Mater et magistra* stresses continuity also in the issue of private property:

> What, then, of that social and economic principle so vigorously asserted and defended by Our predecessors: man's natural right to own private property, including productive goods? Is this no longer operative today, or has it lost some of its validity in view of the economic conditions We have described above? This is the doubt that has arisen in many minds. There is no reason for such a doubt to persist. The

right of private ownership of goods, including productive goods, has permanent validity.

(§ 108, 109)

Equitable distribution of property is once more suggested as the solution:

It will not be difficult for the body politic, by the adoption of various techniques of proved efficiency, to pursue an economic and social policy which facilitates the widest possible distribution of private property in terms of durable consumer goods, houses, land, tools and equipment (in the case of craftsmen and owners of family farms), and shares in medium and large business concerns.

(§ 115)

John's successor, Paul VI, states it clearly, in the encyclical *Populorum progressio* of 1967: 'Private property does not constitute for anyone an absolute and unconditional right' (§ 23).

John Paul II, in the early years of reign, still seeks to establish continuity by taking up the position of Paul VI in *Laborem exercens* (1981). We read:

From this point of view the position of 'rigid' capitalism continues to remain unacceptable, namely the position that defends the exclusive right to private ownership of the means of production as an untouchable 'dogma' of economic life.

(§ 14)

Laborem exercens was published just a few years after John Paul II had assumed office. To some extent, the encyclical might already have been prepared under his predecessor. The next social encyclical, *Centesimus annus*, marking the hundredth anniversary of *Rerum novarum*, can be read as a striking departure from the more progressive views of the 1960s and 70s. The emancipatory spirit now has given way to the new post-socialist neoliberalism. When reading *Centesimus annus*, one gets the impression that this encyclical not only reflects the new atmosphere but also gives the changed *Zeitgeist* a helping hand. This encyclical, issued after the collapse of the socialist experiment in the Soviet Union and in Eastern Europe, does not only celebrate Leo XIII as the founder of Catholic social doctrine. It also renews this doctrine, relegating the changes his immediate predecessors had introduced to the wastebin of history. *Centesimus annus* identifies two key elements of Leo's social doctrine, namely the dignity of the worker and the right to own private property. If dignity is defined as self-exertion, it is rather a bargain for the employer:

Indeed, the key to reading the Encyclical is the dignity of the worker as such, and, for the same reason, *the dignity of work*, which is defined as follows: 'to exert oneself for the sake of procuring what is necessary for the various purposes of life, and first of all for self-preservation'. . . . Another important principle is undoubtedly that of the *right* to '*private property*'. The amount of space devoted to this subject in the Encyclical shows the importance attached to it.

(§ 6, emphasis in the original)

How much *Centesimus annus* (length: 22,355 words) was a departure from *Laborem exercens* (length: 27,457) becomes clear if we look at the concordances for *ownership*. (The concordances are supplied by the Vatican web page: www.vatican.va/. The first number is the number of the concordance, the second number refers to the chapter, and the third to the paragraph; I have removed concordance lines extracted from the commentaries.)

Laborem exercens (23 citations):

```
 1  3,11|    it by eliminating private ownership of the means of production.
 2  3,12|    with work the question of ownership, for the only means that
 3  3,12|  bear fruit, man takes over ownership of small parts of the various
 5  3,14|    owners. Thus the issue of ownership or property enters from
 6  3,14|     the Church's teaching on ownership, on the right to private
 7  3,14|      in the way the right to ownership or property is understood.
 8  3,14|   in the Church's teaching, ownership has never been understood
 9  3,14|   concerns in a special way ownership of the means of production.
10  3,14|    of public or collective ownership-is that they should serve
11  3,14|  exclusive right to private ownership of the means of production
12  3,14|          proposals for joint ownership of the means of work, sharing
13  3,14|  the sphere of the right to ownership of the means of production.
14  3,14|      elimination of private ownership of the means of production.
15  3,14|associating labour with the ownership of capital, as far as possible,
16  3,15|    the principle of private ownership of the means of production
17  3,15|    system in which private ownership of these means has been
18  3,15| reason in favour of private ownership of the means of production.
19  3,15|    the principle of private ownership-in our own time we even
20  3,15|   the system of "socialized ownership" has been introduced-nevertheless
21  4,17|   situation of "socialized" ownership of the means of production).
22  4,19|  one in a system of private ownership of the means of production
23  4,19|       or in a system where ownership has undergone a certain"
24  4,20|  defective in the system of ownership of the means of production
```

Centesimus annus (16 citations):

```
 1  1,6|     mainly considers is land ownership.18 But this does not mean
 2  1,6|    dominated by collective ownership of the means of production,
 3  1,6|   of hindrances to private ownership in many parts of the world,
 4  3,24|  to private initiative, to ownership of property and to freedom
 5  4,30|       the right to private ownership, he affirmed with equal
 6  4,30|  the legitimacy of private ownership, as well as the limits which
 7  4,30|   Private property or some ownership of external goods affords
 8  4,32|     exists another form of ownership which is becoming no less
 9  4,32|  much more on this kind of ownership than on natural resources.~
10  4,33|  ;    it are excluded from ownership and are reduced to a state
11  4,41|      of production and ownership, that is, giving them a
12  4,41|   of values, so that the ownership of things may become an
13  4,43|  to private initiative and ownership is to be found in this activity.
14  4,43|   chain of solidarity. Ownership of the means of production,
15  4,43|  among working people.87 Ownership of this kind has no justification,
16  4,43|  free gift of self, so too ownership morally justifies itself
```

Laborem exercens has ten occurrences of *ownership of (the) means of production*, *Centesimus annus* has only two. Here are the most telling citations in an enlarged context:

> (LE 9) This concerns in a special way ownership of the means of production. . . . They cannot be *possessed against labour*, they cannot even be *possessed for possession's sake*, because the only legitimate title to their possession – whether in the form of private ownership or in the form of public or collective ownership – is *that they should serve labour*, and thus, by serving labour, that they should make possible . . . the right to common use of them.

> (LE 11) From this point of view the position of 'rigid' capitalism continues to remain unacceptable, namely the position that defends the exclusive right to private ownership of the means of production as an untouchable dogma of economic life.

> (LE 14) Therefore, while the position of 'rigid' capitalism must undergo continual revision, in order to be reformed from the point of view of human rights, both human rights in the widest sense and those linked with man's work, it must be stated that, from the same point of view, these many deeply desired reforms cannot be achieved by an *a priori elimination of private ownership of the means of production*. For it must be noted that merely taking these means of production (capital) out of the hands of their private owners is not enough to ensure their satisfactory socialization.

> (LE 19) Thus, *the principle of the priority of labour* over capital is a postulate of the order of social morality. It has key importance both in the system built on the principle of private ownership of the means of production.

> (CA 14) Ownership of the means of production, whether in industry or agriculture, is just and legitimate if it serves useful work.

It is obvious that *Laborem excercens* is at odds with the current situation. LE 9 proclaims that ownership of the means of production always has to serve labour, and this is reiterated in LE 19. LE 11 calls ' "rigid" capitalism' 'unacceptable', while LE 14 states that it must 'be reformed' from a human rights perspective and seems to seriously consider the notion of 'socialization' in a situation where the workforce would profit from it. But *Centesimus annus* tells us that the ownership of the means of production is 'just and legitimate if it serves useful work'. We are not told what constitutes 'useful work'. Is it work that generates a profit for the owner of the factory?

For *property*, we find 12 citations in *Laborem exercens*, as compared to 24 in *Centesimus annus*:

Laborem exercens:

```
1   3,14|       the issue of ownership or property enters from the beginning
2   3,14|          on the right to private property even when it is a question
3   3,14|       the right to ownership or property is understood. Christian
4   3,14|           the right to private property is subordinated to the right
5   3,14|      labour. As mentioned above, property is acquired first of all
6   3,14|       these means as a separate property in order to set it up in
7   3,14(22)|           On the right to property see Summa Th., II-II, q.
8   3,14(22)|   On the social function of property see Summa Th., II-II, q.
9   3,14|        . They cease to be the property of a certain social group,
10  3,14|         owners, and become the property of organized society, coming
11  3,14|       of production into State property in the collectivist system
12  3,14|          to "socializing" that property. We can speak of socializing
```

Centesimus annus:

```
1   1,4|        taken shape. A new form of property had appeared - capital;
2   1,4|        time, another conception of property and economic life was beginning
3   1,6|            and is the exclusive property of him who acts, and, furthermore,
4   1,6|        of the right to "private property".16 The amount of space
5   1,6|        well aware that private property is not an absolute value,
6   1,6|        that the type of private property which Leo XIII mainly considers
7   1,6|      adduced to safeguard private property or to affirm the right to
8   1,6|        of the right to private property. As a result of these changes
9   1,7|         with the right to private property, Pope Leo XIII's Encyclical
10  1,10|      which the right to private property is reaffirmed, is devoted
11  1,11|       a sound view of private property, work, the economic process,
12  2,12|      the suppression of private property, Leo XIII arrived at the
13  2,12|        to do away with private property, contending that individual
14  2,12|      should become the common property of all . . .; but their contentions
15  2,13|        an opposition to private property. A person who is deprived
16  3,24|     initiative, to ownership of property and to freedom in the economic
18  4,30|      of the right to private property, using various arguments
19  4,30|       later we read: "Private property or some ownership of external
20  4,30|        Of its nature private property also has a social function
21  4,31|       teaching on the right to property and the common destination
22  4,31|        the origin of individual property. Obviously, he also has
23  4,42|   business, the market, private property and the resulting responsibility
24  4,43|   between individual or private property and the universal destination
25  5,48|   individual freedom and private property, as well as a stable currency
```

The citations 7 to 12 in *Laborem exercens* are from footnotes, which do not concern us here. Citations 1 and 3 to 5, however, are worth quoting in a larger context. They all relativize the concept of private property:

> (LE 1) Thus *the issue of ownership or property* enters from the beginning into the whole of this difficult historical process.

> (LE 3) In the latter case, the difference consists in the way the right to ownership or property is understood. Christian tradition has never upheld this right as absolute and untouchable.

> (LE 4) On the contrary, it has always understood this right within the broader context of the right common to all to use the goods of the whole of creation: *the right to private property is subordinated to the right to common use*, to the fact that goods are meant for everyone.

(emphasis in the original)

(LE 5) As mentioned above, property is acquired first of all through work in order that it may serve work.

Private property is only admissible if it serves work, and it is 'subordinated to the right of common use'. This is not the perspective that we gain from *Centesimus annus*. There, most of the citations quote *Rerum novarum*, directly or indirectly. The topic of many of them focuses on the illegitimacy of socialism:

(CA 12) The remedy would prove worse than the sickness. By defining the nature of the socialism of his day as the suppression of private property, Leo XIII arrived at the crux of the problem.

(CA13) (*Rerum novarum*) 'Socialists encourage the poor man's envy of the rich and strive to do away with private property.'

(CA 16) The second factor in the crisis [in the socialist countries] was certainly the inefficiency of the economic system, which is not to be considered simply as a technical problem, but rather a consequence of the violation of the human rights to private initiative, to ownership of property and to freedom in the economic sector.

(CA 24) In the light of today's 'new things', we have re-read *the relationship between individual or private property and the universal destination of material wealth.* Man fulfils himself by using his intelligence and freedom. In so doing he utilizes the things of this world as objects and instruments and makes them his own. The foundation of the right to private initiative and ownership is to be found in this activity.

CA 16 and 24 do away with the old presumption that private property is the result of work. Private property is now the result of free, unbridled private initiative, allowing entrepreneurs to use all their intelligence to make them rich. Socialism had to fail because it did not guarantee this 'human right'.

The new social doctrine that *Centesimus annus* has to offer, is perhaps best summed up in this quotation:

Organizing such a productive effort, planning its duration in time, making sure that it corresponds in a positive way to the demands which it must satisfy, and taking the necessary risks – all this too is a source of wealth in today's society. In this way, the *role* of disciplined and creative *human work* and, as an essential part of that work, *initiative and entrepreneurial ability* becomes increasingly evident and decisive.

(§ 32)

The new social doctrine also rejects the welfare state. Instead of providing material assistance to those in need, people should be given moral support, which not only comes much cheaper but also encourages them to take care of themselves:

However, excesses and abuses, especially in recent years, have provoked very harsh criticisms of the Welfare State, dubbed the 'Social Assistance State.' Malfunctions and defects in the Social Assistance State are the result of an inadequate understanding of the tasks proper to the State. . . . By intervening directly and depriving society of its responsibility, the Social Assistance State leads to a loss of human energies and an inordinate increase of public agencies, which are dominated more by bureaucratic ways of thinking than by concern for serving their clients, and which are accompanied by an enormous increase in spending.

(§ 48)

4.2 Work

Work was not yet a moral value held in high esteem in 1891 – the year of the first social encyclical *Rerum novarum* by Leo XIII. It was viewed as a necessary penance for mankind (or at least the poorer part of mankind). Paragraph 8 makes this quite clear: 'Those who do not possess the soil contribute their labour.' This is the consequence of the Fall (of Man), which appears to afflict only the lower classes: 'To suffer and to endure, therefore, is the lot of humanity; let them strive as they may, no strength and no artifice will ever succeed in banishing from human life the ills and troubles which beset it' (§ 18). Thus workers and their employers have different responsibilities:

> Of these duties, the following bind the proletarian and the worker: fully and faithfully to perform the work which has been freely and equitably agreed upon; never to injure the property, nor to outrage the person, of an employer; never to resort to violence in defending their own cause, nor to engage in riot or disorder; and to have nothing to do with men of evil principles, who work upon the people with artful promises of great results, and excite foolish hopes which usually end in useless regrets and grievous loss. The following duties bind the wealthy owner and the employer: not to look upon their work people as their bondsmen, but to respect in every man his dignity as a person ennobled by Christian character.

(§ 20)

In *Quadragesimo anno* (1931), Pius XI reflects on the effect *Rerum novarum* had: 'Feeling themselves vindicated and defended by the Supreme Authority on earth, Christian workers received this Encyclical with special joy' (§ 13). He also responds to those who ask if it would not be more just if all, the rich as well as the poor, would have to work:

> And in this connection We must not pass over the unwarranted and unmerited appeal made by some to the Apostle when he said: 'If any man will not work neither let him eat.' For the Apostle is passing judgement on those who are unwilling to work, although they can and ought to.

(§ 57)

Apparently there are also some people who are not under the obligation to work. This attitude was widely accepted in the Western world. In E. M. Forster's novel *Howard's End*, published in 1910, it is the fact that he has to work that creates an abyss between Leonard Bast and the propertied Wilcox family, and even the Schlegel sisters who have to struggle hard on their small income to survive without work. To be forced to work for one's living (unless it was a gentlemanly profession as that of a barrister), constituted an irreconcilable class barrier well until after the First World War. But then our common perception of work began to change. Earlier perceived as drudgery, it now became a fundamental value. The first sentence of the Italian constitution of 1947 states: 'Italy is a democratic republic based on labour' (www.oefre.unibe.ch/law/icl/it00000_.html, translation by the Italian Embassy in London). Since then, praiseworthy persons, including royalty, millionaires and popes, are characterized uniformly as hardworking from early morning to late at night: 'There is no doubt that Prince Charles works hard and his diary is usually filled up to two years in advance' Western Mail 14 November 2006. Thus it is no longer the issue of who has to work that is discussed in the social encyclicals but the question of a just wage. Remuneration has to be just. But what is just? As we have seen in the preceding section, property has been fairly consistently described, in all the relevant encyclicals, as the result of work. Can we infer that if people only work hard enough they will become members of the propertied classes, and perhaps even own their own means of production? The encyclical *Mater et magistra* by John XXIII (1961) tells us:

> We therefore consider it Our duty to reaffirm that the remuneration of work is not something that can be left to the laws of the marketplace; nor should it be a decision left to the will of the more powerful. It must be determined in accordance with justice and equity; which means that workers must be paid a wage which allows them to live a truly human life and to fulfil their family obligations in a worthy manner.
>
> (§ 71)

Rerum novarum already mentions 'some little savings' that a 'thrifty' person can accumulate, supposing he earns enough:

> If a workman's wages be sufficient to enable him comfortably to support himself, his wife, and his children, he will find it easy, if he be a sensible man, to practice thrift, and he will not fail, by cutting down expenses, to put by some little savings and thus secure a modest source of income.
>
> (§ 46)

Quadragesimo anno first seems to support claims for a larger share of the value workers produce (the keyword is *thrift*, again):

> Therefore, with all our strength and effort we must strive that at least in the future the abundant fruits of production will accrue equitably to those who are rich and will be distributed in ample sufficiency among

the workers – not that these may become remiss in work, for man is born to labour as the bird to fly – but that they may increase their property by thrift.

(§ 61)

Later in this encyclical, however, it seems that the wage has to be sufficient to support the family, only as long as, within their capacity, women and children contribute to the family income:

> In the first place, the worker must be paid a wage sufficient to support him and his family. That the rest of the family should also contribute to the common support, according to the capacity of each, is certainly right, as can be observed especially in the families of farmers, but also in the families of many craftsmen and small shopkeepers.

(§ 71)

Pacem in terris (1963), too, does not foresee the creation of property through remuneration for one's work. We read:

> The worker is likewise entitled to a wage that is determined in accordance with the precepts of justice. This needs stressing. The amount a worker receives must be sufficient, in proportion to available funds, to allow him and his family a standard of living consistent with human dignity.

(§ 20)

This message is largely repeated in the Pastoral Constitution *Gaudium et spes* (1965), which also reminds us that not only the costs of subsistence, but also many other factors have to be taken into account:

> Finally, remuneration for labour is to be such that man may be furnished the means to cultivate worthily his own material, social, cultural, and spiritual life and that of his dependents, in view of the function and productiveness of each one, the conditions of the factory or workshop, and the common good.

(§ 67)

Laborem exercens reminds us once more that property is the result of work: 'As mentioned above, property is acquired first of all through work' (§ 14.3). Yet it also suggests that the remuneration for work should be sufficient to provide for future needs, as well:

> Just remuneration for the work of an adult who is responsible for a family means remuneration which will suffice for establishing and properly maintaining a family and for providing security for its future.

(§ 19.3)

To ask for more is not considered appropriate. Employers will also be glad to read: 'Union demands cannot be turned into a kind of group or class "egoism" ' (§ 20.4). Is not every petition for a wage increase egoistical?

Things changed after the collapse of socialism. The excessive generosity of the preceding decades was not to last. We are not surprised to read that, according to *Centesimus annus*, the worker again cannot hope for more than the necessary subsistence for present and foreseeable needs. The capacity to build up property does not seem to be part of a just remuneration for one's work.

> These objectives include a sufficient wage for the support of the family, social insurance for old age and unemployment, and adequate protection for the conditions of employment.
>
> (§ 34)

However, this encyclical makes us aware of another kind of property which had been previously overlooked:

> In our time, in particular, there exists another form of ownership which is becoming no less important than land: *the possession of know-how, technology and skill.*
>
> (§ 32, emphasis in the original)

The question, though, is to whom does this new kind of property belong? The people who have it are described in this encyclical as 'the firm's most valuable asset' (§ 35). To possess the necessary know-how and skill does not make a person rich. Wealth, we read in *Centesimus annus*, is reserved for the entrepreneurs, for those who turn the capabilities of 'the firm's most valuable asset' into profit:

> Organizing such a productive effort, planning its duration in time, making sure that it corresponds in a positive way to the demands which it must satisfy, and taking the necessary risks – all this too is a source of wealth in today's society. In this way, the *role* of disciplined and creative *human work* and, as an essential part of that work, *initiative and entrepreneurial ability* becomes increasingly evident and decisive.
>
> (§ 32)

Finally I will investigate the question whether work is seen as a duty or a right in the encyclicals. Is it possible to trace the caesura between natural law and human rights in this context, as well? As already said, work is viewed as an obligation in *Rerum novarum* and in *Quadragesimo anno*. In *Rerum novarum*, Leo XIII quotes Genesis: 'In the sweat of thy face shalt thou eat bread' (§ 34) and Pius XI says in *Quadragesimo anno*: 'for man is born to labor as the bird to fly' (§ 6). The Second World War initiates a process of change. In his 1941 Pentecost Address Pius XII explains:

> The individual duty to work given by nature consequently corresponds to the natural right of the individual to ensure one's life and those of one's family members through work. (translated from the German text, *Texte* 1992: 130 f., my translation)

To John XXIII, work is still embedded in natural law, but in *Pacem in terris* he does not postulate an obligation to work:

> If we turn our attention to the economic sphere it is clear that man has a right by the natural law not only to an opportunity to work, but also to go about his work without coercion.
>
> (§ 18)

Gaudium et Spes (1965), however, refers to the now common combination: 'the duty of working faithfully and also the right to work' (§ 67).

Human rights are mentioned in this context for the first time in *Laborem exercens*:

> While work, in all its many senses, is an obligation, that is to say a duty, it is also a source of rights on the part of the worker. These rights must be examined in the broad context of human rights as a whole, which are conatural with man and many of which are proclaimed by various international organizations and increasingly guaranteed by the individual states for their citizens.
>
> (§ 16.1)

The quote exemplifies well how half-heartedly the Church accepted the concept of human rights. According to this encyclical, human rights remain nothing more than an emanation of natural law; they are not created through democratic proclamation.

In *Centesimus annus*, John Paul II quickly adapts to the changing circumstances due to the end of socialism. In his view, 'the human rights to private initiative, to ownership of property, and to freedom in the economic sector' (§ 24) are more important than 'the right to share in the work which makes wise use of the earth's material resources' (§ 47). Ensuring these rights is the state's responsibility:

> Another task of the State is that of overseeing and directing the exercise of human rights in the economic sector. However, primary responsibility in this area belongs not to the State but to individuals and to the various groups and associations which make up society. The State could not directly ensure the right to work for all its citizens unless it controlled every aspect of economic life and restricted the free initiative of individuals.
>
> (§ 48)

This is the use of language that is popular with employers. The *right to work* remains a human right, but the maintenance of human rights is not primarily state responsibility and therefore not legally enforceable. What remains is the *obligation to work*. Similar to the keyword *property*, the semantic change in major aspects of *work* resembles a spiral. It seems as if the Catholic social doctrine of *Centesimus annus* repeats the underlying attitudes of *Rerum novarum*, but on a sublimated argumentation level. The same is true for the paradigmatic change from natural law to human rights. *Human rights* may

sound more progressive, but in erecting *human rights* on the firm foundation of *natural law*, the Church puts itself in the privileged position of
endorsing just those human rights that it has propagated all along as natural law. The state has to guarantee the right of property and to ensure
favourable conditions for its growth. But the right to work will be left to the
market forces. Human rights only have to be respected where they coincide
with natural law. The democratic character of human rights is successfully
subverted.

5 Modern implications of the discourse of the Catholic social doctrine

The analysis of the diachronic dimension of the discourse of the Catholic
social doctrine allowed us to reconstruct the meaning for our key words
property, natural law/human rights, and *work* within this discourse. One result
is the realization that in the beginning 'property' is viewed as a sacrosanct
right which provides protection against any kind of seizure. Later, after the
Second World War, this inviolability is questioned in the encyclical *Laborem
exercens*. It is no longer discussed in the youngest encyclical *Centesimus annus*
where we suddenly find 'property' redefined, now including 'knowledge',
'technology' and 'skill', thus watering down the original concept to a
homoeopathic dose and defusing the conflict with the democratic value of
equality. In this new sense, everyone becomes a proprietor. We also saw that
the 'property' based on 'natural law' was turned into the 'property based on
human rights'. On the other side, the right to work which was never
covered by 'natural law' (as opposed to the obligation to work) is not fully
recognized as a 'human right'; rather its status is left in limbo and usually
mentioned only in connection with work as a duty. The encyclicals repeatedly assert that property is acquired through work. However, only the
otherwise conservative encyclical *Quadragesimo anno* said that the worker
has a claim on a small portion of the profit that he has created by his
work. This is rather an exception to the often reiterated statements that
wages should normally be based on the needs of the worker and his family
unless the economic situation of the enterprise asks for sacrifice. The gener-
ous offer, made in *Quadrigesimo anno*, of a small piece of land as reward
for the especially industrious and thrifty worker was not maintained by later
encyclicals.

The analysis of the social encyclicals makes it clear that, in ideological
terms, they belong to the moderately conservative camp whose use of
language they reflect as well as their influence. Up to *Centesimus annus*,
this is not the liberal free market economy advocated by Adam Smith;
rather, it is a corporational system where everyone knows his place and
where advancement is merited by the extraordinary display of values and
'secondary virtues' like obedience, industry, sense of duty and modesty.
Unfortunately, it would transcend the limitations of this chapter to extend
our discourse in such a way that it would include relevant texts from the
camp of employers, the political parties they endorse, and judges and other

academics with an affinity to the view of the propertied classes. It is well known from historical accounts that these discourses have influenced each other, and a study of the intertextual links obtaining between these texts could easily demonstrate these connections.

A few observations, however, might point out possible links. The (mainly Protestant) encyclopedia *Die Religion in Geschichte und Gegenwart* ('Religion in present time and in the past') (1960) talks, in its entry on *natural law* ('Naturrecht'), about a 'greenhouselike fast and artificially blossoming natural law renewal since 1945 in Europe' and comments (my translation):

> This unreflected naive natural law fascination [,particularly in Germany, has] had consequences in hardly convincing court rulings more than once. Narrowly defined political as well as confessional views could easily be presented as generally valid natural law statutes and thereby prepared the ground for a neopositivistic reaction, giving it cheap arguments against natural law ideas in jurisprudence in general.

The *Europäische Enzyklopädie zu Philosophie und Wissenschaften* (1990) writes about the influence of Catholic discourse: 'Natural law ideas with neothomistic contents appeared in West German *Bundesgerichtshof* [Highest Federal Appellate Court] jurisdiction and here especially in family and criminal law.' Helmut Rittstieg (1975: 289 ff.) shows that the notion of natural law became important in the context of property as well: 'Especially in the area of property law, natural law argumentation exceeded the measure necessitated by the confrontation with National Socialism.' Rittstieg quotes a 1949 ruling of the *Badische Staatsgerichtshof* [Upper State Court of the state of Baden]. There we read that the basic right of property is founded in 'the general, supranational legal principles, in the legal sense and conscience of all civilized nations'. In a later ruling, it is stated that the right of private property is to remain intact 'as an unwritten, supranational basic right also during times when there is no written constitution'. In 1952, the *Bundesgerichtshof* [Highest Federal Appelate Court] refers explicitly, but wrongly, to Catholic natural law doctrine, when it presents the limits of owners' rights as 'a limitation ever inherent to property'. According to Rittstieg (1975: 298), this is more of an 'ornamental reference', indicating that it must have been argumentatively advantageous to refer to Church doctrine at that time. Later, the attitude towards natural law became more remote. From the 1960s onwards, after the publication of *Mater et magistra*, when the Catholic Church seemed to replace the natural law doctrine by adopting the concept of human rights, most knowledgeable law experts would have subscribed to the views of *Meyers Kleines Lexikon Philosophie* (1987, entry *Naturrecht*, my translation):

> The unscientific character of the natural law concept functioning as a basis for ethical and legal norms prevented the natural law doctrine from being revived. Only the Roman Catholic Church continues to support the doctrine of natural law initiated by God in spite of serious criticism also from within its own ranks.

A good example of the longevity of discourse objects in general and the indestructibility of the natural law argumentation in particular can be seen in the renaissance it had in Germany after the unification. While there is no outspoken dissociation from the word *human rights* whose concept served as a weapon in the ideological battle against the socialist block, the semantic aspect of *human rights*, namely that they are based on a democratic act of sovereign citizens, is tacitly dismissed. A recent trend within conservative branches of legal philosophy as well as political science is now trying to subjugate human rights to natural law. Now it is not the people who decide what is a human right, but the expert, legitimized by the authorities. In the new scenario, natural law and human rights superficially seem to coincide. This has been the Catholic strategy ever since *Mater et magistra*.

Today's natural law renaissance becomes obvious in a supplement of the weekly newspaper *Das Parlament* of 9 August 1991, dedicated to this topic. As a starting point, earlier natural law 'exaggerations' are conceded, for example, the 1954 *Bundesgerichtshof* claims of an objective inalienable moral law which it conjures to forge existing positive law into the 'Christian-western concept of the world'. Arthur Kaufmann comments (1991: 5): 'What was claimed here as natural law is a colourful, often contradictory, and confusing abundance of moral values.' Wolfgang Waldstein in his contribution even cites natural law opponents like Hans-Ulrich Evers (Waldstein 1991: 31, my translation):

> The attempt to establish the perennial guarantee of basic rights (in the German Basic Law) on natural law basis is bound to be a failure because in the legal system of a pluralistic society, it is not possible to accept any natural law due its inherent ideological justifications.

But then, Waldstein points out (Waldstein 1991: 32, my translation):

> Evers' argument of natural law being 'justifiable only in an ideological context' presupposes a natural law which objectively does not exist as an object of cognition beyond the influence of ideologies. If this is true, the question where exactly the inviolable and inalienable human rights come from is unavoidable. This kind of rights can only be pre-constitutional and natural, if they are meant to have the quality 'inviolable and inalienable'.

The significant aspect in the meaning of *human rights* is that they are established by democratic consensus, that they are a civil declaration similar to the *volonté générale* expressed by the citizen as the only sovereign. In the contemporary conservative discourse, this aspect is replaced by the respective aspect valid for natural law, namely the notion that it is not subject to human ruling. Even conservatives can live with this new, post-democratic definition of human rights. This is how Joachim Detjen summarizes it:

> According to general consensus, the dignity and personal freedom of the individual have central meaning as basic rights. . . . Other basic and

human rights form groups around this core in their respective shape as liberal defence rights, as social demand rights, and as democratic equality and participation rights. Complementary to these basic values, there are duties, however, basic duties of the individual towards his equals as well as society as a whole.

(Detjen 1991: 22 f., my translation)

We find the model in *Pacem in terris*:

The natural rights with which We have been dealing are, however, inseparably connected, in the very person who is their subject, with just as many respective duties; and rights as well as duties find their source, their sustenance and their inviolability in the natural law which grants or enjoins them.

(§ 28)

To assert the complementarity of rights and duties also belongs to the natural law concept and is intrinsically foreign to the human rights concept.

Conclusions

Diachronic corpus linguistics, as I see it, attempts to build a bridge connecting discourse and society. It is in their discourse that any group of people come to find their identity, to negotiate common beliefs and attitudes and to attach meaning to their activities. The insatiable quest for meaning is, I think, the very core of diachronic corpus linguistics. But where do we find meaning? I believe it is futile to search for it in the minds of the members of a discourse community. We will only know what they think if they commit their thoughts as a text to the discourse, and we will never know if that text is a faithful reflection of their thoughts. We will not find meaning by comparing what is said in the discourse to some discourse-external reality. The reality out there becomes accessible only through the mediation of the discourse; it remains meaningless unless we, the members of the discourse community, succeed in reconstructing it in the discourse. There is no meaning outside of the discourse.

But how do we find meaning within the discourse? It is comparison that opens our eyes for what is there. What a text says comes to our attention only if we relate it to comparable texts. If we are interested in the Catholic social doctrine, we could compare it to Buddhist, Protestant or Muslim, or to socialist or neo-conservative doctrines. Over the last years, this kind of research has invigorated much (synchronic) corpus linguistics. The complementary approach is to look at change over time. A discourse is never stable. Every new contribution to a discourse will change its state.

Whether we investigate the relationship between discourse and society using synchronic or diachronic corpus linguistics, our work is not concluded once we have extracted the relevant data from our corpus. The generation of relevant concordances and the statistical analysis of this data is never more than a first step. What the evidence means is a matter of interpretation. Without an interpretation any study in corpus linguistics would be incomplete. We would have achieved no more than an accumulation of data. Yet while the assembly of the raw data can claim a certain amount of objectivity (like the preparation of a logarithm table), their interpretation forces us to take a stance, to invite criticism. For interpretation is a dialogic activity. I contribute my interpretation of the concepts 'work' and 'property' in the Catholic social doctrine to the discourse of my peer group, other corpus linguists and people interested in critical discourse analysis. I will have been successful if my contribution leaves traces in some future texts, if they refer to my interpretation, by modifying it, by commenting on it or even by rejecting it. My interpretation and subsequent reactions to it can be understood as new paraphrases of the lexical items *work* and *property*. Therefore meanings are always provisional. Each new paraphrase of a lexical item will affect its meaning.

Acknowledgements

I would like to thank Anna Čermáková, Michaela Mahlberg and Lucinda McDonald for their valuable comments on an earlier draft.

References

Unless stated otherwise, the citations from the encyclicals and other source texts are taken from the web page (English version) of the Vatican: www.vatican.va/phome_en.htm.

Brocker, M. (1992) *Arbeit und Eigentum. Der Paradigmenwechsel in der neuzeitlichen Eigentumstheorie*. Darmstadt: Wissenschaftliche Buchgesellschaft.

Detjen, J. (1991) 'Naturrecht in der pluralistischen Demokratie?' in Supplement to *Das Parlament* (Aus Politik und Zeitgeschichte), 08.09.1991, 19–30.

Europäische Enzyklopädie zu Philosophie und Wissenschaften (1990) Vol. 3. Hamburg: Felix Meiner.

Fagiani, F. (2004) 'Natural law and history in Locke's theory of distributive justice'. *Topoi*, 1983, 3, 163–85.

Fillmore, C. (1982) 'Frame semantics', in *Linguistics in the Morning Calm*. Seoul: Hanshin Publishing, pp. 111–37.

Kaufmann, A. (1991) 'Die Naturrechtsdiskussion in der Rechts- und Staatsphilosophie der Nachkriegszeit,' in Supplement to *Das Parlament* (Aus Politik und Zeitgeschichte), 09.08.1991, 3–17.

Lakoff, G. (1996) *Moral Politics: What Conservatives Know that Liberals Don't*. Chicago: University of Chicago Press.

Locke, J. (1982) *Second Treatise of Government*, ed. by R. Cox. Arlington Heights, Illinois: Harlan Davidson.

Meyers Kleines Lexikon Philosophie (1987) Mannheim: Bibliographisches Institut.

Nozick, R. (1974) *Anarchy, State, and Utopia.* New York: Basic Books.

The Oxford English Dictionary (1933) Volume 1–12. (1st edn), ed. by J. A. Murray, H. Bradley et al. Oxford: Clarendon Press.

Pfürtner, S. and Heierle, W. (1980) *Einführung in die katholische Soziallehre.* Darmstadt: Wissenschaftliche Buchgesellschaft.

Die Religion in Geschichte und Gegenwart (1960) Vol. 4. Tübingen: J. C. B. Mohr.

Rittstieg, H. (1975) *Eigentum als Verfassungsproblem.* Darmstadt: Wissenschaftliche Buchgesellschaft.

Teubert, W. (1996) 'The Concept of Work in Europe', in A. Musolff, C. Schäffner and M. Townson (eds), *Conceiving of Europe: Diversity in Unity.* Aldershot: Dartmouth, pp. 129–46.

—— (2001) 'Corpus Linguistics and Lexicography'. *International Journal of Corpus Linguistics,* Special Issue, 125–54.

—— (2004) 'Writing, hermeneutics and corpus linguistics'. *Logos and Language,* 4 (2003), 2, 1–17.

Texte zur katholischen Soziallehre (1992) (8th and enlarged edn by Bundesverband der Katholischen Arbeitnehmer-Bewegung Deutschlands, KAB). Volume 1: Die sozialen Rundschreiben der Päpste und andere kirchliche Dokumente. Mit Einführungen von Oswald von Nell-Breuning SJ und Johannes Schasching SJ. Bornheim. Ketteler Verlag.

Waldstein, W. (1991) 'Zur Frage des Naturrechts im Grundgesetz und in der Europäischen Menschenrechtskonvention', in Supplement to *Das Parlament* (Aus Politik und Zeitgeschichte), 09.08.1991, 31–7.

White, M. (1987) 'The politics of epistemology'. *Ethics,* 100 (1989), 77–92.

5   On texts, corpora and models of language

Michael Stubbs

Introduction

My two chapters in this book have two main themes. This chapter discusses the implications of empirical corpus study for a general model of language system and language use. The second chapter presents a small empirical case study of English phraseology which illustrates some of these general arguments.

Studies of large corpora provide two main contributions to linguistics. First, they provide many new and surprising facts about language use. This is an important test for an approach to language study: it can help us to learn new things. Second, by looking at language from a new point of view, corpus studies can help to solve paradoxes which have plagued linguistics for at least a hundred years. This is also an important test: whether new empirical data and methods can help to formulate the puzzling relations between language system and language use, and therefore help to restate the conceptual foundations of our discipline. Corpus data and methods provide new ways of studying the relations between language system and language use. If a pattern becomes very frequent in use across very large quantities of text, then it becomes 'entrenched' as part of the system. Frequency in text becomes probability in the system. It is this connection between text and system for which corpus studies can provide detailed empirical evidence.

This chapter discusses the problem which de Saussure formulated in the early 1900s, but which has never been solved in a satisfactory way: the term 'language' is ambiguous. Depending on how we look at it, language is both an abstract system and also the use which a community of speakers make of the system. A related dualism was proposed by Chomsky in the mid-1960s, when he argued that we have to distinguish between an individual speaker's knowledge of a language and their use of this knowledge. Both of these dualisms have turned out to be unsatisfactory. Other scholars have proposed pluralist models which distinguish between the abstract language system (which is social and public), an individual speaker's knowledge of the system (which is psychological and private), language as social action (which is intentional and meaningful) and language as text (which is observable and quantifiable). Since these aspects of language have different properties and are logically distinct, they are not reducible to each other. This chapter traces the history of such concepts with brief discussion of work in the 1600s and 1700s by René Descartes and David Hume, and more detailed discussion of more recent work by John Searle, Karl Popper, Dell Hymes, Michael Halliday, Dan Sperber and Juhan Tuldava.

I use the following presentation conventions. 'Single quote marks' are used for terminology and/or quotes from other authors. "Double quote marks" are used for the meaning of a linguistic expression. Italics are used for word-forms. Small capitals are used for a lexeme or lemma. For example, the lemma KEEP is the class of word-forms *keep*, *keeps*, *kept* and *keeping*.

1 Technologies of observation

Since the early 1600s, in the explosion of knowledge which is often known as the scientific revolution, progress in the natural sciences has depended on technological innovations. Before the invention of instruments such as microscopes, telescopes and high-speed cameras, scientists were oblivious to the existence of many things, simply because they were too small, too far away or too fast-moving to be seen. Ziman (2000: 91) points out that some instruments, such as optical telescopes or just a pair of spectacles, enhance what we can see anyway, whereas others, such as radio telescopes, reveal phenomena which we could otherwise never experience. Wilson (1998: 49) points out that such inventions have extended our grasp of reality beyond 'the tiny sphere attainable by unaided common sense'. And Macfarlane and Martin (2002) discuss the profound effect of optical instruments on the whole development of Western science.

In linguistics, inventions such as tape-recorders and experimental phonetic equipment allow accurate recording and therefore public representation of phenomena which are unobservable without their help. In work which started in the 1960s (Sinclair et al. 2004), but with increasing momentum since the 1990s, further technological advances now provide access to large text collections and allow linguists to record and observe things whose existence was rarely imagined because they could never be directly observed. These advances depend on the ability to store, in computer-readable form, large amounts of data (in 2007 'large' means tens or hundreds of millions of running words), and to use software to search and analyse these data. What was previously invisible, but can now be observed, are patterns across these large data collections and the complex systems which arise as 'emergent phenomena' when small units 'act together in large assemblages' (Wilson 1998: 93–4). We therefore have new ways of studying the relations between recurrent use and emergent system.

Within recent linguistics, especially from the 1960s to the 1980s, it was frequently argued that speakers have privileged access to facts about their native language, and that introspective data are adequate, or indeed the only possible data, for studying language. However, for many areas of language use, introspection provides no interesting evidence. Renouf (1987: 174–5) gives good examples of simple facts which are not accessible to intuition, namely that the most frequent uses of many lexical words are not what speakers think of as their core meanings. For example, the most frequent use of KEEP is not "to put and store" (*where do you keep your jewellery?*), but uses such as: *the doors were kept permanently locked* or *they were kept awake*. Sampson (1996) provides a striking grammatical example. Within Chomskyan linguistics, it had often been claimed on intuitive grounds that multiple central embedding in sentences was not a natural linguistic phenomenon and that it simply did not occur. Sampson discovered examples and cites several in his article. One example is:

> In the 18th century, [when [as Linda Colley shows in her book *Britons*], the British national identity was forged in war and conflict with France], our kings were Germans.

He also calculates that such constructions occur at least once per 500,000 running words, and concludes that 'if intuition could get the facts of language as wrong as this', there had to be a better way of 'engaging with the empirical realities of language' (Sampson 1996: 25). In any area of study, data must meet certain criteria: they must be accurate, complete and clearly presented, accessible and searchable. Poor quality data, which are unreliable, unreplicable or incomplete, can be extremely damaging. The reason is expressed in the ironic computing maxim GIGO: garbage in, garbage out.

2 A concrete example: *tolerate*

The most essential technology for corpus study is an aligned KWIC concordance (Key Word in Context). Here is a first short example of the kind of patterns which become visible with a technology which can find all occurrences of a word in a large corpus and display them in a convenient way. The word-form *tolerate* occurs over 600 times in the British National Corpus[1] (BNC). In three-word strings it most frequently co-occurs with a negative and a modal verb: *will not tolerate, could not tolerate, would not tolerate*. A few concordance lines illustrate this pattern and add some more. I extracted all occurrences from the BNC, sorted them alphabetically to the left, and then took every 50th line.

No automatic semantic analysis of such concordance lines is possible, but a concordance presents data in a form which allows the human analyst to see patterns. Most lines have a modal to the left. Several have the word *not* or another negative (*unable*) or a semantic expression of difficulty in accepting something unpleasant (*hard to*). This is empirical evidence for a longer phrasal expression in which the word predictably occurs.

Concordance 5.1 Twelve illustrative concordance lines from the BNC of the patterns around *tolerate*

```
050 scribe it for everybody who can tolerate it, and not to investigate beca
100   essential to him. He couldn't tolerate twenty-four hours in which the
150 dvanced HIV-related illness may tolerate zidovudine better than people w
200  aid might suffer if it did not tolerate an opposition. In return the A
250  telling of tales, you will not tolerate any hitting. Ignoring disputes
300 d and snow that no other plants tolerate (Lamb, 1970; Dodge, 1973). Some
350 art. He had been better able to tolerate it ten years ago, but then he h
400   the fish find this very hard to tolerate. They actually er attack the g
450 ts that society would prefer to tolerate the adverse consequences of rea
500 ainty. One young man, unable to tolerate the thought, burned himself al
550 ish and plants listed here will tolerate a pH of up to 7.5. The temperat
600 ll her so in a manner she would tolerate?" Odette shook her head and sm
```

3 Principles of empirical linguistics

Quantitative information on language use not only reveals new facts, but also helps to solve problems which have been at the heart of the discipline for the last hundred years. In a famous statement, de Saussure (1916) argued that 'far from the object of study preceding the point of view, it is rather the point of view which creates the object'. New observational methods create a new point of view by providing new types of language data. In a statement about this new point of view which has become almost as famous amongst corpus linguists, Sinclair (1991: 100) observes that 'the language looks rather different when you look at a lot of it at once'. Data from large corpora allow linguists to study the meaning of communicative acts in attested samples of language use.

Corpus linguistics is based on two principles of empirical observational study. First, the observer must not influence what is observed. Data and analysis must be independent. What is selected for observation clearly depends on prior hypotheses, as well as on what is convenient and technically possible. Nevertheless, corpus data are part of natural language use and not produced for purposes of linguistic analysis. A sharp distinction must be maintained between introspection as data, which is unreliable, and intuition in interpretation, which is unavoidable (Rundell 2001). Second, repeated events are significant. If a pattern occurs over and over again, in the language use of many different speakers, then it cannot be dismissed as mere performance. The frequent occurrence of lexical or grammatical patterns in a large text collection is good evidence of what is typical and routine in language use. Frequency in the corpus is observable evidence of probability in the system (Halliday 1991, 1992, 1993). Unique events can be described only against the background of what is normal and expected. A major focus of corpus linguistics is therefore to describe what is usual and typical.

Central characteristics of corpus linguistics, as Teubert (1999a, b, 2005) points out, follow from these two principles. It is inherently sociolinguistic: it studies attested texts, which were real communicative acts in a discourse community. It is inherently diachronic: it studies what has frequently occurred in the past. More obviously, it is inherently quantitative. It is surprising how many approaches to language study have dismissed the idea of counting things, and have therefore ignored the fact that some patterns are hundreds or thousands of times more frequent than others because they have been successfully used over and over in the past.

We cannot eliminate subjective factors in observation, but we can make explicit how observations are always constrained by what is possible and/or convenient, and how different aspects of reality are therefore emphasized by available data and observational methods. Concordances make repetitions visible, and corpus linguists tend to emphasize the repetitive and routine nature of language use. However, these repetitions are really there: the technology makes them visible, but does not create them. Sealey and Carter (2004) include examples from corpus linguistics in their robust defence of such realist positions in the social sciences.

Corpus study is empiricist: actual occurrences are the primary object of study and analyses are therefore firmly based in publicly accessible observational data. However, the empirical textual data are evidence of non-observables, both phraseological units of meaning and underlying systems (see Francis et al. 1996, 1998 on pattern grammar). Software tools such as concordances can classify and arrange data and therefore give 'an operational foothold' in a corpus, which then allows 'imaginative, inventive leaps' to abstract explanatory concepts (Botha 1992: 30 citing Hymes and Fought 1975). The argument is not that the essence of language is material observable utterances in a corpus of texts. The texts are only a sample: the traces (products) which remain of cognitive and social communicative events (processes). It is essential to distinguish between the ontology (what you think the essence of language is) and the epistemology (how you think we can discover this essence) (Botha 1992: 3). A materialist epistemology (the methodological principle that data must be observable) does not commit us to a purely materialist ontology (the view that only sense data are real). Corpus data, such as concordance lines, require much interpretation, since we are ultimately interested in abstract units of meaning. This has been the central aim since the beginning of corpus study. In the careful phrasing of Sinclair et al. (2004: 6), there is a relation 'between statistically defined units of lexis and postulated units of meaning'.

In summary: By organizing huge masses of data, technology can make visible patterns which lie outside unaided human perception and which no amount of introspection or manual analysis could discover. Corpus methods can therefore demonstrate order where previously only randomness or idiosyncrasy were visible, and therefore open up research topics which were previously inconceivable. This is one of the rare occasions on which the social sciences have succeeded in 'revealing an invisible world of entities and concepts behind the societal life-world' (Ziman 2000: 230).

4 Rationalism and empiricism, deduction and induction

These comments on ontology and epistemology signal some implications of corpus linguistics for long-standing debates about the nature of knowledge. It is understandable that, by and large, corpus linguists have paid little explicit attention to these debates, since they have preferred to devote their attention to discovering new facts in the vast new resources which large corpora make available. But it is unfortunate, since new empirical corpus data can help to reinterpret old problems. For at least 2,000 years, scholars have disagreed about whether rationalist or empiricist methods are appropriate in language study. The debate goes back to ancient Greece (Robins 1988: 464–5), when some scholars argued that grammar should be based on logical and psychological principles, whereas others argued that grammar should be the observational study of the actual language used by the poets and prose writers. I will pick out just two pairs of opposing positions in this debate: rationalism versus empiricism, and deductive versus inductive methods. This will situate corpus linguistics in a broad historical context and highlight its general implications for these classic problems.

A deductive argument starts from premises, and draws conclusions which must be true if the premises are true. Deductive logic concerns the validity of the argument which relates premises and conclusion. (All students like beer. Bill is a student. Therefore Bill likes beer.) The premises may turn out to be false, but the syllogism is valid.

An inductive argument starts from a sample of individual observations and proposes a generalization which is true of similar cases. (We have seen a lot of students and they all like beer. So, probably a lot of other students also like beer.) However, the observation does not lead logically to this conclusion, and indeed it is not clear how far we can extend the generalization. (All students like beer, or only most?) And perhaps our sample was not a good one: perhaps the cases we observed were not typical.

Deductive reasoning takes place within a closed system, in the sense that all the information is already contained in the premises: implications are merely made explicit by argument. It studies ways in which sentences follow logically from other sentences, and thereby relates propositions (premises) to other propositions (conclusions). The conclusions would be true in all possible worlds, because they depend on the meaning of the words. Deduction can lead to new knowledge only in the sense of a new perspective on old knowledge which is already contained (implicitly) in the premises. However, one of its weaknesses is that it can tell us nothing about the truth of the premises.

Inductive reasoning claims to go beyond the particular starting point to a generalization about cases which we have not observed. It relates individual observations to general statements. This is its strength: we have confidence in the starting point since we have observed these cases to be true, and it tells us something new by going from the particular to the general.

However, this is also its weakness, since we cannot be certain about what we might see in the future.

Deduction and induction are often assumed to be symmetrically related. Deduction starts from premises, and goes from the general to the specific. Induction starts from observations, and goes from the specific to the general. However, this opposition is only apparent. Both deduction and induction assume reliable starting points: either self-evident premises or observed facts. Deductive logic assumes the truth of the premises, and treats only their consequences in a possible world. Inductive logic assumes the reliability of the initial observations in the real world, but since all observations are already interpretations and open to all kinds of potential errors, they can never be certain. If the initial evidence is unreliable, then the conclusions cannot be reliable (Popper 1983: 221–3). The most difficult cases arise when we can observe only a small finite sample but wish to make predictions about a very large population. In the case of language use, it is not clear what would constitute a representative sample of a very large open-ended population.

Within linguistics, these oppositions have characteristic exemplars as follows.

- A rationalist deductive view is adopted by de Saussure and Chomsky. Samples of attested language use are not used as central evidence in investigating the underlying language system. On the contrary, the starting point is a small amount of introspective data from which are deduced characteristics of the system. This work is situated within a French tradition of dualism, as represented by René Descartes in the 1600s.

- An empiricist inductive view is adopted, often implicitly, by most text and corpus linguists such as Firth, Halliday and Sinclair. Large samples of attested language use are interpreted as evidence of probabilistic generalizations. The argument is that a pattern which repeatedly occurs in language use (*parole*) is evidence of a unit in the language system (*langue*). This work rejects dualism in favour of a monist alternative, and is situated within a British empiricist tradition, as represented by David Hume in the 1700s.

My comments below on Descartes and Hume do not provide detailed explanations of these complex sets of work, but they situate corpus studies within these classic debates. Certain general problems of epistemology (the theory of knowledge) may never be definitively solved, but they can be continually reinterpreted as new data and methods of study become available. Corpus study provides new ways of tackling ancient puzzles.

5 Rationalism: Descartes on body and mind

Descartes, working in a French tradition of rationalism, believed that it was possible to use deductive methods in order to arrive at certain knowledge, and his rationalism was closely related to his proposed dualism of body and mind. He argues that human beings are both bodies, which perform actions in the physical world, and minds, which think and feel. In his *Discourse on Method* (1637) he discusses, in a surprisingly modern-sounding argument, whether is it possible to teach a robot to use a human language. Imagine, he says in Part 5 of the *Discourse*, machines whose outward appearance exactly resembles human beings. He concedes that machines might behave in a mechanical and routine way, but argues that they could not react appropriately to unpredictable behaviour from other people. He therefore distinguishes sharply between different aspects of behaviour: external–internal, observable–unobservable, physical–mental and routine–creative. He argues that mental activities cannot be reduced to physical activities, and rejects what is usually called, in twentieth-century discussions, 'behaviourism'. However, Descartes' very clear dualism proposes two contrasting aspects of language which are irreducible to each other and which therefore create their own problems: he cannot explain how body and mind interact. In accounting for the different aspects of language there are two essential questions: we have to show that they are irreducible to each other; but we then have to show how they are related.

Much twentieth-century linguistics is based on these Cartesian dualisms: Chomsky (1966) wrote a book entitled *Cartesian Linguistics.* In this tradition, language is conceived as having two essential aspects. First, it is behaviour, individual and unpredictable in its details. This is *parole* or performance. Second, it is knowledge: this is its underlying organization, which is known unconsciously by native speakers. This has been called 'competence', if we are thinking of an individual speaker, or *langue*, if we are thinking of the system shared by speakers in a discourse community. For de Saussure (1916), *langue* is social and *parole* is individual. For Chomsky (1965), competence is individual, and performance is the category to which the social is relegated, then to be ignored. Cartesian dualisms have also been resisted: Labov (1972: 185 ff.) provides a famous discussion of the de Saussurian paradox, and Hymes (1972) argues that performance is a bucket category which conceals quite different concepts (see section 12 below).

Descartes' position has further characteristics which are relevant to general debates about the nature of language. It is introspective and deductive. Descartes started from a claim to which he believed he had privileged access. He felt that the statement 'I think therefore I am' was certain and could not be denied without logical contradiction, and he tried to deduce further certain statements from this. I am not concerned here with well-known problems with this starting point, only with its characteristics: it starts from an introspective certainty about the private self, and attempts to build a deductive argument which follows logically from this statement.

Corpus linguists work in an essentially different way, using inductive arguments which start from many observations, drawn from a large sample of speakers, and which lead to generalizations which are true of similar cases.[2]

6 Empiricism: Hume on induction

Ideas about inductive reasoning are often traced back to the early 1600s, when Francis Bacon argued that scientific progress must be based on systematic data collection and observation, though he himself admits that some of his main points had been made by Plato. Bacon rejected dogma and authority as sources of knowledge, and criticized deductive reasoning as being similar to spiders making webs of knowledge out of their own substance (Quinton 1980: 26, 55). In its stead, he proposed methodically recording observations, and then proceeding gradually and cumulatively towards general principles. Bacon is often criticized for his naive faith in the possibility of reliable unbiased observation, and for his insistence on the rather timid plodding accumulation of data, as opposed to the leaps of imagination and guesswork which lead to real progress in science (Popper 1983: 222–3).

A more modern tradition is represented by David Hume,[3] who worked in the British empirical tradition of John Locke and George Berkeley. Hume is also concerned with epistemology (the theory of knowledge, its nature and limits), but rejects Cartesian dualism on two grounds. First, he argues that mind is not an immaterial substance, but 'a bundle of perceptions'. Second, he distinguishes clearly between psychological and logical certainty (Popper 1963: 42). Hume's problem is how beliefs can be rationally justified. He admits that there is nothing new about the idea that we learn from experience: 'none but a fool or madman will ever pretend to dispute the authority of experience', and 'it is certain that the most ignorant and stupid peasants – nay infants, nay even brute beasts – improve by experience' (Hume 1748: section 4, part 2). He admits that we cannot avoid jumping to inductive conclusions. It is an unavoidable mental habit, and a perfectly reasonable thing to do, indeed often the only thing to do. But this is a matter of necessary everyday custom and habit, not of logic. He distinguishes clearly between different types of inference, and between the psychological certainty which induction seems to bring, and the impossibility of inductive generalizations providing logical certainty. Any observations we have made were made in the past, but there is no logical reason to assume that the future will resemble the past, since there can always be new cases and new observations, and since any predictions about the future are therefore open to potential counter-example:

> If we be [. . .] engaged in arguments to put trust in past experience, and make it the standard of our future judgement, these arguments must be probable only [. . .]. All our experimental conclusions proceed upon the supposition that the future will be conformable to the past.
>
> (Hume 1748: section 4)

One of Hume's most agressively phrased recommendations about empirical methods is that, when we read a book, we should ask:

> 'Does it contain any abstract reasoning concerning quantity or number?' No.

'Does it contain any experimental reasoning concerning matter of fact and existence?' No. Commit it then to the flames, for it can contain nothing but sophistry
and illusion.

(Hume 1748: closing paragraph)

7 Monism version 1: Bloomfield

For those who see insoluble problems with dualism, there are only two ways
out. A model of language must be based on either fewer or more contrasting elements. Fewer than two clearly means one, and monist positions have
been proposed by Bloomfield and Halliday. Pluralist positions, with three
or four contrasting elements, have been proposed by Popper, Hymes,
Searle and Tuldava.

One strategy to avoid dualism is to abandon the mental and to propose a
view known as 'behaviourism' (and also as 'mechanism' or 'materialism').
An extreme view radically denies the existence of the mind. A less extreme
view concentrates on behaviour, and assumes, for theoretical purposes, that
the mind does not exist. For example, Bloomfield (1933: vii) famously
abandons psychology in favour of 'mechanism', which he calls 'the necessary form of scientific discourse'. Whether Bloomfield really believed that
'we don't have minds' is not important. He was proposing that a scientist
'must proceed as if he held the materialistic view' (1933: 38, see also 142).
Bloomfield argues that language involves observable behaviour, that science has to be based on observable facts, that the mind is unobservable and
therefore inaccessible, and that the admission of mental facts is therefore
an unnecessary complication. Another famous statement along these lines
is: 'The scientific method is quite simply the convention that the mind does
not exist' (Twaddell 1935: 57). We find in American structuralism a corresponding emphasis on recording and analysing texts. For example, Fries
(1940, 1952) based his descriptions of sentence patterns on a corpus of
letters to the US government and on a 250,000-word corpus of recorded
telephone conversations.

Bloomfield's monism and his insistence on observational data were
logically related to his methodological insistence that 'the only useful generalizations about language are inductive generalizations' (1933: 20). In
turn, this view was related to investigations of the native languages of North
America. First, American linguists had no native speaker intuitions on
which they could rely: they had to work with spoken texts produced by
informants. Second, it turned out that these languages had features which
seemed strikingly different from the well-studied Indo-European languages. This led in turn to the view, which seems overstated nowadays, that
'features which we think ought to be universal may be absent from the very
next language that becomes accessible' (1933: 20).

Bloomfield and Twaddell regard monism as an attitude which it is convenient or necessary to adopt. However, people have strong intuitions that
they have mental states, including thoughts, feelings and wishes, and that

language involves essential mental processes of understanding. So, strictly behaviourist views are often felt to be strongly counter-intuitive, even if many people would accept a partly reductionist view that the mind is what the brain does.

8 Monism version 2: Halliday

There is a second version of monism on which much corpus study is based. Firth (1957: 2n) denounces dualisms as 'a quite unnecessary nuisance', and explicitly describes (1935: 53, 1957: 2) his position as monist, and both Halliday (1978: 38, 51) and Sinclair (1991: 103) reject the competence–performance distinction. However, this rejection of dualism is based on a different reductionist argument, that apparent dualisms result from an error in our thinking, namely looking at the same phenomenon from different points of view. The view that behaviour and knowledge are aspects of the same thing also has a long history. Popper (1994: 109) points to Spinoza's argument in the 1600s: if we look at reality from the inside, then it is mind; if we look at it from the outside, then it is matter.

Scholars have tried different analogies in order to try and clarify these difficult ideas. Halliday (1991, 1992, 1993) argues that the weather and the climate are the same phenomenon seen from different time depths. If we are thinking of the next few hours, then we are thinking of the weather, and this perspective determines what kinds of actions we might take, such as going to the beach or packing an umbrella. If we are thinking of the next century, then we are thinking of the climate, and this perspective determines different actions, such as legislating against industrial processes which increase global warming. If the climate changes, then obviously this affects the weather. Conversely, each day's weather affects the climate, however minimally, either maintaining the status quo, or helping to tip the balance towards climate change. Halliday argues that instance and system, micro and macro are two sides of the same coin, relative to the observer's position. Similarly, every instance in a text perturbs the overall probabilities of the system, if only to an infinitesimal extent: the system is inherently probabilistic.

However, Halliday's analogy is not yet quite correct as stated above. 'Weather' refers to short-term events (e.g. the sun is shining, it is windy). 'Climate' has two senses. In one sense, it is a state or a series of events on a very long timescale (e.g. a maritime or continental climate). In another sense, it is a theory, a series of generalizations about what is likely in a geographical area (e.g. the country has a continental climate with hot summers and cold winters). As Halliday and Hasan (2000: 208) argue, 'a climate is a theory of weather'. A systematic theory must be inferred from written records of measurements of temperature, rainfall, and so on, which have been collected over a long time, possibly hundreds of years, and which are therefore accessible to scientists only with the assistance of technologies of observation, measurement and record keeping. It is even clearer that climate is a theoretical concept if one thinks of the debates around climate change: there is no consensus about exactly which factors will determine the climate in the future.

Frequency in the weather leads to probability in the climate. Frequency is a fact about past events, but probability is a prediction about future events. So frequency and probability are not the same, and therefore the weather and the climate are objects of different logical types, which are not reducible to each other. The weather is a series of events, each of which is observable (e.g. it is windy today; thunder clouds are building up). But the climate is neither an event, nor is it directly observable.

9 Pluralism version 1: Halliday reinterpreted

Halliday's analogy can therefore be interpreted as implying not a monist position, but a pluralist position. There are physical events in the world: things happen (e.g. it is very cold today). This can be observed, records can be kept over long periods of time, and a theory can be formulated which allows these events to be predicted (e.g. the average midday temperature in January is 5° centigrade). Popper (1994: 7) argues for a pluralist position in precisely this way, using essentially the same analogy as Halliday. Metereologists make records of changes in temperature. The temperatures are physical states in the world, but the measurements have been selected and the records have been designed by human beings. The sequence of temperatures cannot be directly studied for the patterns it displays, but the record can be. A record can be designed which converts measurements into a form of public knowledge. Local variations in the weather can be directly observed and remembered in a rough and ready way, but records are needed in order to make precise hypotheses about long-term variations in the climate. For serious study, we need systematic records to replace individual human memory. In Popper's terms, events are physical phenomena, the intentions of individual human beings are subjective mental phenomena, and the records, resultant hypotheses and forms of public knowledge are objective phenomena (see section 10 below).

Halliday's analogy is therefore more accurately represented by three relations:

- the weather is analogous to language events (e.g. speech events and speech acts);
- metereological records are analogous to a textual corpus along with normative data (e.g. frequency of vocabulary and other features of language use);
- climate is analogous to a language system.

In analysing language, a further distinction is necessary. The same sentence can be uttered on different occasions by different people. An utterance is a piece of behaviour, and therefore an event in time. But a sentence is a unit of the language system, and is therefore timeless: it stands only in logical relations, such as paraphrase and contradiction, to other sentences (Katz 1981 *passim*). Furthermore, an utterance is never just an instance: it has to be interpreted against a history of language use. Any stretch of language has meaning only as a sample of an enormously large body of text, and represents the results of a process, where each selection (actual) has meaning by virtue of all the other selections which might have been made (potential), but have been rejected (Sinclair 1965: 76–7). The data from large corpora put linguistics in an increasingly good position to address the dualisms of individual and social, small-scale and large-scale, micro and macro. The potential of the system and the actual choice which is made are logically related, but the one is not reducible to the other.

From these remarks it follows that the language system can be seen in three ways:[4] as the cumulative product of the recurrent textual patterns, or as a theory which has been constructed by the linguist, or as the potential of what is possible (see section 15 below).

Linguistics and other disciplines have been constantly beset by the problem of relating the poles of dualisms such as subject and object, internal and external, agency and structure, process and product, *langue* and *parole*, language system and language use, creativity and rules, intended action and unintended consequences. Since concordancers and other software allow millions of words of data to be searched for patterns of language use which otherwise remain invisible, much of the significance of corpus linguistics lies in the possibility of relating these apparent opposites, and several corpus studies now provide precise diachronic demonstrations of these relations. Rissanen (2004) shows how the meaning of the word *side* developed between Old English and Modern English, from the meaning of "part of the body", to locality in relation to inanimate objects (*the side of the house*), to abstract senses (*two sides in a dispute*), to fully abstract relations (*besides* = "in addition to"). Hoffmann (2004) also shows how the meaning of *in view of* was used in the 1600s in a literal sense (*we came in view of the entrance of a wood*), but then developed via repeated pragmatic inferences to abstract causal meanings (*in view of the large number of requests . . .*). Studies of this kind show, in empirical detail, the relation between frequency of use and entrenchment in the system.

10 Pluralism version 2: Searle and Popper

A simple mind–body dualism fails because we need two distinctions: between objective things in the world (body) and individual subjective knowledge (mind), and between individual subjective knowledge and public objective knowledge (Popper 1994: 3 and *passim*). As an alternative to dualist models, different scholars have therefore proposed pluralist models.

A pluralist model which is well known to linguists is developed by Searle (1969: 50 ff.), as follows. There are brute (physical) facts and psychological (individual, mental) facts. But there are also other facts which do not fit this two-way picture, including getting married, being convicted of a crime, and winning a game of baseball. Searle calls these 'institutional facts', because they are not matters of individual opinion, and because they 'presuppose the existence of certain human institutions'. These institutions depend, in turn, on the distinction between regulative and constitutive rules (Searle 1969: 33 ff.). Regulative rules regulate behaviour which can/does exist independently of the rules, such as 'in New Zealand you have to drive on the left'. Constitutive rules, such as the rules of chess, themselves create or define the forms of behaviour. Thus it is only within the constitutive rules which define the social institution of marriage, that uttering a certain sentence counts as a particular kind of promise, which counts as getting married. The fact that two people are married cannot be reduced either to a piece of behaviour (they both uttered some words) or to individual mental feelings or opinions: there is a social reality which is irreducible to either of these other sets of facts. In a more recent book, Searle (1995) develops his work on speech acts into a theory of the construction of social reality.

These concepts have quite a long history in philosophy. For example, Anscombe (1958) distinguishes between 'brute facts' and facts which exist only 'in the context of our institutions'. Suppose, she says, someone orders some groceries. If a grocer brings a bag of potatoes to my house, then this is a brute fact. But there are events which are interpretable only within a set of institutions: these include my ordering the potatoes, the grocer supplying them, my paying his bill, so that I then own them. They also include unobservable facts, such as conventions involving trust between people (e.g. money) and social relations (e.g. ownership), and speech acts. It is a brute fact that I produce an utterance (e.g. *Could you send me ten pounds of potatoes*), but this hardly expresses the point of the utterance and the reciprocal obligations which it triggers. Rawls (1955) argues that there are rules of practices which are logically prior to particular cases. We can only talk of someone ordering and paying a bill for a bag of potatoes, if we presuppose the institutions of money, buying and selling, and property.

A comprehensive view of language must therefore be based on at least a three-way distinction. Depending on how we look at it, language is

[1] utterances: events, realized by actual physical behaviour
[2] individual knowledge: personal competence
[3] social knowledge: shared across a community

When a large sample of utterances [1] is recorded and made publicly accessible in a corpus, we can observe patterns across the usage of many speakers, and therefore make inferences about knowledge which is shared across a speech community [3]. It is usually argued that de Saussurian *parole* is equivalent to Chomskyan performance. However, whereas Chomskyan competence is individual and psychological, de Saussurian *langue* is interpersonal and social, though de Saussure is notoriously vague on the ontological status of this social knowledge. If we put de Saussure, Chomsky and Searle together, we have a three-part model. The first approximation would be

[1] brute facts: *parole*/performance/behaviour
[2] psychological facts: individual competence
[3] social (institutional) facts: *langue*

In slightly different terms, Popper (1972, 1994) proposes a pluralist theory of knowledge and the body–mind problem. He proposes three spheres of experience:

[1] World 1 is the observable external world of physical bodies with their physical states and processes. It contains objects such as stones, trees and chairs.
[2] World 2 is subjective knowledge. It contains the private, mental states and processes, such as beliefs, feelings and intentions, of individual human minds.
[3] World 3 is knowledge in the sense of the public products of human minds. It contains objects such as the contents of books, arguments and theories.

Searle's distinction (1995: 7) between 'physical particles in fields of force', 'consciousness' and 'social facts' seems to parallel Popper's World 1 of physical facts, World 2 of mental phenomena, and World 3 of autonomous public knowledge. His view of 'an objective world' (1995: 1) is close to Popper's view of 'objective knowledge' (World 3), and his view (e.g. 1995: 37) that many institutional facts depend on prior linguistic forms seems related to Popper's views on the role of written language in creating World 3. However, there are different kinds of objects in World 3. Searle (1995) gives an account of how social facts arise, which is much more detailed than Popper's account of World 3. Popper is mainly concerned with forms of scientific knowledge. One of his favourite examples is prime numbers, which were discovered as an unintended consequence of the number system. As Hardy (1940/1992: 130) puts it:

> 317 is a prime, not because we think so, or because our minds are shaped in one way rather than another, but because it is so, because mathematical reality is built that way.

Searle shows how a much wider range of everyday social phenomena arise due to collective intentionality. There is a further logical difference. Popper's prime numbers continue to exist even if everyone forgets about them: since they were unintended, they do not depend on collective intentionality. Whereas, as Searle points out with reference to the ex-German Democratic Republic, if enough people cease to believe in a state, then it ceases to exist. Nevertheless, the two positions seem compatible or complementary, in so far as they are both proposing a pluralist alternative to mind–body dualisms.[5]

11 Pluralism version 3: Hymes and Tuldava

The three-way distinction proposed by Popper and Searle still does not seem quite right. At least a four-way distinction is needed as follows. Suppose we say:

> 'This text is 500 words long.'

An individual text is the only kind of linguistic object which we can directly observe. We can count the words (word-tokens) and the frequencies of different words (word-types) and observe the actual choice of vocabulary. Our concept of word is due to a long tradition of literacy and on conventions which are not always consistent (cf. *all right* versus *altogether*). But given this tradition, units can be defined with minimal ambiguity, observed and counted. The concept of 'text' is also more complex than this, since a text can itself be regarded as either token or type: it would be an elementary logical error to confuse the text of *Hamlet* (type) with a particular printed copy of it (token) (see section 14.1 below).

> 'This speaker has a large vocabulary: s/he knows many rare words.'

This is a psycholinguistic statement, which refers to something quite different: not word-tokens but word-types, which are stored in the 'mental lexicon' (Aitchison 1987). The knowledge which an individual speaker has is psychological, private and unobservable, though we can make inferences about it via experiments of different kinds. For example, Youmans (1994) infers the size of the vocabulary of various authors from the words which they use in texts.

> 'This speaker has a large vocabulary, but when s/he speaks to young children s/he is careful to use simple words.'

This is a sociolinguistic statement, which makes a further essential distinction between knowledge and use, and assumes that speakers can make inferences about what other speakers know, and act accordingly, unlike Descartes' robot (see section 5 above).

> 'English has a large vocabulary: a large dictionary contains over 150,000 words.'

Knowledge must be knowledge of something, so a fourth distinction is required. The vocabulary of English, which is publicly recorded in dictionaries, does not correspond to the mental lexicon of any individual, since no one knows all the words in a large dictionary. The vocabulary of a language can be constructed only by many lexicographers who work in collaboration and who draw on the texts produced by many language users. In addition, the meaning of the words is not something individual: I cannot decide to use words just to mean what I wish. Although vocabulary in this sense is also not directly observable, word meaning is 'a public state of affairs' (Carr 1990: 42).[6]

12 Hymes on communicative competence

In other work which is well known to linguists, Hymes (1972, 1992) proposes a four-way model which is designed to avoid the oversimplified competence –performance polarization. He distinguishes between whether a sentence is [1] formally possible (= grammatical), and whether an utterance of the sentence is [2] psycholinguistically feasible or [3] sociolinguistically appropriate, and since not all possibilities are actually realized, whether an utterance is [4] frequent. This four-way distinction looks like this:

Language as knowledge:

    what can be said, the creative possibilities of the system
    [1] formally possible: grammatical
    [2] psycholinguistically realizable: feasible

Language as social behaviour:

    what is frequently said, the routine realization of the system
    [3] sociolinguistically appropriate: appropriate
    [4] actually said or written: performed

Corpus study uses evidence from [4] to make generalizations about [1], [2] and [3]. Much linguistics from the 1960s to the 1990s studied what is possible in the language system. Corpus linguistics studies what is probable in language use.

This distinction is simple to illustrate with isolated cases. For example, maps in city centres in Britain often have a red dot and the sentence *YOU ARE HERE*. Similar maps in Germany could have the sentence *SIE SIND HIER* (= "you are here"). This would be perfectly grammatical, but by and large it is not used. Such maps usually have the word *STANDORT* (= "place where you are standing"). Mel'čuk (1998: 26) gives similar examples. The rules of English allow the form *DO NOT PARK HERE*, but the form *NO PARKING* is preferred.[7]

13 Tuldava on potential and actual, process and product

Hymes' dimensions [1] to [4] are similar to distinctions made by Tuldava. This work is less well known, largely because it was written mainly in Russian and only recently translated into German. Tuldava (1998: 13 ff.), from which Figure 5.1 is adapted, makes two sets of distinctions, between the potential of the system (what is formally possible) and the actual realization of the system (what occurs), then between dynamic aspects of language use (process) and static aspects of language (product). These aspects can vary independently, giving us four ways of looking at language.

What I now have to show is that these four aspects of language are objects of different logical types and therefore not reducible to each other, but that they are nevertheless logically related and interact in clear ways. We are starting from four distinct things:

potential			
dynamic process	COMPETENCE	SYSTEM	static product
	DISCOURSE	TEXT	
actual			

Figure 5.1 Process and product, potential and actual. Based on discussion in Tuldava (1998: 13 ff.), but using different terminology. I have read a German translation of Tuldava's Russian-language original.

- a language system
- speakers' knowledge of this system
- their use of the system
- the possible record of this use, in a written text, a tape-recorded conversation, etc.

The logical distinctions and the logical relations between these four aspects of language are discussed in the next two sections.[8]

14 Text, discourse, competence, system: logical distinctions

14.1 Text

Since only text is directly observable, this is the basic data for corpus linguistics. Technology changes what is empirically observable, and with computational help we can observe patterns across long texts and text collections, such as which recurrent word-sequences are frequent in many different texts.

For many purposes, the concept is unproblematic. A written text or a transcribed spoken text consists of a sequence of word-forms (word-tokens) which occur with different frequencies in particular distributions. Of course, as noted above, the units which we count are based on the conventions of written language, which are often inconsistent, especially in representations of spoken language (e.g. *I want to go* versus *I wanna go*). More seriously, a central finding of corpus studies is that the units of language use are longer phraseological units. When we study collocations, we study the occurrence of a node word in a given span, which is measured in orthographic words, but the study of collocations leads to the discovery of multi-word units, which should, logically, be used to measure the span. There is currently no solution to this problem.

The term 'text' is ambiguous between an individual text which fulfils some pragmatic function, such as a shopping list or a poem, and 'text' as a mass noun. It is 'text' in this mass sense which is sampled in a corpus. The term 'text' is also ambiguous between token and type. A written text such as a personal letter is likely to exist as a single material object, but the 'same' text can exist in different copies, as different tokens of a type. In *Fahrenheit 451*, a dystopic novel by Ray Bradbury, books are burned, but the text remains in the memories of some readers. A copy of an individual written text is a material World 1 object: my copy of *Hamlet* has some of the famous quotes underlined, but this is only one copy (token) of a text (type) which exists in many different forms in World 3. For some kinds of linguistic analysis (e.g. counting the rare words it contains), it hardly matters whether we are thinking of a text as token or type. However, some texts, such as a personal letter, which exist as just one token, are unlikely to have any measurable influence on the system. Others, such as literary classics which exist in thousands of copies and are studied over and over again by many people, are likely to have a distinct influence. Some of their features may be widely known by many speakers in the form of well-known phrases, such as *to be or not to be*. Arguably such texts should be more heavily weighted in text corpora: this is taken into account in corpus design, but rarely in any clearly quantified way in corpus analysis.

A text is a static product whose structures we can study: a set of traces which are the result of a dynamic intentional process which involves agency. This leads to problems of interpretation which arise in several disciplines. For example, a historian must try to interpret the past on the basis of very incomplete textual records and documents of various kinds, which were written for different purposes by people with different interests. Text and corpus study share this central problem of hermeneutics.

Caveats.

14.2 Discourse

The term 'discourse' is used in several ways. I use the term here as follows. When people use language in some speech event (e.g. to make a telephone call or write a postcard), they engage in intentional social interaction, which consists of spatio-temporal events in the world. Discourse is intentional and meaningful social action, which cannot be reduced to physical behaviour or its traces in text. Since we cannot directly observe meanings, we can observe only superficial aspects of events such as a telephone call. In addition, we can study events systematically only in their recorded form as resultant products (text). Consider, for example, how difficult it was to study speech before the invention of tape-recorders. There is therefore an essential distinction between text as product and discourse as process. Austin (1962) began the modern discussion of how speakers use language to perform actions which have motives, goals and intentions, and whose success depends on the social institutions in which they are performed: you have to occupy a certain social role before you can fire an employee, launch a ship, baptize a baby, and so on. Austin introduced the term 'illocution' to refer to the speaker's intended meaning, and 'perlocution' to refer to the effect on the hearer. Searle (1969) developed the concept of intentional social acts, and Grice (1975) proposed a theory of how this coordination is possible, by pointing out how much is not contained in the words which are spoken/written, but is derived from processes of rational inference.

So, text is product (static, fixed) and discourse is process (dynamic, interactive). Text is 'the language that people produce' and discourse is 'the way this is processed'. Discourse is 'the pragmatic process of meaning negotiation'. Text is 'its product' (Verdonk 2002: 18; Widdowson 2004: 8).

Discourse, in the sense of meaningful interactive events which involve agency, is the aspect of language which is ignored by both de Saussure and Chomsky. It is, however, the only aspect of language which normally makes sense to speakers, since it is only at this level that speakers themselves can explain why they do things: they describe, promise, complain and all the rest. Discourse is the level at which it makes sense to talk about illocutionary cause and perlocutionary effect. Clearly a text does not cause anything: only the understanding of a text can cause an effect (Sperber 1996: 63). For example, to say that 'she complained that he had insulted her' is to describe communicative events from a user's point of view in terms of illocutionary acts.

Much discourse is an intentional process involving agency, but intentions are not observable and the concept is highly problematic.[9] A major finding of corpus studies is the pervasive routine of most language use. We can recognize illocutionary forces precisely because they are often expressed in recurrent conventional forms which continually circulate in the social world and do not depend on the intention of the speaker for their correct interpretation. For example, the largely fixed phrase *it's not the end of the world* is often used when A has suffered some unpleasant setback, and B is expressing their concern, reassurance and sympathy, saying that it could be worse and that A should not be too disappointed. It is a conventional way of expressing a speech act. New technologies allow us to document in empirical detail the repetition which is essential to the functioning of language.

A text, in the sense of a token of a text, is a thing in the material world, and discourse in the sense of intentional social action is an event in the material world, even if all we can observe is its products. Two other essential aspects of language, competence and the language system, are neither things nor events.

14.3 Competence

Competence is the aspect of language which has been theorized by scholars such as Chomsky, who have emphasized language as the mental capacity of individual speakers, irrespective of its actual use in social settings. Competence is knowledge. It is private, mental and individual, a relatively stable state which, in Chomskyan terms, is the result of parameters in phonology and syntax having been set during language acquisition. In its wider Hymesian sense of communicative competence, it refers also to our knowledge of how to use language appropriately in social settings.

Individual competence has been of little direct interest to corpus studies, which have concentrated on the recurrent patterns which are evidence of norms of usage across a community of speakers.

14.4 System

Knowledge has to be knowledge of something. It is knowledge of the language system and how it is used. Knowledge and system are logically distinct: no individual speaker knows the whole system; there are always more words to learn, more styles and text-types to become competent in. The system is inter-subjective. It is autonomous since it always predates the individual speaker, who is born into a community which already uses the language (Marx 1852). The system is not reducible to individual knowledge or even to the sum of all individual knowledges, since the system includes probabilities. It depends on the discourse and texts produced by speakers, but not by any individual speaker. It precedes, and is therefore independent of, every individual, since if one individual speaker dies, this makes no difference to the system. Even if the last native speaker dies, the system can be learned by new speakers in future, if a sufficient amount of text has been recorded in some way (an example is Cornish). The concept of a system, something with holistic properties distinct from its components, is the most frequent concept in the natural and social sciences (Ziman 2000: 146).

15 Text, discourse, competence, system: logical relations

I have tried so far to establish that there are four aspects of language which are autonomous and irreducible to each other:

[1] system	shared social norms:	what is possible and probable
[2] competence	individual cognition:	what a speaker knows
[3] discourse	joint action:	what speakers mean/understand
[4] text	record of behaviour:	what speakers have done in the past

I now have to discuss how [1] to [4] are logically related.

A text is the product of a process: the trace of intentional linguistic behaviour. A transcription of a spoken conversation and a handwritten letter are the traces of behavioural events. We can look at a text as a static product (what has been chosen), and count the frequency of items in it. Or we can look at it, from a different point of view, as the outcome of a dynamic process of linguistic behaviour in time, which involves a constantly changing choice of new and old vocabulary (Youmans 1991; Stubbs 2001b: 133–40).

It is the relation between text and system which has been of most interest to corpus linguists. A text is a realization of the language system: a set of actual choices from the large potential of what is possible. Frequency in a

V. important

text is evidence of probability in the system (Halliday 1991, 1992, 1993). The system is a theoretical construct since it is unobservable and can be identified only via its effects in texts. Nevertheless it exists only by virtue of its effects. As Bhaskar (1998: 45) puts it, it is 'a structure irreducible to, but present only in its effects'. As de Saussure recognized, the relation between *langue* and *parole* is asymmetrical: the system is essential to the existence of the text, but no individual text is essential to the existence of the system.

One part of the language system is the vocabulary. This consists of a timeless list of word-types, including word-forms, lemmas and/or multi-word lexical items. This is a static inventory of what is possible. If a phrasal unit becomes frequent in usage, then it eventually becomes part of the system: 'entrenched' as cognitive linguists say (e.g. Croft and Cruse 2004: 111); or 'grammaticalized' as historical linguists say (e.g. Hopper and Traugott 1993). The maintenance of a language system depends on the production of texts, but it does not consist of texts, and cannot be reduced to texts. The system is an emergent phenomenon: an unintended product of recurrent language use. Phrasings which have been successful in the past become entrenched via a process of natural selection (Popper 1994: 12–14). This is what corpus studies have been very successful in showing: how recurrent collocations can stabilize over time into units of the language system (see the studies cited above by Hoffmann 2004 and Rissanen 2004).

The system predates any individual text: it provides the means required to produce a text. A text is then the result of specific choices made in discourse. Texts do not create the system, but they maintain it as the result of recurrent choices which are made in many texts, and change it slowly over time (cf. the climate/weather analogy). The system is the unintended consequence of the relations of recurrence in mass behaviour. The system exists only because its components interact, but it is not reducible to its components. As Bhaskar (1998: 27–8) puts it, *army* is not the plural of *soldier*.

The system is the cumulative result of patterns of textual phenomena which are widely and fairly homogeneously distributed in the speech community. It cannot be observed directly, but norms of use can be inferred from observing texts. Of course, texts do not do or cause anything: it is speakers who reproduce patterns. In order to explain why some units get successfully copied and replicated, and therefore to explain how the system emerges and is maintained, we would have to explain what makes some units both useful and memorable. Speakers intend to communicate with each other, but they do not intend to produce and maintain a language. The language system is the unintended product of the joint discourse of many speakers. There is little discussion in corpus studies of the psychological implications of points such as these (though see Hoey 2005). Indeed, there is little discussion in corpus linguistics as to what constitutes an explanatory hypothesis, perhaps even little recognition that this is necessary. Grammaticalization studies (e.g. Hopper and Traugott 1993) probably come closest to genuinely explanatory accounts of the emergence of linguistic units over time.

Sentences are types: timeless units of the language system. They are not events: they do not occur. Utterances are tokens: units of discourse, which occur in time and space, and which both are caused by mental intentions, about which we know very little, and have perlocutionary causal effects. The system predates the individual language learner: the individual is always born into a community which already speaks the language. In addition, the system is not known in its entirety by any individual. For example, no single person knows the whole vocabulary of the language, but speakers can learn new words, and draw on this vocabulary if required. Similarly, they can, if required, learn the syntax required for formal written styles (e.g. in legal documents). The language system is inter-subjective, social and public. Linguistic competence is individual, mental and private.

As discussed above (section 9), it follows that system can be interpreted in three ways, which are distinct but compatible. The system is:

[1] what emerges from the cumulative language behaviour of the speech
     community;
[2] what is potential and possible;
[3] what is hypothesized by the linguist, in order to account for [1] and [2].

The evidence for the hypotheses is the recurrent textual patterns which are traces of the discourse processes.

Competence is knowledge of types, such as lemmas and sentences. Discourse produces utterance tokens: these are events which exist in World 1. The linguistic competence of an individual exists in World 2. The language system is a World 3 object. An individual text, such as specific spoken utterances or an individual written text, is also a World 1 object. However, texts can only be interpreted against norms, so, as soon as we start to discuss the meaning of a text, we are considering it as a World 3 object.

16 Motivating the four-part model

We now have a four-part model, which distinguishes four aspects of language. Depending on how we look at it, language is system, competence, discourse or text. This linguistic model can be further motivated by showing that it is a specific example of a more general model and that the same distinctions also hold elsewhere, in both linguistic and non-linguistic domains.

16.1 Potential and actual, process and product

As Tuldava (1998) points out, his four distinctions (see section 13 above) resolve into two oppositions:

- potential (system and competence)   and actual (discourse and text);
- process (competence and discourse)   and product (system and text).

Admittedly we now have two dualisms. However, they embody very general contrasts which hold for other academic disciplines (see section 16.6 below, on geology). Their different logical properties are not reducible to each other, but they relate dynamic human agency and static linguistic structure, two aspects of language which are often not well integrated in models of language. For example, neither de Saussurian structuralism nor Chomskyan generativism has any concept of individual human agency, whereas Austinian and Searlian speech act theory is strong on human agency and intention but weak on detailed descriptions of linguistic form.

16.2 Potential and actual: constraints on language use

In an early pre-corpus study of phraseology, Pawley and Syder (1983) point out that speakers do not make full use of the grammatical potential of their language. With reference to Hymes' four-way model (see section 12 above), Partington (1998: 18) notes that the 'formally possible' dimension refers to context-free aspects of language, whereas the other three dimensions are context-bound and increasingly powerful refining mechanisms on what is actually said or written. The grammar specifies what could potentially occur, but this is constrained by what is psychologically feasible, sociolinguistically appropriate, and actually frequent in the discourse community. It is this last aspect of language use for which corpora provide data.

16.3 Ordered ontological properties: physical, spatial, temporal and logical

System and competence are functional and structural categories which do not necessarily have any further ontological implications (Botha 1992: 95–6). They are abstract systems which are hypothesized in order to explain features of observable language use. In addition, these ontological properties of language are hierarchically related.

- A text (token) has physical, spatial and temporal properties. It can lie on my desk.
- Discourse has spatial and temporal properties. It happens; it consists of events.
- Competence has temporal properties. It is knowledge which develops during language acquisition, and it dies with the speaker.
- The language system has neither physical nor spatio-temporal properties, but it has necessary logical properties, such as relations of entailment and contradiction between its words and sentences. The same holds for a text in its abstract sense.

Katz (1981: 186) cuts the cake in a slightly different way, but makes similar distinctions. And Popper (1994: 29) makes a further point: although the system is timeless, it has a temporal history. It has evolved over time as an unintended consequence of many speakers using the language in predictable ways. It is this connection between textual routine in the past and system in the present for which corpus studies can provide empirical evidence (see Rissanen 2004; Hoffmann 2004, cited above).

16.4 The analogy with the system of natural numbers

These ontological distinctions hold, *ceteris paribus*, for a different domain:

- the system of natural numbers;
- my limited knowledge of this system;
- my use of the system (e.g. to work out how much I owe the bank on my mortgage);
- the record of this calculation (e.g. on the back of an envelope).

The system itself has properties which are independent of us. For example, prime numbers exist whether we understand them or not. Individuals' knowledge of the system is very variable. People can use the system for many different purposes, such as calculating a bet on a horse race or calculating the national debt. If we have a written representation of a calculation we may be able to work out what the calculation was and what it was for. Again Katz (1981: 77) makes rather similar points.

16.5 The analogy with games

These ontological distinctions also hold, *ceteris paribus*, for the domain of games. This is one of the most famous analogies of all, discussed by de Saussure and Wittgenstein (Harris 1988). The following aspects of chess are not reducible to each other:

- the rules of the game of chess (the system);
- my knowledge of the rules (which might be incomplete);
- a game between me and an opponent on a particular occasion (which would reveal that my skill in using the rules is very low);
- a record of the game in a standard notation.

As Wittgenstein argues, games and languages are institutions: they are not something which happens once, but are realized by recurrent social practices (Wittgenstein 1953 e.g. §§ 199, 202; Harris 1988: 97). The system itself has properties which are independent of us. Only a few grand masters can come anywhere close to understanding all the implications of the rules in use. Individuals' knowledge of the system is very variable, and their skilful use of the system is extremely variable. I personally might not know all the rules. For example, I could play chess quite successfully for some time before my opponents notice that I apparently do not know the particular rule, which is not used in many games, which allows pawns to take other pieces 'en passant'. The rules are logically distinct from my knowledge of them, and my knowing the rules is clearly distinct from my being able to use them skilfully. If we have a written representation of a specific game, for which different formalisms are available, we may be able to work out the motivations behind various moves, even if we could not have seen this at the time.

As with all analogies, there are features of chess which do not quite fit the case of a language. For example, the rules of chess can be stated comprehensively and quite briefly: there are then simply no more rules to cite. We can be certain of all the rules of chess but probably never of all the rules of a language. But the whole point of a simplified analogy is to simplify.

16.6 The analogy with geology

Consider, as a final analogy, the parallels between corpus linguistics and geology. Both disciplines are based on an assumed relation between process and product. In both cases, traces in the present are empirical evidence of general patterns in past events: unobserved processes must be inferred from their observable products (Love 1991; Ziman 2000: 95).

1. Geologists are interested in processes which are not directly observable because they take place across vast periods of time.
2. What is observable is the products of these processes: e.g. individual rocks and geographical formations.
3. These products are the observable traces of general processes which have often taken place a long time in the past. Geological change may be measured in millions of years.
4. The products are highly variable because any specific instance is due to local environmental conditions.
5. Nevertheless, these variable products are due to highly general processes of destruction, such as erosion, and construction, such as sedimentation.

The analogies to corpus study are striking:

1. Corpus linguists are interested in processes which are not directly observable because they are realized across the language use of many different speakers.
2. What is observable is the products of these processes: e.g. utterances and recurrent word combinations. Technology changes what is empirically observable: concordancers and other software reveal patterns across large corpora.
3. These products are the observable traces of general processes which have emerged over long periods of time. Language change may take hundreds of years.
4. The products are highly variable because any specific token is due to local sociolinguistic contexts.
5. Nevertheless, these variable products are due to highly general processes of collocation and colligation, probability, expectation and pragmatic inference.

16.7 Epistemic methods and areas of language study

16.1 to 16.6 are ontological arguments for the autonomy and irreducibility of these four aspects of language and a brief statement of some of their logical relations. The four-way model is a crude way of cutting the cake, since each of the four domains can be sub-divided, and each requires complex theories. Nevertheless, these areas correspond to recognized areas of language study and provide a schematic cognitive model of empirical linguistics. To this can be added related epistemic statements about the characteristic or necessary methods of studying these ontologically distinct objects:

- The system is the area which is tackled by all dictionaries and grammars and different aspects have been famously theorized by de Saussure and Halliday. It has typically been studied with structuralist and normative concepts.
- Competence is the area whose importance and complexity was perhaps first fully recognized by Chomsky. It has typically been studied with introspective, and sometimes experimental, methods.
- Discourse is the area which, for linguists, was opened up by Austin, Searle and Grice, but it includes many approaches to hermeneutics, which studies not only how individual texts should be interpreted, but how interpretation is possible. It must be studied with a wide range of hermeneutic methods.
- Text provides the essential primary observational data for corpus studies. Only recorded text can be studied with quantitative, statistical methods, and only textual data is directly observable.

17 Summary and implications

The language system depends on implicit collective agreement: it is public and social, but not directly observable. Competence is individual knowledge: it is private and largely unconscious, and therefore not directly observable. Discourse is intentional behaviour: it is interactive and therefore also social. Text is the trace of these different underlying factors: the observable product which can be studied with empirical methods. We can now state what a corpus is and how the study of corpora can contribute to solving some of the classic problems which I have discussed. Linguists design corpora as records of linguistic behaviour. A corpus therefore does not fit into the four-way schema above, because it is not something that a speaker does or knows. It is neither a linguistic system, nor linguistic knowledge, nor linguistic behaviour, but a sample of behaviour, designed according to a theory of language variation, so that we can make inferences about typical language across many different speakers and writers. When we record utterances and collect them in a corpus, we create a new kind of World 3 object. It is often objected that a corpus is mere performance data, but this is a shorthand formulation which disguises important points. Utterances are actual behaviour, spoken or written: intentional acts performed by individuals. A corpus is not itself the behaviour, but a sample of behaviour, recorded in a form which is useful to researchers. An utterance is an event in time, but a corpus is not an event.

De Saussure (1916: 171) distinguished syntagmatic and paradigmatic (associative) relations. A syntagmatic relation holds between items *in praesentia*, which co-occur in a linear string. A paradigmatic relation is a potential relation between items *in absentia*, which have a psychological reality. In an individual text, we can observe neither repeated syntagmatic relations nor any paradigmatic relations at all. Tognini-Bonelli (2001: 2–3, 2004: 18) shows how these are the two things which concordances make visible. Suppose we have a concordance of a word or pattern from a large general corpus. A text is designed to be read as a whole, linearly, from left to right. A concordance is designed to be read as a series of fragments, vertically, from top to bottom. On the horizontal axis of a single concordance line we can observe only a single instance of syntagmatic relations and no paradigmatic relations at all. On the vertical axis we can observe what frequently co-occurs syntagmatically, and how much constraint there is on the paradigmatic choices. Co-occurrences become visible, especially if the concordance lines are re-ordered alphabetically to left or right.

The horizontal axis of the concordance provides individual fragments of attested communicative acts. A single concordance line is a fragment of language use (*parole*) from an individual speaker. It is part of a meaningful speech act (discourse), which has been extracted from a real communicative situation. The vertical axis reveals the repetitions which make up a social practice across a speech community. A set of concordance lines is a sample of language use from many different speakers. Frequency of occurrence in the corpus is evidence of a social norm. The concordance lines provide evidence of a recurrent social practice, by revealing formal patterns or tendencies in the language system (*langue*). These points from Tognini-Bonelli help to make explicit what we can observe in a corpus and what this tells us about the relations between text, discourse and system. Individual competence does not fit, and we see why corpus linguists have tended to ignore questions about individual knowledge of system and use. The model of language must take competence into account, but corpus methods are not well suited to studying it.

Concordance 5.2 An illustrative sample of concordance lines for the word-form *endure*

```
01  st that smokers will have to endure 12-hour flights by becoming
02  d can remember having had to endure a certain amount of misery
03  ng that Romania still had to endure a period of austerity. Rome
04  ht find himself compelled to endure a spartan existence; unlike
05  so that the rider has had to endure a steady worsening of the t
06  erced family audience has to endure an hour of his old cine fil
07  the 1,700 prisoners have to endure constant noise from the Gar
08  dertake forced labour and to endure dehumanizing captivity in t
```

```
09  t workers in El Paso, Texas, endure difficult conditions, and c
10  e felt he had been forced to endure during the last three years
11  nd the animals often have to endure hours trapped in the midst
12  lame. At last, when he could endure no more, her jerked his hand
13  in a dark and cold place, to endure patiently sorrow and weakne
14  ans, for they were forced to endure the indignity of having ano
15   over, one finds it easier to endure those tedious weekly audien
16  s will be painful for her to endure, and for you to witness, bu
```

The formal patterns which are made visible on the vertical axis have led to one of the main discoveries of concordance studies: that words occur in predictable longer lexical units as in the illustrative sample of concordance lines for the word-form *endure* in Concordance 5.2. Speakers use this word when they are talking about someone being forced to endure something unpleasant for a long time. The evidence for this meaning is in the repeated co-selections to left and right. To the left is usually either the words *HAVE* to or variants such as *BE* forced to. To the right are descriptions of unpleasant situations (e.g. *constant noise* or *dehumanizing captivity*) and frequently also an expression of a time period (e.g. *12-hour flights* or *the last three years*). Not all uses of the words explicitly contain all these features, but a set of concordance lines across a corpus provide repeated examples. There are many examples of the analysis of patterns which are associated with different lexical items in Hunston and Francis (2000) and Sinclair (1991).

Such methods allow corpus linguists to discover patterns which are otherwise invisible: what is expected, predictable, usual, normal and typical in language use. We have as yet only the outlines of a theory which can relate system and use, but we have methods for studying patterns which are stable across the language use of many speakers, and which therefore offer new ways of studying the material base of many of society's activities. One of the most elegant defences of such study is by Burrows (1987: 2–3), who talks of 'evidence to which the unassisted human mind could never gain consistent, conscious access'.

When Chomskyan linguistics took a decisive step away from studying behaviour and its products, to studying the underlying cognitive system, this led to the discovery of many new facts about language. Equally, when corpus linguistics took a decisive step towards the study of patterns across large text collections, this also led to the discovery of many new facts. The approaches are currently often seen as being in opposition, and the dualisms are perpetuated, but the long-term aim must be to integrate the insights from different approaches.

At one level, corpus studies have provided many new and surprising facts about language use. In addition, they suggest ways out of an ontological problem which has been repeatedly raised, but never satisfactorily solved, by some of the greatest thinkers of modern linguistics, including de Saussure, Chomsky, Hymes, Labov, Halliday and Searle. I am not so naive as to think that I have solved this problem. However, I do think that empirical corpus data can provide new ways of formulating the puzzling relations between language system and language use, and can therefore provide new ways of stating the conceptual foundations of our discipline.

Acknowledgements

This article started life as Chapter 10 of my book *Words and Phrases* (2001, Blackwell), but has been considerably adapted, revised and expanded. Several friends and colleagues seemed to think the argument was worth attempting, and, even if they were just being tactful, I am grateful for their encouragement. For critical comments, which expressed various degrees of scepticism about earlier drafts, I am very grateful to Guy Cook, Andrea Gerbig, Naomi Hallan, Michaela Mahlberg, Amanda Murphy, Kieran O'Halloran, Bettina Starcke and Wolfgang Teubert.

Notes

1. The British National Corpus (BNC) is a corpus of 100 million running words: 90 million from written texts and 10 million from transcribed spoken texts. For further details, see Aston and Burnard (1998) and the BNC website at www.natcorp.ox.ac.uk/.
2. Stubbs (2007) discusses the surprising disagreements between the meanings of words, especially their evaluative connotations, as recorded in four corpus-based dictionaries.
3. There are useful short accounts of Bacon's ideas by Quinton (1980), and of Hume's ideas by Noonan (1999).
4. I am grateful to Wolfgang Teubert for discussion of this point.
5. Limitations to Popper's work in this area are his rudimentary conception of language (Botha 1992: 188), which makes no reference to any work on language functions since Bühler (1934), and his lack of a clear theory of how Worlds 1, 2 and 3 interact. For further discussions of Popper, see Leech (1983: 48–56), Carr (1990) and Botha (1992: 183 ff.). For similar ideas, see Ziman (1978: 106–8) on [1] the material domain of the external physical world, [2] the mental domain of perceptions and thoughts and [3] the 'noetic' domain, which depends on language in order to create and maintain knowledge as a social institution. Ziman refers to Popper and to similar ideas in Polanyi (1958). Giddens' (1984: 8–12) discussion of the importance of the unintended consequences of intentional actions for a theory of the social world also comes close to Popper's views. Unfortunately, the major theorists, Popper, Searle and Giddens, do not refer to each other's work, and, as far as I know, no systematic comparison of their ideas has appeared.
6. It would be interesting to develop these points with reference to Wittgenstein's (1953) arguments on the impossibility of a private language. Wittgenstein said many things which are of central importance to an empiricist approach to language use. One of his most famous

statements, which is implied in much corpus linguistics, but rarely accurately cited or acknowledged is: 'The meaning of a word is its use in the language' (1953: § 43). As far as I know, these connections between Wittgenstein's radical empiricism and corpus linguistics have never been discussed in detail.

7. Stubbs (2001a) gives a more complex example of the different preferred uses and connotations of BE and GET passives.

8. Brown and Yule (1983: 26) discuss the text–discourse distinction: the data for discourse analysis are 'the record (text) of a dynamic process in which language was used as an instrument of communication in a context by a speaker/writer to express meanings and achieve intentions (discourse)'. Lyons (1995: 20–1, 35, 235) discusses the process–product distinction: for example, he argues that *parole* denotes the 'products of the use of a language-system', and that the term 'utterance' has both a product-sense and a process – sense (1995: 235). He proposes a 'system–process–product trichotomy' (1995:22).

9. This criticism of Austin is made by Cameron and Kulick (2003: 126–9), citing Derrida. In addition, Duranti (1997) summarizes anthropological criticisms of the Austin/Searle/Grice tradition on the grounds that individual intention is an unanalysed Western notion and not a universal.

References

Aitchison, J. (1987) *Words in the Mind. An Introduction to the Mental Lexicon.* Oxford: Blackwell.

Anscombe, G. E. M. (1958) 'On brute facts'. *Analysis,* 18, 4: 69–72.

Aston, G. and Burnard, L. (1998) *The BNC Handbook. Exploring the British National Corpus with SARA.* Edinburgh: Edinburgh University Press.

Austin, J. L. (1962) *How to Do Things with Words.* Oxford: Clarendon.

Bhaskar, R. (1998) *The Possibility of Naturalism. A Philosophical Critique of the Contemporary Human Sciences.* (3rd edn). London: Routledge.

Bloomfield, L. (1933) *Language.* New York: Holt, Rinehart and Winston. (Page references to British edition, London: Allen and Unwin, 1935.)

Botha, R. P. (1992) *Twentieth Century Conceptions of Language. Mastering the Metaphysics Market.* Oxford: Blackwell.

Brown, G. and Yule, G. (1983) *Discourse Analysis.* Cambridge: Cambridge University Press.

Bühler, K. (1934) *Sprachtheorie: Die Darstellungsfunktion der Sprache.* Jena: Fischer.

Burrows, J. F. (1987) *Computation into Criticism. A Study of Jane Austen's Novels and an Experiment in Method.* Oxford: Clarendon.

Cameron, D. and Kulick, D. (2003) *Language and Sexuality.* Oxford: Blackwell.

Carr, P. (1990) *Linguistic Realities. An Autonomist Metatheory for the Generative Enterprise.* Cambridge: Cambridge University Press.

Chomsky, N. (1965) *Aspects of the Theory of Syntax*. Cambridge, Mass.: MIT Press.
—— (1966) *Cartesian Linguistics. A Chapter in the History of Rationalist Thought*. New York: Harper and Row.
Croft, W. and Cruse, D. A. (2004) *Cognitive Linguistics*. Cambridge: Cambridge University Press.
Descartes, R. (1637) *Discours de la Méthode*. Leyden: Publisher unknown.
Duranti, A. (1997) *Linguistic Anthropology*. Cambridge: Cambridge University Press.
Firth, J. R. (1935) 'The technique of semantics.' *Transactions of the Philological Society*, 36–72.
—— (1957) 'A synopsis of linguistic theory, 1930–1955'. *Studies in Linguistic Analysis*. Special Volume, Philological Society. Oxford: Blackwell. pp. 1–32.
Francis, G., Hunston, S. and Manning, E. (1996, 1998) *Grammar Patterns*, vols 1 and 2. London: HarperCollins.
Fries, C. C. (1940) *American English Grammar*. New York: National Council of Teachers of English.
—— (1952) *The Structure of English*. London: Longman.
Giddens, A. (1984) *The Constitution of Society. Outline of the Theory of Structuration*. Oxford: Polity.
Grice, H. P. (1975) 'Logic and conversation', in P. Cole and J. L. Morgan (eds), *Speech Acts. Syntax and Semantics*. Volume 3. New York: Academic Press, pp. 41–58.
Halliday, M. A. K. (1978) *Language as Social Semiotic. The Social Interpretation of Language and Meaning*. London: Edward Arnold.
—— (1991) 'Corpus studies and probabilistic grammar', in K. Aijmer and B. Altenberg (eds), *English Corpus Linguistics. Studies in Honour of Jan Svartvik*. London: Longman, pp. 30–43.
—— (1992) 'Language as system and language as instance', in J. Svartvik (ed.), *Directions in Corpus Linguistics. Proceedings of Nobel Symposium 82 Stockholm, 4–8 August 1991*. Berlin: Mouton, pp. 61–77.
—— (1993) 'Quantitative studies and probabilities in grammar', in M. Hoey (ed.), *Data, Description, Discourse. Papers on the English Language in Honour of John McH Sinclair on his Sixtieth Birthday*. London: HarperCollins, pp. 1–25.
Halliday, M. A. K. and Hasan, R. (2000) 'System and text'. *Text*, 20, 2: 201–10.
Hardy, G. H. (1940/1992) *A Mathematician's Delight*. Cambridge: Cambridge University Press.
Harris, R. (1988) *Language, Saussure and Wittgenstein. How to Play Games with Words*. London: Routledge.
Hoey, M. (2005) *Lexical Priming. A New Theory of Words and Language*. London: Routledge.
Hoffmann, S. (2004) 'Are low frequency complex prepositions grammaticalized?' in H. Lindquist and C. Mair (eds), *Corpus Approaches to Grammaticalization in English*. Amsterdam: Benjamins, pp. 171–210.

Hopper, P. J. and Traugott, E. (1993) *Grammaticalization*. Cambridge: Cambridge University Press.

Hume, D. (1748) *An Enquiry Concerning Human Understanding*. Edinburgh. (Harvard Classics, Collier and Son, 1910.)

Hunston, S. and Francis, G. (2000) *Pattern Grammar. A Corpus-driven Approach to the Lexical Grammar of English*. Amsterdam: Benjamins.

Hymes, D. (1972) 'On communicative competence', in J. Pride and J. Holmes (eds), *Sociolinguistics*. Harmondsworth: Penguin, pp. 269–93.

—— (1992) 'The concept of communicative competence revisited', in M. Pütz (ed.), *Thirty Years of Linguistic Evolution*. Amsterdam: Benjamins, pp. 31–58.

Katz, J. J. (1981) *Language and Other Abstract Objects*. Oxford: Blackwell.

Labov, W. (1972) 'The study of language in its social context', in *Sociolinguistic Patterns*. Philadelphia: University of Pennsylvania Press, pp. 183–259.

Leech, G. N. (1983) *Principles of Pragmatics*. London: Longman.

Love, A. M. (1991) 'Process and product in geology'. *English for Specific Purposes*, 10: 89–109.

Lyons, J. (1995) *Linguistic Semantics. An Introduction*. Cambridge: Cambridge University Press.

Macfarlane, A. and Martin, G. (2002) *The Glass Bathyscaphe*. London: Profile.

Marx, K. (1852) 'Der 18te Brumaire des Louis Napoleon. Die Revolution', in K. Marx and F. Engels, *Werke*. Volume 8. Berlin: Dietz, 1960.

Mel'čuk, I. (1998) 'Collocations and lexical functions', in A. P. Cowie (ed.), *Phraseology. Theory, Analysis, and Applications*. Oxford: Oxford University Press, pp. 23–53.

Noonan, H. W. (1999) *Hume on Knowledge*. London: Routledge.

Partington, A. (1998) *Patterns and Meanings. Using Corpora for English Language Research and Teaching*. Amsterdam: Benjamins.

Pawley, A. and Syder, F. H. (1983) 'Two puzzles for linguistic theory', in J. C. Richards and R. W. Schmidt (eds), *Language and Communication*. London: Longman, pp. 191–226.

Polanyi, M. (1958) *Personal Knowledge. Towards a Post-Critical Philosophy*. London: Routledge and Kegan Paul.

Popper, K. R. (1963) *Conjectures and Refutations. The Growth of Scientific Knowledge*. London: Routledge and Kegan Paul.

—— (1972) *Objective Knowledge. An Evolutionary Approach*. Oxford: Clarendon.

—— (1983) *Realism and the Aim of Science*. London: Routledge.

—— (1994) *Knowledge and the Body-Mind Problem*. London: Routledge.

Quinton, A. (1980) *Francis Bacon*. Oxford: Oxford University Press.

Rawls, J. (1955) 'Two concepts of rules'. *The Philosophical Review*, 64: 3–32.

Renouf, A. (1987) 'Moving on', in J. Sinclair (ed.), *Looking Up. An Account of the COBUILD Project in Lexical Computing*. London: Collins, pp. 167–78.

Rissanen, M. (2004) 'Grammaticalization from side to side', in H. Lindquist and C. Mair (eds), *Corpus Approaches to Grammaticalization in English*. Amsterdam: Benjamins, pp. 151–70.

Robins, R. H. (1988) 'Appendix: History of linguistics', in F. J. Newmeyer (ed.), *Linguistics: The Cambridge Survey*. Volume 1. Cambridge: Cambridge University Press, pp. 462–84.

Rundell, M. (2001) 'Corpora, evidence and intuition'. Corpora List, 1 November 2001. http://torvald.aksis.uib.no/corpora/2001-4/0080.html.

Sampson, G. (1996) 'From central embedding to empirical linguistics', in J. Thomas and M. Short (eds), *Using Corpora for Language Research*. London: Longman, pp. 14–26. Reprinted in G. Sampson (2001) *Empirical Linguistics*. London: Continuum, pp. 13–23.

Saussure, F. de (1916) *Cours de Linguistique Générale*. Paris: Payot.

Sealey, A. and Carter, B. (2004) *Applied Linguistics as Social Science*. London: Continuum.

Searle, J. R. (1969) *Speech Acts. An Essay in the Philosophy of Language*. Cambridge: Cambridge University Press.

—— (1995) *The Construction of Social Reality*. London: Allen Lane.

Sinclair, J. (1965) 'When is a poem like a sunset?' *Review of English Literature*, 6, 2: 76–91.

—— (1991) *Corpus, Concordance, Collocation*. Oxford: Oxford University Press.

Sinclair, J., Jones, S. and Daley, R. (2004) *English Collocation Studies. The OSTI Report*. London: Continuum. (First published 1970.)

Sperber, D. (1996) *Explaining Culture: A Naturalistic Approach*. Oxford: Blackwell.

Stubbs, M. (2001a) 'Texts, corpora and problems of interpretation'. *Applied Linguistics*, 22, 2: 149–72.

—— (2001b) *Words and Phrases. Corpus Studies of Lexical Semantics*. Oxford: Blackwell.

—— (2007) 'Inferring meaning: text, technology and problems with induction', in R. Köhler and A. Mehler (eds), *Aspects of Automatic Text Analysis*. Berlin: Springer, pp. 233–53.

Teubert, W. (1999a) 'Corpus linguistics: a partisan view'. www.solaris3.ids-mannheim.de/ijcl/teubert_cl.html. (Accessed 24 November 1999.)

—— (1999b) 'Korpuslinguistik und Lexikographie'. *Deutsche Sprache*, 27, 4: 292–313.

—— (2005) 'My version of corpus linguistics'. *International Journal of Corpus Linguistics*, 10, 1: 1–13.

Tognini-Bonelli, E. (2001) *Corpus Linguistics at Work*. Amsterdam: Benjamins.

—— (2004) 'Working with corpora', in C. Coffin et al. (eds), *Applying English Grammar. Functional and Corpus Approaches*. London: Arnold, pp. 11–24.

Tuldava, J. (1998) *Probleme und Methoden der quantitativ-systemischen Lexikologie*. (Translated from Russian original, 1987.) Trier: Wissenschaftlicher Verlag.

Twaddell, W. F. (1935) 'On defining the phoneme', reprinted in M. Joos (ed.), *Readings in Linguistics*. Washington: American Council of Learned Societies, 1957, pp. 55–80.

Verdonk, P. (2002) *Stylistics*. Oxford: Oxford University Press.

Widdowson, H. G. (2004) *Text, Context, Pretext. Critical Issues in Discourse Analysis*. Oxford: Blackwell.

Wilson, E. O. (1998) *Consilience. The Unity of Knowledge*. London: Abacus.

Wittgenstein, L. (1953) *Philosophical Investigations*. Oxford: Blackwell.

Youmans, G. (1991) 'A new tool for discourse analysis: the vocabulary management profile'. *Language*, 67, 4: 763–89.

—— (1994) 'The vocabulary management-profile, two stories by William Faulkner'. *Empirical Studies of the Arts*, 12, 2: 113–30.

Ziman, J. (1978) *Reliable Knowledge. An Exploration of the Grounds for Belief in Science*. Cambridge: Cambridge University Press.

—— (2000) *Real Science*. Cambridge: Cambridge University Press.

6 Quantitative data on multi-word sequences in English: the case of the word *world*

Michael Stubbs

Introduction

In my first chapter in this book, I discussed the implications of empirical corpus study for a general model of language use and language system. In this chapter, I present a small empirical case study of English phraseology in order to illustrate how quantitative data on recurrent language use can help to identify phrasal units of meaning in the language system. The general method is inductive, in the sense that we start with a large corpus, and use search software in order to automatically extract patterns which are invisible without such help. We then try to formulate generalizations about these patterns. For example, do frequent words and the phrases in which they occur tend to have particular evaluative functions in language use? Phraseology and corpus study are intimately related, because it is scholars who have studied texts and corpora who have been struck by the large amount of recurrent phraseology which characterizes normal language use. If you study individual, isolated, invented sentences, then – obviously, by definition – you cannot see the phenomenon of recurrent multi-word units. If you study texts and corpora, in particular concordance data, you can hardly miss it. So, we find many attempts to automatically extract recurrent phrasal units from large corpora.

In discussions of phraseology the term 'fixed phrase' is often used. However, empirical work on large corpora does not support a concept of fixed phrases, but rather of recurrent phrasal constructions, which are combinations of lexis and grammar, and which typically consist of a partly fixed lexical core plus other variable items. The form of these constructions can be specified as combinations of collocation and colligation (co-occurring words and grammatical categories) and their meanings can be specified as often evaluative communicative functions. This view of phraseology has been developed in detail by John Sinclair and others, including Gill Francis, Susan Hunston and Rosamund Moon.

This chapter uses data drawn from the British National Corpus (BNC) and from an associated database which is described in detail below. As a case study I analyse the word *world* in order to illustrate how evidence of phrasal constructions can be extracted from large corpora. The word *world* is one of the most frequent nouns in the BNC. However, it is frequent partly because it occurs in many semi-fixed phrases (e.g. *Third World, Second World War*) and evaluative phrasal constructions (e.g. *one of the world's most gifted scientists; the most natural thing in the world*). In both of these cases, there is a strong tendency for the meaning of the string to be non-compositional, in the sense of at least partly semantically opaque.

I use the following presentation conventions. 'Single quote marks' are used for terminology and/or quotes from other authors. "Double quote marks" are used for the meaning of a linguistic expression. Italics are used for word-forms. Small capitals are used for a lexeme or lemma. For example, the lemma KEEP is the class of word-forms *keep, keeps, kept* and *keeping*. Diamond brackets enclose collocates of a node word or phrase, e.g. *world's most* <*beautiful, famous, important*>, or frequencies e.g. *the rest of the world* <483>. Slashes separate alternatives, e.g. *one/some of the world's most*. Round brackets enclose optional items, e.g. *in the whole (wide) world*. A hash is used to indicate a variable word in a phrase. For example, in *the world's most # NOUN*, the # is often realized by a positive evaluative adjective such as *advanced, beautiful, expensive, important, popular*.

1 Introductory examples

My illustrative case study starts with a little puzzle. The word *world* is one of the top ten nouns in the BNC. It occurs something over 54,000 times, over 500 times per million running words. This is intuitively rather odd, since it seems unlikely that speakers keep referring so frequently to the external world. However, the explanation is quite simple: the word is frequent because it occurs in frequent phrases. This feature of word frequency is noted by Summers (1996) and Sinclair (1999).

Obviously, some of these phrases do refer to the external world. They are idiomatic and conventional but otherwise unremarkable, in so far as they largely mean what they say. If you know the meaning of the constituent words, then you can usually understand the phrases. Examples with their frequencies in the BNC include:

- the rest of the world <483>; from all over the world <225>; in many parts of the world <75>; the other side of the world <62>

But even these phrases are not always completely semantically transparent. If Australia are playing cricket against *the rest of the world*, then this means selected players from other cricket-playing countries.[1] In other cases, however, the literal denotation of "world" is weakened. Several of the most frequent two- and three-word phrases are the names of places, institutions, events and so on. Examples with their frequencies include:

- World War <3,813>, World Cup <2,157>, Second World War <1,620>, Third World <1,696>, World Bank <861>, World Champion <392>

In such expressions, the word often does not quite have its full literal meaning. The expressions are not fully compositional (semantically transparent), since the whole is different from the intersection of the parts. Knowing the meaning of the two words *third* and *world* does not tell you the meaning of the expression *Third World*. In other cases again, a longer phrasal construction has a text-internal function of comparison and emphasis. In the following examples, although the word can be interpreted literally, its phraseology has evaluative functions. The semantic denotation of the individual word is weakened and the pragmatic meaning of the multi-word sequence is strengthened.

- one of the <u>world</u>'s   finest hotels
- one of the <u>world</u>'s   most gifted scientists
- one of the richest countries   in the <u>world</u>
- some of the best players   in the <u>world</u>
- the most natural thing   in the <u>world</u>

These related phrasal constructions consist of combinations of obligatory lexis (the noun phrase *the world*) and grammar (a superlative adjective), together with small variations in the content words and the grammar. Most examples are positive evaluations, and only a few are negative. Examples of adjectives following *one/some of the of the world's (most)* include:

- largest, leading, top, greatest, great, finest, major, best, biggest
- beautiful, famous, important, powerful, expensive, advanced, successful, popular
- worst, poorest
- dangerous, endangered.

The approximate structures are:

- one/some of the world's   + superlative ADJ   + NOUN
- (one/some of) the   + superlative ADJ   + NOUN + in the world

I say 'approximate' because these structures are not entirely fixed. For example, the BNC contains infrequent instances of the more emphatic variants *in the whole (wide) world*:

- my favourite person   in the <u>whole</u> world
- the best   in the <u>whole</u> world
- the best job   in the <u>whole wide</u> world

Such phrases are not strictly truth-conditional, but are rather examples of conventional ways of expressing an evaluative meaning. We have what Sinclair (2004: 290) describes as 'a single lexical choice whose realisation is [several] words long and within which there is some variation'. Finally, there are also cases which will be discussed in more detail below (section 3) of longer recurrent phrases with clearly pragmatic meanings, such as:

- all the time in the world <50>; with the best will in the world <38>; it's not the end of the world <13>

In summary so far: The word *world* is frequent because it occurs in frequent longer phrasal constructions many of which are not entirely semantically transparent. Some of these shorter constructions inhabit the grey area between noun phrases and names. Many others are conventional ways of expressing evaluation or other pragmatic meanings. These evaluative functions are one aspect of text organization (Mahlberg 2005), since evaluating something focuses attention on it, contrasts it with something else, and emphasizes its importance in the text.

2 Phrases in English: the PIE database

There are now available several excellent interfaces to the BNC, which can extract recurrent phraseology. As the primary source of data for this chapter I have used a database called PIE (Phrases in English) which has been developed by Fletcher (2003–06) and which is available at http://pie.usna.edu. The terminology and main concepts used in this database are as follows:

n-gram:	a recurrent uninterrupted string of orthographic word-forms
p(hrase)-frame:	a recurrent n-gram with one variable lexical slot
PoS-gram:	a recurrent string of part of speech tags
A hash # is used for a variable word-form in a p-frame.	

PIE allows the user to extract recurrent sequences of words, specified by length (1 to 8) plus any combination of lexis and syntax (defined by BNC grammatical tags). In any slot, from 1 to 8, the user can specify nothing, or a word-form or pattern, and/or a part of speech tag. For example, given these two patterns, where ? stands for a single character and * stands for any string of characters or none,

(a) kn?w*
(b) kn?w* + VERB

pattern (a) would return *know, knows, knew, knowledge,* etc. and pattern (b) would exclude the noun *knowledge.* Any combination of these patterns can be specified for any of the slots.[2] In addition one can include or exclude any of the specifications: for example, one can extract 3-grams which end in *world* but do not begin with a preposition, thus excluding *in the world.*

In extracting recurrent phrases from PIE, we can start from either of two extreme points or any point in between. We can start from selected individual words and study their typical co-text, or from recurrent empty n-grams and study their typical content. So we can do what I have started to do in my example with *world*: extract n-grams and p-frames which are specified by length plus any combination of lexis and syntax. If we do things this way round, then we can investigate the hypothesis that frequent words are frequent because they occur in frequent phrasal constructions which have frequent and predictable functions in text. Alternatively, we can extract recurrent phraseology directly: we can extract the most frequent n-grams, p-frames and PoS-grams without further specifications of lexis or syntax. In a different study (Stubbs 2006) I use this second strategy. It turns out, for example, that the most frequent 4-grams in the BNC are the beginnings of prepositional phrases (e.g. *in the middle of*, *as a result of*), that their lexis falls into a small number of semantic sets (mainly spatial, temporal and causal), that they frequently have text-structuring functions, and that there are clear differences between the most frequent 4-grams in written and spoken text-types.

In summary: PIE allows the user to identify the most frequent recurrent strings in the BNC. We can then use these data to formulate hypotheses about their communicative functions, and therefore try to explain why this phraseology is frequent. In other words, PIE can provide a great deal of evidence for phrasal constructions in the sense of a unit of meaning which combines collocation and colligation and which usually has a pragmatic function.

3 Exploring the PIE database: an informal start

It is often useful to start in a relatively informal and exploratory way, by extracting some patterns and following up some ideas which look intuitively interesting. This probably provides examples of phenomena which have been identified in other studies, probably confirms some ideas which we already have, but probably also generates some new ideas. Here are four examples.

1. PIE allows us to search for PoS-grams. If we search just for the most frequent 2-PoS-grams consisting of NOUN + NOUN, we discover that the most frequent is *World War* <3,813> and that *World Cup* <2,157> is in the top ten.
2. PIE also allows us to search for combinations of individual words and word classes, and this might suggest several further patterns and corresponding hypotheses to study. Examples are the top 2- and 3-grams which consist of [1] *world* + NOUN or [2] ADJECTIVE + *world* or [3] *world's* + ADJECTIVE or [4] *world's most* + ADJECTIVE:

   [1] world <war 3,813, cup 2,157, bank 861, champion 392, championship 311>
   [2] world <third 1,696, real 666, outside 623, Arab 610, whole 426>
   [3] world's <largest 317, first 176, biggest 159, greatest 113, leading 112>
   [4] world's most <famous 36, powerful 17, successful 16, beautiful 15, important 15>

3. PIE allows us to identify recurrent n-grams up to length 8. The most frequent 8-gram[3] containing *world* in any position is *it's not the end of the*

world <13>. This is not very frequent, but if we search for some variants, we discover that there are around 45 cases where *the end of the world* <157> is preceded by a negative. In Concordance 6.1 are 20 lines which have been intuitively selected to provide particularly clear empirical evidence of how the phrase is used. Collocates to the left are evidence that the construction has the pragmatic function of expressing concern, reassurance and sympathy (01, 07, 09, 17, 18). Someone has suffered something unpleasant such as failure (08), disease (11) or a row (14), but is being reassured that it could be worse or is determined not to be worried (04). There are two examples (13, 19) in which the phrase is preceded by the words *disappointing but.* Two examples of this co-occurrence in such a small sample is statistically very unlikely. A larger corpus could be checked to see whether the canonical use is: *it's disappointing, but it's not the end of the world.*

Concordance 6.1 20 selected concordance lines: negative plus *the end of the world*

```
01   with motherly concern. "Well, it ain't the end of the world, ducks. It 'appens
02    promotion. It wouldn't necessarily be the end of the world, though it would se
03   he power to sack her, that would not be the end of the world. Tenuous as her ty
04    be, it will not worry me. It won't be the end of the world. Hill's hope is to
05   as sick as a parrot, but it wouldn't be the end of the world. I'd live off my w
06   actical part of her said it wouldn't be the end of the world. She wasn't broke
07     r. "Cheer up, boy," said Tom. "It ent the end of the world." But to Willie it
08   ies you've had. Show her failure isn't the end of the world." Child Consultants
09   He said reassuringly, "Angel, it isn't the end of the world." "It is for me,"
10   , but it wasn't unexpected and it isn't the end of the world. "You always have
11    blems. Diabetes mellitus does not mean the end of the world. With a little com
12   decay does set in, it's not necessarily the end of the world, or the window. Ne
13   ion it would be "disappointing, but not the end of the world" if he were left ou
14   er, they will realise that a row is not the end of the world and will learn that
15   oughts to square the damage. "It's not the end of the world," he said. "Not af
16     aud." "My God," Sally said. "It's not the end of the world," Harriet exclaimed
17   't look so glum!" she added. "It's not the end of the world." And off she went
18   sica, sympathetically. "Look, it's not the end of the world, love. They may ha
19   eux. "It's disappointing, but it's not the end of the world," said Burke. "We
20   won't always get it right, but it's not the end of the world if you don't. Your
```

4. Amongst the most frequent 8-grams is also *he had all the time in the world* <4>. This is less frequent again, but it is easy to find other variants. In the top dozen 5-grams is *the time in the world* <50>. All 50 occurrences are immediately preceded by *all.* Here are 20 lines which have been intuitively selected to provide particularly clear empirical evidence of how the phrase is used. The co-text can sometimes provide direct evidence of the meaning of an expression, and here the expression is preceded by several other expressions which closely paraphrase it: *we've got time* (04), *we don't have to rush* (05), *there was no hurry* (11), *no need to hurry* (16). Several occurrences are preceded by *as if* or *as though* or by other expressions which imply that perhaps only a pretence is involved: *with the air of* (19) and *giving the impression of* (20).

Concordance 6.2 20 selected concordance lines: *all the time in the world*

```
01  Oh for the patience of a Saint and All the Time in the World "I'd really like
02   's all right." She'd got all day. All the time in the world, in fact. "Please
03  ed the door Munro added, "We've got all the time in the world, Jack. So has Ste
04  ot sure we've got time." "I've got all the time in the world." "The brief vers
05  We d on't have to rush. We've got all the time in the world." "That would be
06  houts .) As if you hadn't both got all the time in the world! (Polite) Could
07  ps lingering on hers as if they had all the time in the world. Dimly Merrill he
08  n Namibia in July last year Gus had all the time in the world to admire the Afri
09  s kiss was leisurely as if they had all the time in the world to explore each ot
10  ack into her walk as though she had all the time in the world, she paused to rub
11   tools. There was no hurry. I had all the time in the world. I also went out
12  kissed her lingeringly as if he had all the time in the world and she felt a shu
13   agers too. I saw the way you had all the time in the world to chat to the pat
14  pping from his own cup as if he had all the time in the world. Corbett tasted t
15  The trial was over. He should have all the time in the world. But it wasn't as
16   's no need to hurry because we have all the time in the world. We are going to
17  egan to kiss her slowly, leisurely, all the time in the world at his disposal.
18   finitely patient and gentle, taking all the time in the world to skilfully lead
19  n and, with the air of someone with all the time in the world, set about checkin
20  giving the impression of a man with all the time in the world. "So much to do,
```

Neither of these expressions (*it's not the end of the world* and *all the time in the world*) is very frequent, though the fact that such long strings of words recur at all is statistically extremely unlikely. They are clearly semi-fixed phrases which are immediately recognizable to native speakers as idiomatic ways of expressing common pragmatic meanings. As emphasized, I have selected both these sets of concordance lines intuitively, in order to illustrate important principles which are well known from other studies. The phraseology around a word often stretches quite a long way to left and/or right, and the co-text therefore often provides a lot of evidence of the meaning of words and phrases. In addition, since semantic features are shared across stretches of text, this contributes to the textual cohesion.

4 Exploring the PIE database: a more formal way

These examples illustrate, informally, some important ideas, but we require also a more systematic way of collecting data on the most frequent phraseology around the word *world*. A first essential criterion for a discovery method is that it should be replicable: given the same corpus data, different researchers should be able to extract the same data on recurrent phrases. They may not arrive at the same interpretation of the data, but as a matter of principle, we should avoid using introspection as data, even if we cannot avoid using intuition in the analysis (Rundell 2001). A second criterion is that the data should be comprehensive, down to a frequency cut-off point. The cut-off has to be set at a level of delicacy which is realistic, but it is ultimately arbitrary. This restriction is justified on practical grounds, since the most frequent phrases are likely to be of most interest to language learners, and on theoretical grounds, since what is typical should receive more prominence.[4]

In other words, these examples of individual phrasal units are illustrative.

They are a necessary intermediate goal in investigating the best way to represent such extended units of meaning. However, we have to move beyond individual examples if we want to provide a comprehensive description of phraseology in English, such as would be required in compiling a phraseological dictionary. We require a systematic method of extracting the most frequent recurrent strings from a large corpus: this could then provide the evidence for the underlying phrasal units of meaning. PIE provides a way of doing this. It allows us to specify n-grams by length (e.g. 8-, 7- and 6-grams together), a node word or pattern, and a cut-off frequency (e.g. at least ten occurrences in the 100 million-word BNC). We can then extract all recurrent n-grams with the node at each position. With 8-grams this looks like Figure 6.1.

If necessary, we can check on whether these 8-grams are parts of longer phrasal constructions by looking directly at concordance lines. We repeat the procedure for n-grams of length 7 down to 2. We check whether this procedure has missed recurrent units by manually inspecting a random sample of raw concordance lines sorted to left and right. Given the 54,000 occurrences of *world*, every fiftieth line would give 20 pages of data which could be inspected manually.

We have to work down from longer to shorter multi-word sequences. For example, the 6-gram *the end of the second world* is frequent, but only because is it part of a recurrent 7-gram *the end of the Second World War*. The 2-gram *World War* is frequent, mainly because it is part of a recurrent variable 3-gram *Second World War, World War One*, etc. though we may decide to identify *World War* as an independent unit.[5] Similarly, we may wish to identify *in the world* as a unit: it is a frequent conventional way of emphasising a comparison. But we will certainly wish also to identify longer constructions in which it typically occurs (e.g. *the most natural thing in the world*). Although these decisions involve subjective interpretation, they are based on observable and replicable corpus data which can be reinterpreted by others.

5 A more systematic analysis of *world*

Native speakers are quite unable to generate, from their intuition alone, comprehensive lists of the most frequent uses of frequent words. However, although native speakers have no intuitive access to such information,

```
world xxxxx xxxxx xxxxx xxxxx xxxxx xxxxx xxxxx    min freq = 1C
xxxxx world xxxxx xxxxx xxxxx xxxxx xxxxx xxxxx    etc
xxxxx xxxxx world xxxxx xxxxx xxxxx xxxxx xxxxx
xxxxx xxxxx xxxxx world xxxxx xxxxx xxxxx xxxxx
xxxxx xxxxx xxxxx xxxxx world xxxxx xxxxx xxxxx
xxxxx xxxxx xxxxx xxxxx xxxxx world xxxxx xxxxx
xxxxx xxxxx xxxxx xxxxx xxxxx xxxxx world xxxxx
xxxxx xxxxx xxxxx xxxxx xxxxx xxxxx xxxxx world
```

Figure 6.1 Searching for *world* in each position of recurrent 8-grams

when they see automatically generated lists of recurrent n-grams, they immediately recognize idiomatic ways of expressing common pragmatic meanings. As Fox (1987: 146) puts it, as soon as they are told what the most frequent uses are, they cannot understand why they did not think of them in the first place: 'the important thing, of course, is that they had not'.

The Appendix lists the recurrent n-grams, from length 8 down to 3, with *world* in each position. Frequency cut-off points are clearly arbitrary, but can always be lowered to give a more delicate description. And there is a trade-off between the length of a phrase and its frequency (Mason 2005): each increase in the length of an n-gram will reduce its frequency and shorter n-grams will usually be more frequent than the recurrent longer n-grams in which they occur.

The recurrent n-grams listed in the Appendix can be easily grouped, at least into some of the most obvious recurrent phrases. Exactly how such findings should be converted from a list of n-grams into a list of variable phrases, appropriate to different purposes (e.g. a dictionary for advanced learners), is a matter for the intuition of lexicographers and materials designers. The database can provide quantitative evidence, but not the presentation and layout. What follows are some of the most obvious phrases. Alternatives are separated by slashes and alphabetized. Optional items are in round brackets.

the First/Second World War

at/since the end of   }
after/during/in/since   }
the outbreak of   } the First/Second World War
(in) the aftermath of   }
the time of   }

the end of the world
it's not the end of the world
with the best will in the world
all the time in the world
the most natural/easiest/most important thing in the world
the best in the world
the only person in the world who . . .

throughout/around the world
(on/to) the other side of the world
(from/in/to/with) the rest of the world
(in) many/different/other parts of the world
(in) this/any part of the world
(from) all over the world
(in) the First/Third World

(one/some of) the world's great/largest/leading/most
of its kind in the world
of/in/to the world

in the world of
the world of work
in the real world
the outside world

the World Cup
the World Bank (and the International Monetary Fund)
the IMF and the World Bank
(the) World Wide Fund for Nature

per cent of the world's (population)   [where # = number]

In a more detailed description, we can also check if some of the phrases have a restricted distribution in different texts and text-types, and therefore use both frequency and range as criteria of typicality. In addition, we can calculate the contribution of different phrases to the frequency of the individual word: *world* <ca 57,500>, *in the world* <5,885 = a little over 10 per cent>, *the world's* <5,530 = a little under 10 per cent>, *World War* <3,800 = 6.5 per cent>, etc.

6 Problems for analysis: variable and related patterns

A problem in interpreting such data is to see the wood for the trees. We want to identify frequent and typical patterns of use. This means respecting variant patterns and not implying that we are dealing with 'fixed phrases'. However, as is always the case with lexical data, some patterns are so much more frequent than others that they can be taken as canonical. Sinclair proposes the strong hypothesis that for each unit of meaning there is one canonical form plus variants. If it was possible to specify these phrasal units plus prototypical variants, then we would have 'the ultimate dictionary' (Sinclair et al. 2004: xxiv). Part of this problem is relatively simple, since, as I have done above, we can set a frequency cut-off and resolutely ignore occurrences below this point. We will probably find later, in a more delicate analysis, that rare instances fall into the categories established for the frequent cases (Sinclair 2004: 275, 281–2, 294).

The problem of identifying the boundaries of recurrent phrasal constructions is more difficult,[6] given that patterns can be nested within each other. Longer strings can contain shorter strings. For example, we might want to take any of the following instances as realizations of a recurrent pattern:

since	the end of	the Second	World War
since		the Second	World War
	the end of	the Second	World War
		the Second	World War
			World War
	the end of		

Then how should we relate constructions which vary due to different lexical realizations of a semantic set? For example, it would seem reasonable to regard a frame such as:

- the world 's most # NOUN

as a phrasal construction, since the variable is usually realized by one of a small set of positive evaluative adjectives: *advanced, beautiful, expensive, important, popular, powerful, successful.* Judgements of semantic similarity are subjective, but such cases are often not very difficult: if the realizations are similar, then the software makes them easy to see.

A second problem is that other patterns have a family resemblance to the patterns with *world.* For example, the following string is quite frequent in the BNC:

- one of the SUPERLATIVE ADJ (+ NOUN) in the { geographical expression }

Examples include:

- one of the oldest   in the city
- one of the best   in the country
- one of the worst   in the developed world
- one of the finest   in the region
- one of the largest in the world

Most attested examples are clearly evaluative, such as:

- the inflation rate is already one of the <u>highest</u> in the European Union
- our crime rate is one of the <u>lowest</u> in the country

But how abstract should patterns be allowed to be? We can identify a grammatical frame with typical lexis which provides a frequent idiomatic way of expressing evaluation. But if we cast the net a little wider still, we find further expressions which also seem intuitively to be related, but where the formal similarity is now becoming rather stretched. Examples include:

- one of the <u>wettest</u> areas <u>on earth</u>
- for the <u>first</u> time <u>in my life</u>

There are families of related constructions which express related semantic and pragmatic meanings. It is a basic finding, and now a premise, of pattern grammar (Hunston and Francis 2000) that words which share a pattern also share a meaning. But it is not known how best to formalize repeated but variable events in a way which reveals relations between phrasal constructions within a structured taxonomic network (Tognini-Bonelli 2001: 89; Croft 2001: 25).

Then to what extent can/should other types of abstract patterns be identified? For example, the 3-gram *into the world* occurs around 325 times in the BNC. Many instances, but a minority, are part of a larger construction which the Cobuild dictionary identifies as 'if a woman brings a child <u>into the world</u>, then she gives birth to a baby'. But this pattern is too variable to be found by searching for recurrent n-grams: the 3-gram may be preceded by different forms of the lemmas BRING and/or CHILD or BABY, all in different possible positions relative to the 3-gram. No particular realization is likely to occur very often, so the pattern remains largely invisible in output from the software. An additional common use is in religious texts: *he has sent his son into the world.*

The tools in PIE are very good at providing quantitative information on recurrent strings which have limited formal variation. However, no tools do everything, and they provide only intermediate data. The methods discussed in this chapter can find recurrent multi-word-strings which have a pre-set length and which consist of adjacent words within a fairly short span.

7 A more detailed analysis of an extended lexical unit

Here is a more detailed analysis which illustrates the problem of phrasal boundaries. One of the most frequent 7-grams in the BNC (see Appendix) is *the most natural thing in the world*. All 38 occurrences are given in Concordance 6.3, ordered alphabetically to the left. But let us use a little bit of native speaker intuition in order to find related patterns. The concordance gives all 123 occurrences of *thing in the world*, and shows related phrasal units. The most frequent is *the most natural thing in the world* <38>. But 119 occurrences out of 123 are preceded by a superlative: exceptions are 97, 99, 113, 114. The other most frequent are *the easiest thing* <23>, *the most important thing* <10>, *the last thing* <9>, *the simplest thing* <4>. Most are positive evaluations, and only a few are negative (*the hardest damn thing, the most difficult thing, the most terrible thing, the worst thing*). A rather small number of modifying adjectives occur, and several are pairs of antonyms: *easiest* <23>, *simplest* <4> versus *hardest* <1>, *most difficult* <2>, and *best* <2> versus *worst* <3>. And several are approximate synonyms: *natural, ordinary, reasonable, usual.*

Concordance 6.3 All concordance lines: *thing in the world*

```
001 she thought it was the most astonishing thing in the world." Sacco bit his lip
002 t. "Having a good body is not the best thing in the world," Cindy told More! ma
003 ste our lives on trash. why is the best thing in the world tied to the least las
004 ou, coming off coke is the hardest damn thing in the world, and you're real luck
005   three ping-pong balls. "Most difficult thing in the world to flush," he said.
006    ault. It was surely the most difficult thing in the world to appear sincere whe
007      but I mean Ford Escorts are easiest thing in the world to drive Oh yeah!
008 ended together as if it was the easiest thing in the world, forming a new, three
009 hty? "Becoming a parent is the easiest thing in the world. Being a good parent
010 er much thought. It is not the easiest thing in the world to enter a closed ord
011   off. They meant well, but the easiest thing in the world to do is to put diffi
012 her class. It ought to be the easiest thing in the world." "You haven't spoke
013 color Dreamcoat : "It's not the easiest thing in the world to be Phillip Schofie
014 es (certainly by me), it is the easiest thing in the world to write a review of
015 t at night when it would be the easiest thing in the world. All her agitation o
016 ritten put the pen down and the easiest thing in the world to have a but if you
017    just not listening. Oh. The easiest thing in the world to take off that ques
```

```
018  oming and, in theory, it is the easiest thing in the world to stop - you just st
019  ld have thought it would be the easiest thing in the world to write a file on hi
020  er to "relax, as if it were the easiest thing in the world to do? Not only is i
021  t like that, you see. It's the easiest thing in the world you see as she says
022  repared to take the strike The easiest thing in the world is to say" Yes" espec
023  bout that. She said, it is the easiest thing in the world, she said, to just sa
024  e that. It would have been the easiest thing in the world take me into another
025  mmediately that it would be the easiest thing in the world to listen for informa
026  very aware that it would be the easiest thing in the world to embrace him again,
027  Espana. It would have been the easiest thing in the world for the softly spoken
028  d surely relaxing should be the easiest thing in the world, lazing in the jewel -
029   pleasure. Somehow, it was the easiest thing in the world to imagine, though it
030  ist as though it's the most fascinating thing in the world. I notice a greasy s
031  l do doctor told me Epsom, the finest thing in the world is salt, you ca
032   ere? ? Yes. Yes. . It was the finest thing in the world. Mm mm. It the met
033  I'd probably think it was the greatest thing in the world." Actually, none of
034  tly as though it was the most important thing in the world. "One of them toffs
035  ll at once it seemed the most important thing in the world that he should know t
036  belief that love is the most important thing in the world. In my third term
037  , where feelings are the most important thing in the world. I want to get out t
038  him. "My family is the most important thing in the world to me. "Unless every
039  tionship with God is the most important thing in the world: I believe that each
040  brains." "She said the most important thing in the world was little frogs livi
041  is right. Youth is the most important thing in the world. Oh, why did you pai
042  stman and it's still the most important thing in the world. It's the only thing
043  said? He said that the most important thing in the world, I mean our world, is
044  "His feelings aren't the only important thing in the world." "He knows that. L
045  back into my eyes. ": is the important thing in the world. And arguing for wha
046  up my own stud farm here. And the last thing in the world you'd want would be t
047  can't do anything else. It's the last thing in the world he wants to do. It's
048  he end of the Benefit. It was the last thing in the world I wanted to do, but I
049  th that often hid its humour. The last thing in the world she needed was to be
050  ed and she could hardly chew. The last thing in the world she might have expect
051  ith heart-stopping suddenness, the last thing in the world she wanted was to be
052  ren. It was mikva night, and the last thing in the world that she felt like do
053  daren't think of the future. The last thing in the world she had thought of be
054  gave him the impression "that the last thing in the world that lie wished was e
055  "  went on Robert. "It is the loneliest thing in the world to wake up in the mid
056  am married to the most perfectly lovely thing in the world. It isn't strange to
057  re we understand that it's not the main thing in the world to conduct all Americ
058  and sang as if it was the most natural thing in the world. "I'll not leave th
059  aved as though it were the most natural thing in the world. We all spent the ne
060  omposed, as if it were the most natural thing in the world that Mrs McLaren's wh
061  if it were the easiest and most natural thing in the world. "I'm Nick," he said
062  and did what was still the most natural thing in the world for a 20-year-old gir
063  to sound as if it was the most natural thing in the world that we should be sit
064  round them. It seemed the most natural thing in the world. When he gently push
065  for a second it seemed the most natural thing in the world when the ships airloc
066  , make love as if it's the most natural thing in the world *, and lie down to di
067  smiling as if it were the most natural thing in the world that Carrie and Nick
068  ildren, is by no means the most natural thing in the world. There are no unambi
069  wayside) as if it were the most natural thing in the world ("indeed it is, it is
070  t and squatted down as the most natural thing in the world. There was a silence
071  om the idea that it is the most natural thing in the world for parents and child
072  hen, as though it were the most natural thing in the world, she heated up a kett
073  airs and moaning about the most natural thing in the world. He'd seen women giv
074  p for argument. "It's the most natural thing in the world. I read an article i
075   moonlight to Raynor. The most natural thing in the world: and had we but world
076  delight, and it seemed the most natural making her way
                                                      thing in the world to be
077  t seem as if this were the most natural thing in the world for a boy and his owl
078  baby and make it look the most natural thing in the world - another skill some
079  e found that it seemed the most natural thing in the world to her when she was s
```

```
080  ng fire. As if it was the most natural thing in the world he said, "God bless y
081  ire up here, it seemed the most natural thing in the world that cousins should w
082  to enter as if it were the most natural thing in the world. How can he? How ca
083  demanding music appear the most natural thing in the world. For some I know thi
084  anguages as if it were the most natural thing in the world. And so for these ch
085  ouble." As if it were the most natural thing in the world, he put his arms roun
086   talking, as if it was the most natural thing in the world. I knew you wanted m
087  the end of a phrase as the most natural thing in the world. There are other del
088  Robyn thought, it were the most natural thing in the world. Had he forgotten ho
089  familiar, as if it was the most natural thing in the world. "Ross:" she gasped
090  with the Exiles seemed the most natural thing in the world. Making no attempt t
091  s though all this were the most natural thing in the world. It is only upon ref
092  You are learning to do the most natural thing in the world. This is what your b
093  lmly as though it were the most natural thing in the world to have a wedding dre
094   It was as if it were the most natural thing in the world: (Speer, 1970: 18; i
095  larmed. It had seemed the most natural thing in the world. Lightness, that was
096    mash his first brew. THE MOST NATURAL THING IN THE WORLD The only ingredients
097    such thing in the world. There was no thing in the world for an explanatory pr
098    bly afflicted. It was the most obvious thing in the world that that man had a b
099    entails the existence of more than one thing in the world. But consider now th
100  e, I will," I said as if it was the one thing in the world I wanted to do. "Oh
101  ally appears to me that almost the only thing in the world which other men do bu
102  u see." As if it was the most ordinary thing in the world, Lindsey found hersel
103   e you have not. It is the most pitiful thing in the world. It was dead, shrive
104  I mean it's it's not the most pleasant thing in the world but it's certainly fu
105  thought was right for the most precious thing in the world to me. Remember, alw
106  ugh she were saying the most reasonable thing in the world, but her lips were nu
107  , as though it were the most reasonable thing in the world, but she saw that her
108  be, not a "text", but another "sensory, thing in the world (Sontag 1967, pp. 165
109   fact - it would have been the simplest thing in the world for the ICC to announ
110   iteroles, or flambes being the simplest thing in the world. They are recipes fo
111   and a fissure eruption is the simplest thing in the world but, unfortunately, i
112  And I had a slight mishap, the simplest thing in the world, really, when I was u
113  is to talk of some thing - either some thing in the world, which the word stand
114  on", there was none. There was no such thing in the world. There was no thing
115  was alone, and it was the most terrible thing in the world. But then you picked
116  cause they are doing the most unnatural thing in the world, which everyone tells
117  factly as though it were the most usual thing in the world. "They hide a number
118  und as though it was the most wonderful thing in the world. "Please," she said
119  inside your heart is the most wonderful thing in the world. I have been a lucky
120  ue," said Masklin. "The most wonderful thing in the world," said Grimma. "No.
121  n't rise sooner, because 'tis the worst thing in the world for the complexion; n
122  n stage. Jacko added: "It is the worst thing in the world to let fans down."
123  ing a new book - but "work is the worst thing in the world". "I hear that anyon
```

Most occurrences of the largest subset, *the most natural thing in the world,* follow phrases such as *as if it was/as though it were* or similar phrases which express hypothetical meanings (*appear, idea, look* and *seemed*). The canonical pattern is:

- as if it were the most natural thing in the world.

It might seem as if the extended phrasal construction could be internally analysed into segments which have paradigmatic alternatives, analogously perhaps to <u>invented</u> examples such as *as if it was the most desirable car in the showroom* or *she seemed the most intelligent student in the class.* However, as Sinclair (1991: 110, 113) argues, the <u>attested</u> examples quoted above are semi-preconstructed and carry additional attitudinal meanings, and it is therefore 'unhelpful to attempt to analyse grammatically any portion of text which appears to be constructed on the idiom principle'.

A dramatic increase in the quantity of data plus the ability to search the data very fast and redisplay concordance lines in different ways, alphabetically or by frequency, creates a significant change in the quality of the data. The key techniques are: concordancing a large number of texts in KWIC format, permuting and redisplaying node words in concordance lines, extracting recurrent fixed word-strings or variable collocational frameworks, and calculating the strength of attraction between coselected words (this last technique is not discussed here).

These techniques make recurrent patterns easy to recognize. Exactly what we can observe with concordance lines from a large general corpus is well discussed by Tognini-Bonelli (2001, 2004):

> on the horizontal syntagmatic axis we have:
> a single instance of *parole*
> in the form of a fragment of a meaningful speech act
> which has been extracted from an individual text/speaker
> which originally occurred as a piece of natural communicative behaviour
> on the vertical paradigmatic axis we have:
> evidence of *langue*
> in the form of repeated formal patterns
> which have been extracted from language use across a speech community
> and which have been displayed artificially by the linguist.

In an individual instance of *parole*, it is impossible, by definition, to observe repetitions. But concordance lines which are extracted from many texts and displayed in an appropriate way reveal repetitions. We can then observe two things: exactly repeated word-strings (n-grams) which are identifiable by the software, without human intervention, and evidence for more abstract semantic patterns which are identifiable via subjective judgements about semantically related word-sets.

We have empirical evidence of the relations between the poles of the dualisms which have plagued linguistics for a hundred years: instances of language use versus generalizations about the language system, individual speech acts versus social practice, and meaning versus form.

8 Sinclair's model of extended lexical units

One of the main theoretical proposals to come out of corpus studies is Sinclair's model of extended lexical units. The nature of this corpus-driven model usefully emphasizes a central feature of corpus analysis: empirical quantitative evidence is given a qualitative interpretation which becomes the basis for a powerful model of phrasal units of meaning. In retrospect, with the benefit of hindsight, it is evident how the technologies of observation and analysis have led to this model, but it was the ability to see these implications which required the stroke of genius. Sinclair (1998, 2005) proposes an extended unit of meaning with the following structure.

[1] COLLOCATION is the relation between the node word and individual word-forms which co-occur frequently with it.

[2] COLLIGATION is the relation between the node word and grammatical categories which co-occur frequently with it.

[3] SEMANTIC PREFERENCE is the relation between the node word and lexical sets of semantically related word-forms or lemmas.

[4] SEMANTIC PROSODY is the discourse function of the unit: it describes the speaker's evaluative attitude.

Relations [1] to [4] are increasingly abstract:

[1] Collocates are word-tokens: individual word-forms which are directly observable in texts. With computational help, we can discover which word-forms most frequently co-occur with a node word.

[2] Colligation refers to word-classes, which are not directly observable: they are abstractions based on the behaviour of the word in the class. The classes are often small, and may be closed: for example, there is a small, finite number of quantifiers in English. But grammatical classes are not entirely formal sets. They shade into semantic classes: for example, "negative" may be realized by exponents such as *not, hardly* and *refuse.*

[3] Semantic preference refers to what has traditionally been known as a lexical field: a class of words which share some semantic feature. Corpus study provides much empirical data on which words belong to which fields. This will relate to the topic of the surrounding co-text: what the text is about. Such a class is also abstract: its statement involves judgements about semantic similarity. It will have frequent and typical members, but will usually be open-ended.

[4] Semantic prosodies are a generalization about the motivation for speaking, and therefore related to concepts of speech act and illocutionary force. Their realization is even more open-ended and typically has great lexical variability. Indeed it may not be realized at all if the unit is highly conventionalized, but there will be observable evidence in recurrent collocates in repeated examples in the corpus. Semantic prosodies have pragmatic and textual functions. For this reason, I prefer the term 'discourse prosody' (but terminology is not important).

Collocation is the lowest and most specific level in the model. Individual words contrast paradigmatically with each other and these individual collocates make the lexical units fit into the surrounding co-text. Semantic/discourse prosody is the highest level. This is the reason for the choice of the lexical unit: the attitudinal/pragmatic meaning of the unit.

It is also possible to specify position and positional mobility, and to specify the strength of attraction between node and collocates, though there is considerable debate about which statistics are appropriate (Evert 2004). We should also specify distribution in text-types: whether the lexical unit occurs widely in general English, or whether it is restricted to broad varieties, such as journalism or technical and scientific English, or to specialized text-types, with a narrow speech act function, such as recipes or weather forecasts.

In summary: We can state the structure of extended lexical items, with their canonical forms and most frequent variants, as follows:

[1] collocation   tokens   co-occurring word-forms
[2] colligation   classes   co-occurring grammatical classes
[3] semantic preference topics   lexical field, similarity of meaning
[4] discourse prosody   motivation   communicative purpose

Much twentieth-century linguistics has assumed that lexis is not amen-able to systematic treatment, because the vocabulary is merely 'a list of basic irregularities' in a language (Bloomfield 1933: 274). For much of Chomskyan linguistics, it is syntax which is claimed to be concerned with general rules, whereas lexis is largely dismissed as being concerned with isolated and idiosyncratic facts. However, Sinclair's elegant model inte-grates lexis fully within the traditional concerns of linguistic theory. A lexical unit consists of lexical, syntactic, semantic and pragmatic com-ponents. Relations [1] to [4] correspond to the classic distinctions which were drawn by Morris in the 1930s (Morris 1938). Syntax deals with how linguistic signs relate to one another (here collocation and colligation), semantics deals with how linguistic signs relate to the external world (here lexical sets and the phenomena they denote), and pragmatics deals with how linguistic signs relate to their users (here expression of speaker attitude).

[1] collocation   lexis   }
[2] colligation   syntax   } relations between linguistic signs
[3] semantic preference semantics   relations between signs and the
                                     world
[4] discourse prosody   pragmatics relations between signs and
                                     speakers

For example, *the end of the world* (see section 3 above) collocates with words such as *disappointment, failure, worry*, colligates with negatives, and has a semantic preference for words in the lexical field of "reassurance". The resulting construction *it's not the end of the world* is used when the speaker wants to express a guarded encouragement: "it may look bad, but it could be worse, so cheer up!"

9 Previous work: case studies of individual words

The present chapter is not, of course, the only analysis of the phraseology around high-frequency nouns. The following are three excellent case stud-ies. Goldberg (1996) studies one frequent use of the word *way*. She points out that the *make one's way* construction often implies that someone has to overcome some external physical or social barrier (*he made his way cautiously along the lake; he bought his way into the club*). Lenk (2000) studies collocational patterns around the word *time*. Amongst many other observations, she points out that the phrase *all that time* may express the speaker's dismay at how long something has taken (*he hasn't been paid all that time*). Lavelle and Minugh (1998) study a second construction around the word *time*. The *high time* construction is used when a speaker is advocating a desirable change or approving a change which has already taken place (*it's high time that we stopped this charade; it was high time for a fresh interpretation*). All three articles make acute observations about the meanings of individual 'stabilized expressions' (Lenk's term) which have conventional non-compositional and evaluative meanings (semantic prosodies). But they do not propose a quantitative method which would allow us either to describe the overall phraseology of the individual words, or to develop a comprehensive listing of all the units of meaning in the language, or to make functional generalizations about the phraseology of subsets of the vocabulary, such as frequent nouns. A move in this second direction is made by Mahlberg (2005). She starts from an observation by Halliday and Hasan (1976), who call such words 'general nouns' and point to their cohesive textual functions. She then uses corpus data to investigate the phrasal uses of a larger set of high-frequency nouns. She points out that they are often characterized by local textual functions, including evaluation: *one of the greatest in modern times; the best buy of the past year* (Mahlberg 2005: 153, 157).

Many corpus-driven case studies have improved the analysis of individual words and phrases and greatly refined the concept of collocation and colligation. Work has of course not stopped at case studies of individual expressions: analyses have been built into the pattern grammars of Francis et al. (1996, 1998), where the relation between similar patterns and similar meanings is clearly shown. Such studies show that the micro-patterns around individual words are more detailed than we could previously imagine. However, corpora can also show macro-patterns, since we can quantify how often patterns of different kinds occur, and draw generalizations by 'inspect[ing] the whole corpus in a single process', as Krishnamurthy (2000: 41) recommends. These comments suggest how work in phraseology can be developed. I conclude with some proposals for research projects.

10 Research projects

One general aim of work on routine and idiomatic language use is to identify the main recurrent phrasal constructions in English and to explain why they are frequent. I have illustrated automatic methods which are good at extracting recurrent strings with limited formal variation. These methods can analyse very large amounts of corpus data, and provide quantitative evidence which was previously invisible. However, there is no purely automatic way of identifying phrasal units of meaning. The question is not: Do the methods tell us everything we want to know about phraseology? Clearly no. But are they better than trying to discover patterns by introspection? Clearly yes. A major criterion is that the results should be comprehensive, down to a given frequency cut-off. As noted above (section 4), this restriction is justified both on theoretical grounds (what is typical should receive more prominence) and on practical grounds (e.g. beginning language learners should start with the most frequent and most useful phrases).

A description of a phrasal construction must state its internal and external features and provide:

a structural analysis	of its canonical forms and internal variants
a functional analysis	of its meaning and communicative purpose
a taxonomic analysis	of its relation to other phrasal constructions
a distributional analysis	of the text-types in which it frequently occurs.

(I have not discussed this last point in this chapter.) One functional hypothesis is that frequent words are frequent because they occur in frequent phrasal constructions, and that many of these constructions express essential pragmatic meanings, including discourse functions of managing information.

My illustrative case study of the word *world* is part of a medium-term project on the feasibility of the methods. This work is proceeding in stages: detailed studies of individual cases; studies of sets of words, such as high-frequency 'general' nouns (Mahlberg 2005), and nouns from semantic sets (Lindquist and Levin 2005); and studies of grammatical constructions (Stubbs 2006). Most of the most frequent words in the language are grammatical (function) words, but some lexical (content) words (i.e. nouns, lexical verbs and adjectives) do occur amongst the top 200 or so words in word-frequency lists. The top ten verbs[7] and adjectives (word-forms) in the BNC are as follows:

- said, make, made, get, see, going, go, take, know, came
- other, new, good, old, different, local, small, great, social, important

Many of the top ten verb-forms are frequent because of their use in longer n-grams (e.g. *make a mistake*, *take place*), and many of the top ten adjectives are comparative and/or evaluative and therefore have textual functions.

Such studies are intermediate stages on the way to a long-term goal which must be to identify all the phraseological units of meaning in the language, and the examples in this chapter can therefore be linked into a research programme which has various aspects:

1. Description/theory. The concept of phrasal constructions is entirely compatible with the premise of 'construction grammar', that constructions have 'unique semantic, pragmatic and grammatical properties' (Shibatani and Thompson 1996: vii). This comparison is sometimes

made in passing (e.g. Lenk 2000; Legallois 2005) but I do not know of any studies which attempt to compare systematically the concepts of 'extended lexical unit' (e.g. Sinclair 1998) and 'construction' (e.g. Croft 2001: 18). The similarity is particularly interesting, since scholars who have started from quite different theoretical assumptions and worked within quite different methodological traditions have arrived at similar conclusions about how to model units of meaning.

2. Description/applications. Phrasal constructions are best described rather differently within linguistic theory, in dictionaries for non-native learners and in teaching materials. Different levels of detail and different presentations are appropriate for professional linguists and for language learners. An approach based on frequency can, in principle, handle these differences quite easily: learners might initially require just the most frequent prototypical exponents of the most frequent constructions, whereas linguists might require a much more delicate description. However, the best ways of presenting information remain to be investigated.

3. Text analysis. I have claimed that many frequent phrasal constructions have textual functions of evaluation and information management. However, the methods of extraction remove these constructions from their discourse contexts. The hypothesis must also be studied from the other end, by identifying them in specific texts and studying their function in longer stretches of text and in different text-types. Studies of phraseology must combine corpus analysis (which phrasal constructions are frequent in the corpus?) and textual analysis (how do these constructions organize individual texts?).

If we are interested primarily in theory, then empirical quantitative data about recurrent phrasal constructions can help solve a long-standing and difficult problem in linguistic theory by providing crucial evidence about the nature of units of meaning. If we are interested primarily in practice, empirical quantitative data about recurrent phrasal constructions can help with designing a new type of dictionary which would list phrasal units with their canonical forms, their frequent variants and their often evaluative meanings (Sinclair et al. 2004: xxiv). This would have far-reaching implications for lexicography and language teaching.

Acknowledgements

Previous much shorter versions of this paper were given at the Victoria University of Wellington in New Zealand, at the Catholic University of Milan in Italy, at the University of Aalborg in Denmark, and at the conference on Phraseology 2005, Louvain-la-Neuve in Belgium. I am grateful to colleagues on these occasions and also to Kieran O'Halloran for critical comments. My main debt is to Bill Fletcher, who developed the database which I have used for most of my analysis.

Notes

1. I am grateful to Kieran O'Halloran for this example.
2. This description of PIE gives only a very abbreviated summary of its power. For some functions, it is possible to use these relatively simple pattern-matching conventions, or to use fuzzy matches, or to use the much more powerful pattern-matching language known as 'regular expressions', which allows patterns to be defined using the alternatives AND, OR and NOT. For example, the pattern 'smel(l|ls|t| led| ling)' would expand as the word-forms *smell* or *smells* or *smelt* or *smelled* or *smelling*, and therefore as the lemma of the verb SMELL.
3. The BNC tagging splits *it's* into two words, so *it's not the end of the world* is an 8-gram.
4. PIE has a built-in cut-off frequency of three or more for realizations of an n-gram or p-frame.
5. Some illustrative frequencies are: *World War* <3,813>, *Second World War* <1,620>, *First World War* <1,021>, *World War Two* <591>, *World War One* <288>.
6. For a detailed attempt to solve the problem of indeterminate boundaries of collocational units, see Daudaravičius and Marcinkevičienė (2004).
7. If the same verb-forms with different PoS-tags (e.g. finite base versus infinitive) are collapsed, the top ten occur in a different frequency order.

References

Bloomfield, L. (1933) *Language.* New York: Holt, Rinehart and Winston. (Page references to British edition, London: Allen and Unwin, 1935.)

Croft, W. (2001) *Radical Construction Grammar.* Oxford: Oxford University Press.

Daudaravičius, V. and Marcinkevičienė, R. (2004) 'Gravity counts for the boundaries of collocations'. *International Journal of Corpus Linguistics,* 9, 2: 321–48.

Evert, S. (2004) *The Statistics of Word Co-occurrences.* Doctoral dissertation. University of Stuttgart.

Fletcher, W. (2003–06) *PIE: Phrases in English.* [Database] http://pie.usna. edu.

Fox, G. (1987) 'The case for examples', in J. Sinclair (ed.), *Looking Up. An Account of the COBUILD Project in Lexical Computing.* London: Collins, pp. 137–49.

Francis, G., Hunston, S. and Manning, E. (1996, 1998) *Grammar Patterns,* vols 1 and 2. London: HarperCollins.

Goldberg, A. E. (1996) 'Making one's way through the data', in M. Shibatani and S. A. Thompson (eds), *Grammatical Constructions.* Oxford: Oxford University Press, pp. 29–53.

Halliday, M. A. K. and Hasan, R. (1976) *Cohesion in English*. London: Longman.

Hunston, S. and Francis, G. (2000) *Pattern Grammar. A Corpus-driven Approach to the Lexical Grammar of English*. Amsterdam: Benjamins.

Krishnamurthy, R. (2000) 'Collocation: from silly ass to lexical sets', in C. Heffer and H. Sauntson (eds), *Words in Context*. [CD-ROM] Discourse Analysis Monograph 18. Birmingham: University of Birmingham.

Lavelle, T. and Minugh, D. (1998) 'And high time too: a corpus-based study of one English construction', in H. Lindquist et al. (eds), *The Major Varieties of English*. Papers from MAVEN 97. Växjö: Acta Wexionensia 1: 213–26.

Legallois, D. (2005) 'La grammaire de construction et la grammaire contextualiste'. Paper presented at Phraseology 2005, Louvain-la-Neuve, October 2005.

Lenk, U. (2000) 'Stabilized expressions in spoken discourse', in C. Mair and M. Hundt (eds), *Corpus Linguistics and Linguistic Theory*. Amsterdam: Rodopi, pp. 187–200.

Lindquist, H. and Levin, M. (2005) 'Foot and mouth: the phrasal patterns of two frequent nouns'. Paper presented at Phraseology 2005, Louvain-la-Neuve, October 2005.

Mahlberg, M. (2005) *English General Nouns: a Corpus Theoretical Approach*. Amsterdam: Benjamins.

Mason, O. (2005) 'Automatic identification of English multi-word units'. Paper presented at Phraseology 2005, Louvain-la-Neuve, October 2005.

Morris, C. W. (1938) 'Foundations of the theory of signs', in O. Neurath, R. Carnap and C. W. Morris (eds), *International Encyclopedia of Unified Science*. Chicago: Chicago University Press, pp. 77–138.

Rundell, M. (2001) 'Corpora, evidence and intuition'. Corpora List, 1 November 2001. http://torvald.aksis.uib.no/corpora/2001-4/0080.html.

Shibatani, M. and Thompson, S. A. (eds) (1996) *Grammatical Constructions*. Oxford: Oxford University Press.

Sinclair, J. (1991) *Corpus Concordance Collocation*. Oxford: Oxford University Press.

—— (1998) 'The lexical item', in E. Weigand (ed.), *Contrastive Lexical Semantics*. Amsterdam: Benjamins, pp. 1–24.

—— (1999) 'A way with common words', in H. Hasselgård and S. Oksefjell (eds), *Out of Corpora. A Study in Honour of Stig Johansson*. Amsterdam: Rodopi, pp. 157–79.

—— (2004) 'New evidence, new priorities, new attitudes', in J. Sinclair (ed.) *How to Use Corpora in Language Teaching*. Amsterdam: Benjamins, pp. 271–99.

—— (2005) 'The phrase, the whole phrase and nothing but the phrase'. Plenary lecture presented at Phraseology 2005, Louvain-la-Neuve, October 2005.

Sinclair, J., Jones, S. and Daley, R. (2004) *English Collocation Studies. The OSTI Report*. London: Continuum. [First published 1970.]

Stubbs, M. (2006) 'Quantitative data on multi-word sequences in English: the case of prepositional phrases'. Paper given at the conference on idioms, Berlin-Brandenburgische Akademie der Wissenschaften, 2–4 November 2006.

Summers, D. (1996) 'Computer lexicography: the importance of representativeness in relation to frequency', in J. Thomas and M. Short (eds), *Using Corpora for Language Research*. London: Longman, pp. 260–6.

Tognini-Bonelli, E. (2001) *Corpus Linguistics at Work*. Amsterdam: Benjamins.

—— (2004) 'Working with corpora', in C. Coffin et al. (eds), *Applying English Grammar. Functional and Corpus Approaches*. London: Arnold, pp. 11–24.

Appendix

All 7- and 8-grams which occur more than ten times, with *world* in any position.

the end of the Second World War	103	7
at the end of the Second World	39	7
at the end of the Second World War	39	8
the end of the First World War	39	7
the most natural thing in the world	38	7
with the best will in the world	38	7
on the other side of the world	32	7
the outbreak of the Second World War	29	7
since the end of the Second World	26	7
since the end of the Second World War	26	8
the outbreak of the First World War	21	7
by the World Wide Fund for Nature	20	7
and the World Wide Fund for Nature	17	7
at the end of the First World	14	7
at the end of the First World War	14	8
the World Wide Fund for Nature and	14	7
's not the end of the world	13	7
all the time in the world to	13	7
had all the time in the world	13	7
it's not the end of the world	13	8
the World Bank and the International Monetary	13	7
the World Bank and the International Monetary Fund	13	8
were the most natural thing in the world	13	8
World Bank and the International Monetary Fund	13	7
# per cent of the world's population	12	7
in the aftermath of the First World	12	7
in the aftermath of the First World War	12	8
of one of the world's most	12	7
the aftermath of the First World War	12	7
to the other side of the world	12	7
of the World Wide Fund for Nature	11	7
the easiest thing in the world to	11	7

the time of the First World War	11	7
their understanding of the world of work	11	7
the most important thing in the world	10	7
the only person in the world who	10	7

All 6- and 7-grams which occur more than 25 times.

the World Wide Fund for Nature	115	6
end of the Second World War	103	6
the end of the Second World	103	6
the end of the Second World War	103	7
one of the world's most	98	6
in other parts of the world	79	6
# per cent of the world 's	75	6
in many parts of the world	75	6
the other side of the world	62	6
and the rest of the world	53	6
with the rest of the world	53	6
is one of the world's	51	6
all the time in the world	50	6
in this part of the world	46	6
from the rest of the world	44	6
to the rest of the world	44	6
one of the world 's largest	41	6
at the end of the Second World	39	7
end of the First World War	39	6
in the rest of the world	39	6
most natural thing in the world	39	6
the best will in the world	39	6
the end of the First World	39	6
the end of the First World War	39	7
the most natural thing in the world	38	7
with the best will in the world	38	7
in different parts of the world	35	6
of the rest of the world	34	6
on the other side of the world	32	7
of one of the world's	31	6
one of the world's great	31	6
one of the world's leading	31	6
some of the world's most	31	6
outbreak of the Second World War	29	6
the outbreak of the Second World	29	6
the outbreak of the Second World War	29	7
the IMF and the World Bank	28	6
as one of the world's	27	6
of its kind in the world	27	6
in any part of the world	26	6
since the end of the Second World	26	7

All 5- and 6-grams which occur more than 50 times.

the rest of the world	483	5
one of the world 's	401	5
of the Second World War	283	5
during the Second World War	279	5
from all over the world	225	5
after the Second World War	215	5
of the First World War	197	5
BBC summary of world broadcasts	186	5
of the world 's most	164	5
the end of the world	157	5
in the Second World War	145	5
in the First World War	139	5
other parts of the world	138	5
since the Second World War	128	5
World Wide Fund for Nature	127	5
during the First World War	125	5
after the First World War	121	5
the World Wide Fund for	119	5
the World Wide Fund for Nature	115	6
end of the Second World	103	5
end of the Second World War	103	6
the end of the Second World	103	6
before the First World War	98	5
one of the world 's most	98	6
some of the world 's	92	5
the best in the world	92	5
# per cent of the world	89	5
many parts of the world	87	5
per cent of the world 's	87	5
the Second World War and	83	5
in other parts of the world	79	6
of the world 's largest	78	5
# per cent of the world 's	75	6
in many parts of the world	75	6
this part of the world	69	5
before the Second World War	68	5
since the Second World War	68	5
of the world 's population	66	5
other side of the world	62	5
the other side of the world	62	6
the First World War and	57	5
different parts of the world	55	5
and the rest of the world	53	6
is one of the world	53	5
with the rest of the world	53	6
is one of the world 's	51	6
after the Second World War	50	5
all the time in the world	50	6
the time in the world	50	5

All 4- and 5-grams which occur more than 200 times.

the Second World War	1,537	4
of the world 's	1,264	4
the First World War	972	4
all over the world	716	4
rest of the world	500	4
parts of the world	486	4
the rest of the world	483	5
one of the world	412	4
one of the world 's	401	5
in the world of	353	4
the world 's most	349	4
in the Third World	344	4
the world 's largest	310	4
part of the world	295	4
of the Second World	286	4
of the Second World War	283	5
during the Second World	279	4
during the Second World War	279	5
in the real world	239	4
from all over the world	225	5
after the Second World	216	4
after the Second World War	215	5
of the First World	210	4
in the world and	208	4

All 3- and 4-grams which occur more than 500 times.

of the world	5,988	3
in the world	5,885	3
the world 's	3,400	3
Second World War	1,620	3
the Second World	1,554	3
the world of	1,540	3
the Second World War	1,537	4
of the world 's	1,264	4
the First World	1,048	3
around the world	1,036	3
First World War	1,021	3
the First World War	972	4
to the world	840	3
the World Cup	829	3
the Third World	811	3
over the world	753	3
the world and	731	3
all over the world	716	4
the outside world	602	3
the world is	580	3
throughout the world	577	3

the real world	572	3
for the world	542	3
the World Bank	541	3
and the world	521	3
rest of the world	500	4

7 Lexical items in discourse: identifying local textual functions of *sustainable development*

Michaela Mahlberg

Introduction

Both of my chapters in the present book deal with aspects of the relationship between lexis and text. This chapter takes a more lexical point of view by concentrating on one specific phrase; the following chapter starts from a more textual point of view and focuses on the study of literary texts. Both approaches are embedded in a corpus theoretical framework that sees the study of meanings in corpora based on insights into contextual patterns. The analysis of words in context has led to in-depth characterizations of lexico-grammatical patterns and distributions of linguistic features across different types of texts. However, texts in corpora may be just parts of texts, and even if they are full-length texts they are decontextualized from the situations in which they were used. Thus with an increase in objectivity resulting from huge amounts of data comes a loss of detail with regard to functional features of texts in situations of use. Recent developments in the use of corpora stress the potential of corpus linguistic methodologies for the study of social meanings, ideologies and the construction of social reality. The present chapter aims to explore how meanings can be studied both on the basis of concordance lines and with regard to textual features. Local textual functions are identified that contribute to the description of social aspects of meaning. The example that is discussed is the phrase *sustainable development* studied in a corpus of newspaper articles. Section 1 begins by providing the corpus linguistic context in which the present study is set. Section 2 looks at the issue of localness from the point of view of texts and from the point of view of lexical items as cultural key words. Section 3 describes the corpus and the methodology for the analysis of *sustainable development*. Section 4 presents the results of a concordance analysis to describe groups of different meanings associated with *sustainable development*. Section 5 provides details on the subsections of the corpus and the distribution of *sustainable development* across different types of newspaper articles. Section 6 relates the meanings identified in section 5 to different sections in the corpus. Finally, section 7 returns to the corpus linguistic starting point.

1 A corpus linguistic starting point

In a recent discussion of the state of the art in corpus analysis, Stubbs (2006) outlines links between corpus work and classic questions of social theory. He observes that 'many corpus-based case studies are restricted to individual schemas, such as *budge*,[1] and not related to wider lexical fields in the language' (Stubbs 2006: 32); and he illustrates how corpus analysis can aid the identification of meanings which play a part in 'the routine transmission of cultural knowledge' (Stubbs 2006: 33). Among his examples are ways of talking about 'groups of people', such as *band, bunch, crowd, relatives, friends*, that relate to the location of people in the social world. The typical phrases in which these words occur reveal the attitudes and evaluations that play a part in the social discourse.[2] For the link between corpus analysis and social theory, issues of both corpus methodology and corpus theory play a central role. When Hunston (2002) looks at the use of corpora in the study of ideology and culture, she concludes her discussion by pointing out that '[b]ecause data in corpora is de-contextualised, the researcher is encouraged to spell out the steps that lie between what is observed and the interpretation placed on those observations' (Hunston 2002: 123).

Although corpus linguistics is still often treated as a methodology in the first place, an approach that Tognini-Bonelli (2001) describes as 'corpus-based', we can argue in favour of theoretical positions in corpus linguistics; such an approach would be what Tognini-Bonelli (2001) views as 'corpus-driven'. Theoretical issues in corpus linguistics have been raised mainly by Sinclair (2004),[3] Hunston and Francis (2000), Stubbs (2001), Tognini-Bonelli (2001), Teubert (2005) and Hoey (2005), but also others that can be seen as working in a neo-Firthian tradition. The link between language and society receives particular attention in the work of Teubert (e.g. 2004, and the present volume) that is less interested in extensive quantitative data than in hermeneutic approaches to and interpretations of corpus data in its social and historical contexts. Generally, however, theoretical discussions in corpus linguistics seem to centre on the nature of units of meaning and the interplay between lexis and grammar. The textual dimension of meanings and relationships between lexical items still leave us with many open questions. Although corpus linguists refer to fundamental work by J. R. Firth (e.g. 1957) to stress the recurrent nature of social contexts, in corpus linguistic practice social aspects of meaning seem to receive attention mainly in the design and compilation of corpora or in studies on the variation of linguistic features across different types of texts. As Stubbs (2006) points out, the link between corpus findings and social theory still needs closer investigation.

The present chapter does not claim to tackle high-level social theoretical questions; its aim is to argue that the types of descriptive categories we apply to interpret corpus data have an impact on the extent to which we can investigate social aspects of meanings. This section outlines the theoretical context in which the present chapter is set. The arguments summarized here are discussed in more detail in Mahlberg (2005). They form the basis for the analysis of *sustainable development* in the present chapter. The next chapter further develops the arguments within the realm of literary stylistics.

Even authors who see themselves placed towards the corpus-driven end of the spectrum in corpus linguistics and who may share assumptions and similar basic concepts, may also place different emphasis on specific arguments with differing implications. Therefore, it is important that I briefly summarize what for me seem to be the fundamental arguments in corpus linguistics:

1. Language is a social phenomenon.
2. Meaning and form are associated.
3. A corpus linguistic description of language prioritizes lexis.

These three points can be taken as key pillars of a corpus theoretical framework (see Mahlberg 2005). They can provide a basis for further claims and a context that accommodates more detailed observations. Theories organize arguments in explanatory hierarchies and characterize relationships between claims on different levels. As key pillars of a corpus theoretical framework, the above points are related to one another in the following way. The focus on the social dimension of language sees language as action. The members of a discourse community interact, and language is one form of their social behaviour. Meanings are the ways in which words are used; and repeated patterns of usage can be recorded in corpora and make patterns of meanings visible. If the same formal features are repeated, we are able to notice them as patterns and we can describe the meanings that tend to go with them. If we take the position that the patterns in a corpus are patterns of lexical items that can be observed in a bottom-up fashion, we need descriptive categories that are adequate to characterize these patterns. The descriptive categories have to be less general than systematic distinctions meant to account for the whole of a language. In a corpus theoretical approach, a grammar is seen as a set of generalizations about the behaviour of words in texts, and these generalizations have to be related to the texts on which they are based. Such a grammar is less general than a description of syntactic phenomena, and it is preferably organized in a flexible way (cf. Mahlberg 2005) so that different local points of view are possible. Thus lexical categories can link in with the social aspects of language via the texts in the corpus.

A descriptive category within this corpus theoretical framework is the concept of 'local textual functions' (Mahlberg 2005). Local textual functions are 'textual' as they describe the meanings of lexical items in texts. They pay close attention to similarities between lexical items and/or meanings in specific groups of texts. The functions are 'local' in that they do not claim to capture general functions, but functions specific to a (group of) text(s) and/or specific to a (group of) lexical item(s).

The concept of local textual functions becomes clearer when we see it in relation to three other ways of looking at the meaning of a word, illustrated in Figure 7.1. Firstly, we can look at a word in isolation from any textual context. Sinclair (2005a: 21) uses the term 'residual meaning' to describe a meaning that a word retains when cited: '[w]ithout any support from a cotext, each individual word still yields one or more meanings when cited'. In contrast to its residual meanings there is the 'text meaning' of a word that depends on the configurations and patterns of coselection in a particular text. Both of these types of meaning are difficult to capture on the basis of corpora. Residual meanings may be better described with regard to cognitive and psycholinguistic processes. In this sense they may be related to the theory of lexical priming (Hoey 2005) which says that the meaning of a word depends on the language experience of the speaker of a language and the encounters that s/he has had with that word. Still, the residual meaning has a further aspect in that it refers to the citation meaning of a word, which raises the question of to what extent individuals are aware of primings and to what extent the citation meaning of a word is related to previous encounters with the word in a range of communicative contexts. The text meaning of a word is similarly complex. In a text a word can mean virtually anything depending on its context, and the interpretation by an individual reader/listener plays an important role. Safer ground for corpus linguistics is the examination of a large number of textual contexts to identify repeated patterns. Thus in Figure 7.1, the text meaning and the residual meaning are placed at two ends of a continuum illustrating different facets of meaning that can be described.

The concept of the 'lexical item' describes meanings that are different from residual meanings in that contextual features around a core are taken into account. Sinclair (2004) introduces the categories of collocation, colligation, semantic preference and semantic prosody as increasingly abstract descriptive categories to characterize components of units of meaning.[4] At

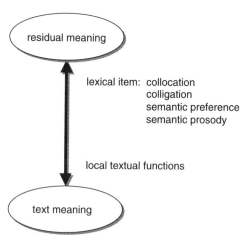

Figure 7.1 Levels of description for the meanings of a lexical core

the same time, the characterization of a lexical item is based on generalizations across a number of texts, thus its description needs not be as detailed as the description of the meaning of a word in one single text (its text meaning). From the level of collocation to semantic prosody the descriptive components of a lexical item become increasingly abstract and move from the fixed core of the item towards its boundaries. Collocation is a very concrete category and accounts for the actual repetition of words on the textual surface around the core. The component colligation introduces a level of abstraction with reference to grammatical categories. Semantic preferences interpret the context of the core in terms of shared semantic features, and finally the semantic prosody accounts for attitudinal or pragmatic meanings. The semantic prosody is the most variable and often most difficult component to describe. Sinclair (2004: 34) characterizes it as being close to the 'function' of an item and playing an important role 'in the integration of an item with its surroundings'. As the description of the lexical features moves further outwards, we come to the concept of local textual functions. Local textual functions do not account for as much detail on the lexico-grammatical level as the description of a lexical item. They come closer to the textual components of meanings that are associated with lexical items. However, descriptive categories to characterize local textual functions do not automatically draw on the tools of textlinguistics or discourse analysis; the labels that are used are more *ad hoc*, as demonstrated in later sections.

Examples of local textual functions that I have discussed previously are, for instance, patterns to talk about people, or patterns to talk about time (cf. Mahlberg 2005, 2006). These local textual functions were identified on the basis of the Bank of English as a large general corpus, and the social aspects of the meanings were thereby of a general nature. The present article explores another dimension of localness by focusing on a single phrase in a smaller and more specific corpus.

2 Localness – texts and key words

It is a truism that the meanings and functions that can be identified by means of a corpus analysis depend on the selection of texts that make up the corpus. With the social dimension as a key point in a corpus theoretical approach, it seems important that criteria for the collection of texts are determined by external factors in the first place. As Sinclair (2005b: 1) puts it: 'The contents of a corpus should be selected without regard for the language they contain, but according to their communicative function in the community in which they arise.' This approach can help to avoid bias and circularity in the corpus analysis. However, texts in corpora are decontextualized. Thus, as Hunston (2002) points out, corpora are not automatically suited for the study of texts in their social context:

If a corpus is composed of a number of texts, corpus search and processing techniques, such as word-lists, concordance lines and lists of collocations, will tend to obscure the character of each text as a text. Each individual example is taken out of context – that, in a sense, is the point.

(Hunston 2002: 110)

The way in which an analysis of corpus data can be related to social situations depends on the information that is available on the origins and contexts of the texts. If the texts in a corpus are selected according to transparent criteria and information on their contexts is stored together with the texts, corpora can provide useful insights into meanings that are relevant to a society and indicative of the ways in which society creates itself. Textual functions that can be identified are, for instance, evaluative functions that characterize a specific point of view on aspects of society.

The linguistic discipline that typically deals with the characterization and construction of society through language is critical discourse analysis (CDA). CDA investigates social structures and power relationships and how they shape and are shaped by language. CDA studies attitudes, opinions and ideologies expressed through language. In contrast to corpus linguistics, CDA tends to focus on in-depth studies of small collections of texts. Thus critical discourse analysts may not readily accept corpora as useful resources. Ideologies, however, can be difficult to pin down and one of the strengths of corpora is that they can help to discover subtle meanings. Louw (2004) pointedly talks about the potential of 'concordancing spin'. Similarly, Koller and Mautner (2004: 222) see the area of semantic prosody as one that is of mutual interest for corpus linguistics and CDA. In order to link findings to their social contexts, the construction of the corpus is crucial, as Adolphs (2006: 81) stresses: 'When it comes to the study of ideology, the choice of texts is probably the most important factor in the research design process.'

A number of corpus studies have been conducted to deal with aspects of society and the discourses that are represented by specialized corpora. Some examples are Teubert's (2001) analysis of a corpus collected from British Euro-sceptic websites and Partington's (2003) study of White House press briefings. Garzone and Santulli (2004) present a case study on newspaper articles dealing with the events of September 11 and a study on pre-electoral speeches by Berlusconi. Baker and McEnery (2005) investigate discourses of refugees and asylum seekers on the basis of newspaper articles and texts from the United Nations High Commissioner for Refugees website (see also Baker 2006).

When investigating the link between texts that are taken to represent an aspect of society and meanings in these texts, a question that arises is which lexical items are taken to be relevant. One approach is to work with key words generated by the software *WordSmith Tools* (Scott 2004). The basic idea is to compare the frequencies of words in corpus A (which can be just a single text) with the frequencies of the words in corpus B (often a large reference corpus) and identify those words which are comparatively more or less frequent in A than in B. Such key words can reveal patterns of 'aboutness' and stylistic features of texts. Scott (2002: 46) shows how relationships between key words across articles from the *Guardian* 'reflect not so much the world as it is, but rather the way the *Guardian* chooses to display it because of considerations such as newsworthiness'.

Also looking at *Guardian* texts, Tribble (2006) uses key word lists to identify which personalities dominate the news agenda over a particular period of time. For the period 1996–2001 he finds *Clinton, Blair, Milosevic, Bush, Clinton's, Gore, Pinochet, Netanyahu, Putin, Hague, Blair's,* a list that 'summarises the heroes, villains and supporting cast in the period immediately before the 11th September attack on the World Trade Centre in New York, from this newspaper's perspective' (Tribble 2006: 165). A closer look at the collocates of the key words can then 'sort the good guys from the baddies' (Tribble 2006: 165). Key words can also be used in the study of more specific discourses. For instance, Baker (2006) presents a study on political debates on fox-hunting in the British House of Commons and uses key words to distinguish between the speech of people in favour of fox-hunting and those who voted to ban fox-hunting.

Key words that are derived by the *KeyWords Tool* in *WordSmith* (Scott 2004) can provide insights into aspects of social organization and views of the world. Such key words overlap with words that are intuitively regarded as culturally important. The notion of key words relates to Williams' (1983) vocabulary of culture and society, where he explains the social and cultural issues around words such as *unemployment* or *popular*. Similarly, Wierzbicka (1997: 16) points to the importance of certain words as 'focal points around which entire cultural domains are organized'. To illustrate ways in which words can help to explain cultural issues Wierzbicka (1997: 156 ff.) analyses, for instance, the German *Heimat* and *Vaterland* to discuss notions of 'native country'. For words that are intuitively selected a corpus analysis can still make an important contribution to the characterization of their meanings. Stubbs (1996), for instance, discusses cultural key words, and shows how collocations can reveal associations and connotations, and thus the assumptions embodied by cultural key words (Stubbs 1996: 172); among his examples are words from the lexical field of 'work' (Stubbs 1996: 176 ff.). The notion of cultural key words is also further developed in Stubbs (2001).

To study intuitively selected cultural key words on the basis of large corpora is one way to combine corpus linguistic studies with questions of social theory. Another option is to study such key words in specialized corpora, as Teubert's (2001) study on the Euro-sceptic discourse in Britain illustrates. In the following, I want to suggest a further step. *Sustainable development* is selected as a cultural key word, the corpus is purpose-built, and additionally, features of the texts in the corpus play a part in the analysis of the meanings of *sustainable development*.

3 *Sustainable development*: corpus and methododolgy

The phrase *sustainable development* has been chosen because it seems to be becoming increasingly important in our society. In an article that analyses

Shell Reports (for 1999 and 2000), Alexander (2002) argues that the popularity of the phrase *sustainable development* is to some extent due to the fact that it can be exploited by PR and marketing departments. Alexander (2002: 240) describes the reports as an example of 'greenwash'. They try to distract from the real environmental issues and 'over-state their commitment to sustainable development' (Alexander 2002: 251), so that in PR material the phrase can become 'conveniently meaningless' (Alexander 2002: 248).[5]

Even if we do not focus on specialist discourses, such as corporate web pages, there seem to be links to the concept of *sustainable development* in various ways in our everyday lives. Major supermarkets in the UK have recently started to tackle the problem of shoppers using too many plastic bags and efforts are made to cut this waste of resources. On the radio we hear advertisements encouraging us to do more recycling, and some coffee bars advertise their fairtrade coffee with the slogan 'Growing a better future'. Such efforts can be related to the idea of *sustainable development* (from here onwards abbreviated as SD), which is discussed on a number of web pages. The UN's Division for Sustainable Development, for instance, has the following definition at the top of its web page: '[d]evelopment that meets the needs of the present without compromising the ability of future generations to meet their own needs'.[6] This is the definition provided by the Brundtland report, *Our Common Future* (Brundtland 1987: 43). Other important documents dealing with SD are 'Agenda 21', the 'Rio Declaration on Environment and Development' and the 'Statement of Principles for the Sustainable Management of Forests', which were adopted at the United Nations Conference on Environment and Development (UNCED) in Brazil, in 1992. Ten years later, the Rio conference was followed up by the World Summit on Sustainable Development, which was held from 26 August to 4 September 2002 in Johannesburg.

It is difficult to say to what extent or whether at all customers at Tesco would think about SD and the wider political context when trying to save plastic bags. However, SD is associated with different events and major conferences that receive press coverage. Thus SD can be a starting point for a corpus analysis of newspaper articles. The corpus used for the present study focuses on SD in the *Guardian* of 2002, the year of the Johannesburg summit. SD occurs 368 times in about 37.5 million words of *Guardian* text from the year 2002. The articles in which SD occurs were collected to form the Sustainable Development Corpus (SDC); it contains 211 articles and approximately 150,000 words. It is important to note that the noun *sustainability* is used with a similar meaning to *sustainable development. Sustainability* occurs 157 times in the *Guardian* 2002, and 55 times in the SDC, but here the focus is on SD.

The first step of the study is to identify groups of examples that illustrate different aspects of meanings associated with SD. These groups of meanings contain examples whose concordance lines show similar patterning. The criteria for the groups are a combination of repeated surface patterns and similarities in meaning that are not automatically visible through an exact repetition of a sequence of words. In the latter case the context provided by concordance lines was not always sufficient but had to be extended for the analysis. Some concordance lines could be placed into more than one group, but a decision was made for one group. It is clear that these categories cannot be watertight, as the phenomenon they aim to describe is itself fuzzy. I refer to these groups as 'functional groups' in order to stress that they describe meanings of SD that are embedded in textual contexts. In the second step, the texts that make up the corpus are described with regard to their distribution across different sections of the *Guardian*. Finally, the functional groups based on the concordance analysis are discussed in relation to the textual information. In the present study, the concept of local textual functions applies to the meanings of SD that are described on the basis of both lexical information from the concordance lines and textual information that relates to properties of newspaper articles.

4 Functional groups associated with *sustainable development*

The 368 examples of SD fall into 11 functional groups and there are five examples that do not seem to fit well into any of these groups; they are listed as 'other' in Table 7.1 below. Table 7.1 provides an overview of the frequencies of the groups, which are examined in detail below. Because of space limitations, the concordance lines that are given in the description of a group are not necessarily all the examples of that group. The selection, however, is not random; it aims to illustrate the main features on the basis of which a group is defined. The labels for the functional groups are *ad hoc* labels that aim to represent typical features of the examples in a

Table 7.1 Functional groups associated with SD

Group	Number of examples
G1 Conferences	61
G2 Organizations	22
G3 Education	13
G4 Approaches	58
G5 SD requires	24
G6 Working towards SD	74
G7 Leading in SD	10
G8 The need for SD	12
G9 Talking about SD	21
G10 SD means	33
G11 And SD	35
Other	5
Total	368

group.[7] In the present section, the 11 groups are dealt with individually; the relationships between the groups is discussed in section 7.

G1 Conferences and the World Summit

As the texts in the SDC are from the year 2002, it is not surprising that a large number of the examples of SD occur in references to the World Summit. But there were also other conferences on SD, for instance, as demonstrated in line 1, a conference in Mumbai in India at the beginning of 2002. Examples of the World Summit in Johannesburg can take a number of different forms. Of the 61 examples, 35 refer explicitly to the *World Summit on Sustainable Development* with some variation in capitalization, but we also find the *Johannesburg summit on sustainable development* (line 7) or other variations with or without Johannesburg, as in line 2 or line 4.

Concordance 7.1 G1 Conferences (14 of the 61 examples)

```
 1   ext month travelling to India for a sustainable development conference. But
 2   mmit - the UN's world conference on sustainable development. It is the big
 3   lopment pre-Johannesburg meeting on sustainable development draws on many
 4   ng to Johannesburg for the talks on sustainable development can now pay a
 5   rs at the world's biggest summit on sustainable development. Serious
 6   o be had out of the Earth summit on sustainable development in Johannesbur
 7   g before the Johannesburg summit on sustainable development. The US,
 8   e feast of opinions at the summit on sustainable development in Johannesbur
 9    proper name of the World Summit on Sustainable Development (WSSD), will no
10   n the lead-up to the world summit on sustainable development, which opens
11    other than that the World Summit on Sustainable Development was an abject
12   Johannesburg for the World Summit on Sustainable Development as part of the
13    of the Johannesburg World Summit on sustainable development, which is exp
14    Johannesburg at the world summit on sustainable development and another
```

G2 Organizations

Whereas the above group deals with meetings and venues the present group collects names of organizations, groups or commissions on SD. Below are examples of each of the organizations that are mentioned.

Concordance 7.2 G2 Organizations (6 of the 22 examples)

```
 1   oups including Business Action for Sustainable Development (BASD), support
 2   it. The World Business Council for Sustainable Development, a corporate lo
 3   te and the Western Partnership for Sustainable Development - the group org
 4   of the International Institute for Sustainable Development
 5    hon Porritt is chairman of the UK Sustainable Development Commission and
 6   ource," said James Shikwati of the Sustainable Development Network in Nairo
```

G3 Education in and for sustainable development

For some of the examples in this group it is clear from the concordance lines that educational issues are referred to. There are, for instance, new degrees such as an *MSc in Sustainable Development* (line 3) or a whole new field of 'education for sustainable development' or *ESD* (line 2). In other examples more context than a concordance line makes the link to educational issues clearer. Example[8] (1) presents the extended context of concordance line 9 below, which not only mentions *pupils* but also refers to *teachers* and the *curriculum*:

> (1) The English winner was Brixington Junior in Exmouth, Devon, where the *teachers* and *pupils* are trying to bring *sustainable development* issues into the *curriculum* and want to promote sustainable lifestyles in their community.

Concordance 7.3 G3 Education (9 of the 13 examples)

```
1    1 - the foundation certificate in sustainable development - was launched b
2      a pioneering field: education in sustainable development (ESD). It is som
3    rling is developing a new MSc in Sustainable Development for launch in 20
4    sity also offers a new MSc/PgD in Sustainable Development. (marian
5    reate strategies on education for sustainable development. These id
6    el puts it simply: "Education for sustainable development is about the lea
7    ty of evidence that education for sustainable development is being taken s
8    , linked to the objectives of the sustainable development education panel
9    rs and pupils are trying to bring sustainable development issues into the
```

G4 Approaches to sustainable development

SD occurs as a premodifier of nouns such as *test, review, projects, report, criteria, strategy*, which can be interpreted as an indication of systematic approaches to dealing with SD, or of the complexity of SD that requires a well-organized approach, demonstrated in noun phrases such as *principles of sustainable development*. There are also concordance lines that refer to *a new/their approach to, a plan for, policy on sustainable development*. The group further collects examples of jobs and groups dealing with SD, e.g. *the council's head of, chief adviser on*, or *the sustainable development commission*. The latter of these examples shows some overlap with the group 'Organizations' (G2) described above, the difference is that the 'Approaches to SD' group does not include names that are capitalized. Overall the examples in this group share the notion that SD is dealt with in a systematic and/or institutionalized way, which is related to the complexity of the issue of SD. Two examples in this group are part of the address of the government's official website, www.sustainable-development.gov.uk/, that has the title 'Sustainable Development – The Government's approach. Providing guidance on how to pursue a more sustainable future'.

Concordance 7.4 G4 Approaches (18 of the 58 examples)

```
1      e military deals be subject to a "sustainable development" test which mea
2    ill set out the goods subject to a sustainable development review, but wil
3    t prompted Shell to come up with a sustainable development framework, which
4    ch showed off African crafts, and sustainable development projects from ac
5    l report. The government's annual sustainable development report should be
6      in return undertook to introduce sustainable development criteria in the
```

```
7   in Rio in 1992 set the agenda for sustainable development - not just on th
8   nces on the international plan for sustainable development, with critics p
9   andra Fryer, the council's head of sustainable development services, is mov
10  esterday when his chief adviser on sustainable development lambasted the g
11  he government's declared policy on sustainable development, it was agreed i
12  ent must publish what guidance on sustainable development, if any, ministe
13  ction. It urges a new approach to sustainable development. Natural disast
14  ofit-making with the principles of sustainable development. But that's mil
15  an of the government's independent sustainable development commission, ques
16  to allow parliament to ensure that sustainable development is coherent with
17  , give new impetus to the EU's own sustainable development strategy. In par
18                          http://www.sustainable-development.gov.uk) in
```

G5 Sustainable development requires

The examples in this group characterize aspects of *sustainable development* by describing what is *crucial in*, or *vital for* SD, what SD *requires*, or *conditions for* SD. The examples show SD in relation to other social factors and developments. The focus seems to be less on organized and institutional approaches than on characterizations of relationships and a description of what is important to SD. The surface patterns of the meanings in this group are more varied than in the previous group and the borderline with the group 'Approaches to SD' (G4) is fuzzy. Take for instance line 9: *where all decisions are based on sustainable development rather than short time gain and greed*. The fact that decisions are based on SD can be interpreted as an indication of systematic approaches to SD and thus makes the example similar to cases in G4. The context of *short time gain and greed* then adds evaluative meaning.

Although the line between the groups G4 and G5 is not completely clear-cut, the patterns in G4 appear less evaluative but more factual. The factual meaning is reflected in patterns with nouns such as *test*, *report* or *criteria*. If examples in the 'Approaches to SD' group (G4) do not contain such nominal patterns, there is usually some reference to legal or political institutions as in example 2 below (line 16 in Concordance 7.4 above), where we find *the export control bill*, *parliament* and *defence export policy* in the textual context.

(2) India is a timely reminder that the government now needs to reconsider *the export control bill* to allow *parliament* to ensure that *sustainable development* is coherent with *defence export policy*.

Concordance 7.5 G5 SD requires (11 of the 24 examples)

```
1   ial for the world to develop, but sustainable development requires a major
2      Sanitation is important but for sustainable development poor communities
3   stem are necessary conditions for sustainable development." Mr Buit
4   he conditions in place for strong sustainable development", experience els
5   mine how they travel is vital for sustainable development. The case for re
6      planning is a crucial element in sustainable development, yet proponents
7      and GM food companies, "play in sustainable development". As happ
8   e accountability at the centre of sustainable development. Corporate influ
9      where all decisions are based on sustainable development rather than shor
10  about the impact of arms sales on sustainable development. "What the India
11  ct. This effectively subordinated sustainable development to trade. The WS
```

G6 Working towards sustainable development

Group 6 illustrates ways of working towards SD or making an effort to show commitment to SD. Patterns include verbs such as *promote, finance, support, achieve, work towards* or patterns like *commitment to, the declared aim of, a powerful contribution to*. From the concordance lines, however, we cannot automatically assume that the efforts were successful. The *But* that follows SD in line 6, for instance, hints at difficulties in reaching the aim of SD. Furthermore, there are indications that the goal is not necessarily one that is pursued in a self-motivated way, but there can be *a statutory duty* or *legally binding obligations* (lines 1 and 3). Included in this group are also examples that refer to factors that facilitate or hamper progress (lines 10 and 11).

Concordance 7.6 G6 Working towards SD (14 of the 74 examples)

```
1   have a statutory duty to promote sustainable development, but the Departm
2    tial of the internet to promote sustainable development and human rights
3     binding obligations to promote sustainable development. A draft UN code
4    tainability Exchange, promoting sustainable development and dedicated to
5    anies with a deep commitment to sustainable development. Looking down th
6   nments agreed to set off towards sustainable development. But environment
7   ions. The aim is to work towards sustainable development of the region, i
8    to achieve its declared aim of "sustainable development", have mushroome
9   t of a renewed effort to achieve sustainable development. In a lec
10  ade and investment as the key to sustainable development. In its s
11   tions have hampered progress on sustainable development. Result R
12  alls "a powerful contribution to sustainable development". Many were set
13   reate a resource base to finance sustainable development in developing co
14  increase in resources to support sustainable development. They need to be
```

G7 Leading in sustainable development

Group 7 is related to group 6 in the sense that efforts to achieve SD can result in some nations or institutions doing better than others. Success, however, is difficult to evaluate. The US may be regarded as a *world leader* (line 1) and Britain may also be seen as *leading the world in sustainable development* (line 2), or, in contrast, as having a *patchy record* in SD (line 7). The fact that Johannesburg is described as the *Crystal Palace of sustainable development* is another example of how those involved in the strive for SD are interested in their image. The concordance sample below contains all occurrences of this group.

Concordance 7.7 G7 Leading in SD (all 10 examples)

```
1    id. "The US is a world leader in sustainable development. No nation has m
2     of Britain leading the world in sustainable development and environment
3   epartment cannot be a champion of sustainable development." Crucial
4   ute its role as the "champion" of sustainable development across governmen
5    be seen as the Crystal Palace of sustainable development," Mr Malloch-Bro
6    o'burg was the Crystal Palace of sustainable development. Mushrooming gro
7   tre and patchy the UK's record in sustainable development has been over th
8      much so that it has placed its sustainable development record - alongsi
9        should we visit? It's big on sustainable development - a trail around
10   st country in Europe in terms of sustainable development with specific ta
```

G8 The need for sustainable development

Below are all examples of group 8 that evaluate the importance of SD. SD can be regarded as something that is important and needed, or something that does not receive enough attention as in line 10, where the expanded context tells us that SD *was added to the preamble as an afterthought.*

Concordance 7.8 G8 The need for SD (all 12 examples)

```
1    ght farmers reflect the need for sustainable development and concern abou
2    , August 21) states the need for sustainable development but shies away f
3    , is an essay about the need for sustainable development, with artworks c
4    protested that they believed in sustainable development. This is no more
5     e (Sc1, Sc2) The importance of sustainable development and factors affe
6    he former Shell chairman turned sustainable development business bigwig.
7    ant. "We're all really into this sustainable development thing now - it's
8    reinforce the centrality of the sustainable development goal to governme
9    's champion, told Mr Blair that sustainable development was really impor
10   estment and even basic services. Sustainable development was added to the
11   lems, and we know the solution: sustainable development. The issue is th
12   the rest of government, for which sustainable development indisputably isn
```

G9 Talking about sustainable development

The next group contains examples showing that SD is a topic or an issue that people need to be aware of and talk about. There are *plans to raise awareness about* SD (line 1), which may encourage even more *debates around* or *speeches about* SD (e.g. lines 5, 7).

Concordance 7.9 G9 Talking about SD (10 of the 21 examples)

```
1    ous plans to raise awareness about sustainable development. Ringmer Communi
2    t about the environment, but about sustainable development - giving the wo
3    udents a voice in the debate about sustainable development. Bananas
4    t Beckett, chaired a debate titled Sustainable development at the heart of
5    f the international debates around sustainable development were dominated
6    cipators will send a message about sustainable development to Tony Blair i
7    ws of who has given a speech about sustainable development in Africa and h
8    toring human rights. To talk about sustainable development in Africa while
9    t a time when we are talking about sustainable development." The Gre
10   d. Some 217 global issues around sustainable development have been identi
```

G10 Sustainable development means

The fact that people talk about SD is also relevant in references to SD as a *phrase* (line 12 below) or an *umbrella term* (line 15). In some of these cases quotation marks occur, or expressions such as *became known as, call, coining the concept of* (lines 5, 6, 8). The examples in this group can contain definitions that provide information such as the following (line 2 below):

(3) *Sustainable development* means managing growth in the world's economies during the next century in a way that avoids disaster for the

environment, and reduces the intolerable gaps between the haves and the have-nots.

Other examples are more critical of the way in which the term is used, as in example 4 (line 16):

> (4) The widening gap between rhetoric and reality that has transformed *sustainable development* into an irrelevant buzz phrase now threatens to turn the WSSD into tragic farce.

Concordance 7.10 G10 SD means (16 of the 33 examples)

```
1              20020822 <STO><P>Sustainable development is a hollow con
2   they be aiming to achieve? </P><P>Sustainable development means managing
3      difficult areas." He added: "Sustainable development is not yet a ce
4              16 Comment & Analysis: Sustainable development is a hoax: we c
5   to talk about what became known as sustainable development. In some
6   tection, an accommodation we call "sustainable development". We know
7   of this "mainstreaming" challenge. Sustainable development cannot just be d
8   lvation by coining the concept of "sustainable development" (
9    but will not give a definition of sustainable development. The arms
10  I want to set the record straight. Sustainable development - economic, soci
11  go, under the catch-all phrase of sustainable development. This is really
12  l world, and dismissed the phrase "sustainable development". He said it ha
13  "localised poor". Like the phrase sustainable development, they don't tri
14  s succeeded in placing the phrase "sustainable development" firmly in peop
15  issues under the umbrella term of "sustainable development". The iss
16  c and reality that has transformed sustainable development into an irreleva
```

G11 And sustainable development

The final group contains examples where SD is listed together with other concepts such as *environmental change, poverty reduction, human rights*, or SD is contrasted with concepts such as *globalisation* (line 11).

Concordance 7.11 G11 And SD (13 of the 35 examples)

```
1   rstanding environmental change and sustainable development. Science
2    social responsibility, ethics and sustainable development Article 1
3   or Alan Milburn: public health and sustainable development are pretty muc
4   nternational trade, innovation and sustainable development - conferred upo
5   ated with environmental issues and sustainable development. Creative ideas
6    principles on the rule of law and sustainable development" yesterday, the
7    in the alleviation of poverty and sustainable development. The north is n
8   debt relief, poverty reduction and sustainable development," he said.
9   mines fundamental human rights and sustainable development," Kate Allen, A
10   expected figure in business and in sustainable development. His sense of st
11   the process is globalisation, not sustainable development, while the obje
12  st order of communism, rather than sustainable development - would have joi
13  ence and responsibility, including sustainable development and Local Agenda
```

So far the 11 functional groups have been presented in the form of an overview. Section 7 will return to the relationship between the groups. But first, we need to look in more detail at the textual contexts in which the examples occur.

5. *Sustainable development* in newspaper articles

Newspaper articles deal with events or social and political issues that are regarded as newsworthy by journalists and press agencies. News values cover a number of different aspects: 'they include general values about society such as "consensus" and "hierarchy"; journalistic conventions; nature of sources; publication frequency and schedule; and so on' (Fowler 1991: 13). A detailed discussion of news values can be found, for instance, in Bell (1991). Some aspects of newsworthiness that are immediately obvious in the examples are directly related to the selection criteria of the texts in the corpus. All articles are from 2002, the year of the World Summit on Sustainable Development. However, the summit is an event that is not only described as 'taking place'. There are many participants from different countries and different institutional levels. Additionally, SD is an 'umbrella term' (see G10 above) for diverse issues so the event of the summit can be exploited to make news in various ways. Table 7.2 outlines the composition of the SDC and provides information on the distribution of SD across the subsections in the corpus that contain different types of articles.

Newspaper articles are grouped into sections such as 'Home News' or 'Letters to the Editor'. Table 7.2 presents an overview that shows how the articles in the SDC spread over 12 sections. The table does not list all sections that appear in the *Guardian*, only those in which instances of SD occur. Although it is not surprising that the Sport section is missing from the list, the occurrence of SD in Obituaries may not have been immediately obvious. The second column in Table 7.2 gives the number of articles in each section, the third column contains the number of hits per section together with a normalized figure per 1,000 words, the next column gives the overall number of tokens in a section, followed by the average number of words per article in a section, and the average number of hits per article, both rounded to the first decimal. The sections Home News and Features contain the largest number of articles, and the highest number of occurrences of SD appears in Features: Society. The sections, however, do not contain equal numbers of tokens. So when the numbers of hits are normalized to show the number of hits per 1,000 words, Letters to the Editor is the section where SD occurs most frequently. As a detailed study of the present kind is very time-consuming, the numbers are relatively small, and thus quantitative information has to be treated with caution. The main purpose of Table 7.2 is to illustrate a number of different factors that play a role when analysing the meanings and functions of SD.

In addition to text length, another important factor for the analysis of newspaper articles is the time framework that characterizes their publication. This factor is most clearly visible for the section Features: Weekend, which is by definition restricted to specific dates. The final two columns in Table 7.2 introduce another time factor. They provide information on the number of different months that are covered by a section, and give information on the months in which most articles in a section were published.

Table 7.2 Composition of SDC and distribution of SD

Section	Articles	Hits (and hits per 1,000 words)	Overall number of words in section	Average number of words per article	Average number of hits per article	Highest number of occurrences in 1 article	Months covered	Most frequent month
Leading Articles	6	6 (1.7)	3,488	581	1	1	4	Aug (3)
Home News	37	69 (2.8)	25,054	677	1.9	6	8	Aug (22)
Overseas News	28	33 (2.2)	15,307	547	1.2	3	10	Sept (7)
Business	21	33 (2.3)	14,444	688	1.6	4	8	Aug (5)
Obituaries	3	4 (1.7)	2,352	784	1.3	2	3	Jan (1), April (1), Dec (1)
Letters to the Editor	11	12 (6.3)	1,897	172	1.1	2	5	Aug (7)
Features	37	73 (2.3)	31,964	864	2	19	9	Aug (18)
Features: Education	21	41 (3.1)	13,125	625	2	9	11	Sept (6)
Features: Media	2	2 (0.9)	2,129	1,065	1	1	2	July (1), Aug (1)
Features: Society	35	83 (3.2)	26,009	743	2.4	8	11	Aug (8)
Features: Weekend	6	7 (0.7)	9,538	1,590	1.2	2	5	Dec (2)
Features: Travel	4	5 (1.4)	3,626	907	1.3	2	4	Feb (1), May (1), Aug (1), Dec (1)
Total/Overall	211	368 (2.5)	148,933	706	1.7	19	12	Aug (70)

For instance, the articles from the section Home News cover eight months, whereas the articles in Features were published in nine different months and those in Features: Society in 11 different months. In the Home News section 22 of the 37 articles were published in August. Overall, August is the month in which most articles were published. This observation relates to the fact that the World Summit on Sustainable Development was held from 26 August to 4 September. Still, the 211 articles cover all 12 months of the year 2002. In the sections Obituaries, Features: Media, and Features: Travel, there is no month with more than one article, so all months are listed in the column 'Most frequent month'. Further details on the dates of publication that are not explicitly included in Table 7.2, are provided in the discussion below.

The column that has not been mentioned so far is that which indicates the highest number of occurrences of SD in a single article. Here the section Features stands out, which has one article with 19 occurrences of SD. The article was published on October 1 under the headline of 'Comment & Analysis: Can she sustain it?' With 1,221 words it is longer than the average article in this section. It deals with issues of SD that Margaret Beckett (Secretary of State for Environment, Food and Rural Affairs in 2002) has to face at home in the UK. Another factor that has an impact on the description of newspaper articles is their headlines. The phrase SD occurs in headlines of two articles in the SDC, both of which appear in the section Features. However, there are a number of articles that relate to the issue of SD. In the section Home News many headlines refer in some form or other to the summit, e.g. on August 22: 'Act now, bank urges earth summit: Growth must not come at price to planet, report warns'. The analysis of references to SD in headlines would itself make a complex discussion, but within the space of the present article it is not possible to present further details.

Table 7.2 points to tendencies that seem to go together with criteria that are employed to distinguish between 'hard' and 'soft' news. According to Bell (1991: 147) '[h]ard news is news as we all recognize it, and at its core is spot news – tales of accidents, disasters, crimes', as well as political matters such as government announcements or international negotiations. White characterizes the subject matter of hard news as 'events or situations which are construed as threatening to damage, disrupt, or rearrange the social order in its material, political or normative guise' (White 1997: 104). In addition to the negativity that characterizes a hard news story, hard news can satisfy further news values, for instance, by providing facts and figures (facticity), or adding quotes (personalization, eliteness). The structure of hard news is to some extent determined by the time and place and the movement of an event, whereas features can dwell on details of time, place and person (cf. Bell 1991: 198), which can be reflected by the length of the articles.

In Table 7.2, characteristics of hard news seem to apply to Leading Articles, Home and Overseas News, Business, and Letters to the Editor: these types of articles are shorter than the average of 706 words per article for the SDC. In addition to text length these groups of articles (except Business) show strong links to a time frame. The Home News section has three articles on the first day of the summit, 26 August. On the same day, there is a leading article on the summit, and three Letters to the Editor. The Overseas News section focuses more on the end of the summit, with two articles on 4 September and three on 5 September. Business has still five articles in August, but none of them on the first day of the conference. It is worth pointing out that the split into Home and Overseas News is not necessarily due to geographical criteria. Take, for instance, one of the Home News articles published on 26 August. Under the headline 'The earth summit gets under way – with 400 issues still to be resolved', Paul Brown, an Environment correspondent in Johannesburg describes issues of the agenda, protest marches in South Africa and comments by international politicians – an article which would as well fit into the Overseas section.

The feature articles are on average longer, except for the Education articles, and if we focus on the bigger feature sections, they also have a slightly higher average of hits per article. In particular, the article of 1 October, with 19 occurrences of SD, illustrates how a topic can be discussed in detail. With regard to text length, obituaries are more similar to the features, although their average number of hits per articles is lower than that of features. Features are not only longer than hard news, but also spread wider over the year. And their distribution seems to be almost complementary to hard news reporting in the sense that on the first day of the summit, there is no feature article that contains the phrase SD. Obviously, it has to be taken into account that the issue of SD can be talked about without using the term SD. For all observations in this section, it is important to keep in mind how the texts of the corpus have been selected. The observations do not characterize the newspaper sections in general but with reference to the fact that the texts contain the phrase SD at least once.

6 Functional groups and newspaper sections

Quantitative information has to be handled with caution for the SDC. In Table 7.3, the numbers are not normalized because they are very small, but also because various factors that are outlined in Table 7.2 affect their interpretation that cannot easily be figured into a normalization. Additionally, when meanings are counted only one aspect of meaning is captured by the numbers. With these caveats, the following interpretation is exploratory and aims to indicate tendencies of relationships between meanings and newspaper sections.

The most frequent meaning 'Working towards SD' (G6) with 74 occurrences, appears in all sections except Weekend Features. The second most frequent meaning is the 'Conference' (G1) meaning and it spreads across ten of the 12 sections. The ones in which it does not occur are Features: Media, a section that only contains two articles altogether, and

Table 7.3 Distribution of functional groups across newspaper sections

	Total	Lead Art	Home	Over	Busi	Obit	Lett Ed	Feat	Feat Educ	Feat Soc	Feat Media	Feat Week	Feat Trav
G1 Conferences	61	4	11	10	11	0	4	7	3	8	0	1	2
G2 Organizations	22	0	7	2	4	0	0	4	0	5	0	0	0
G3 Education	13	0	0	0	0	0	0	0	11	0	0	2	0
G4 Approaches	58	1	11	5	6	1	1	15	3	13	1	2	0
G5 SD requires	24	1	6	1	1	0	1	3	0	10	0	0	1
G6 Working towards SD	74	1	18	8	3	1	2	15	2	22	1	0	1
G7 Leading in SD	10	0	2	0	1	0	0	2	1	4	0	0	0
G8 The need for SD	12	0	0	1	1	0	1	3	4	2	0	0	0
G9 Talking about SD	21	0	4	0	0	1	0	8	3	4	0	1	0
G10 SD means	33	0	7	0	1	1	1	11	4	8	0	0	0
G11 And SD	35	0	3	6	5	0	2	4	7	7	0	1	0
Other	5	0	0	0	0	0	0	1	3	0	0	0	1
Total	368	6	69	33	33	4	12	73	41	83	2	7	5

Obituaries which are dealt with in more detail below. Both meanings relate to news values in the sense that progress that is or is not made in achieving the goal of SD is recognized as being relevant to our society and topical through the specific event of the World Summit. The 'Working towards SD' (G6) meaning is the most frequent of the meanings in the sections Home News and Features: Society; in Features it shares the top position with the meaning 'Approaches to SD' (G4). The 'Conferences' (G1) meaning leads the table in the sections Leading Articles, Overseas News, Letters to the Editor and Business. As Table 7.2 shows, Business articles are similar to Leading Articles, Home and Overseas News, and Letters to the Editor as far as text length is concerned. Similarities, however, were not equally obvious with regard to the time orientation visible in Table 7.2. Now, the 'Conference' meaning as most frequent meaning in the Business section provides a further aspect of time orientation. The summit is referred to as an upcoming event, but it also links back to political arguments put forward at the conference. In an article of 14 October, for instance, a statement made by the Prime Minister at the summit is quoted with reference to the current debate on common agricultural policy. References to conferences and the summit automatically imply a time orientation, also in features articles. A difference between feature articles and articles in the Business section is that in the three big Features sections other meanings occur more frequently than the conference meaning; additionally the average number of hits per article is higher which points to a tendency that the time reference is less often the central function of SD in an article.

The Features Weekend, Media and Travel only contain a few examples so it is difficult to make specific claims for them. Still, it seems reasonable to look at different feature sections separately and more data will probably reveal clearer patterns. In the present analysis, the most striking point is the relationship between the 'Education' (G3) meaning and the Features: Education. This feature section contains 11 of the 13 examples of the 'Education' meaning. Although one of the texts contains nine occurrences of SD, of which six are instances of the education meaning, the education meaning is still distributed across six different texts in the Education section.

Relationships between meanings and sections of the newspaper also seem to hold for the group 'SD means' (G10). In this group, SD is referred to as a term or a concept and its meaning is either explained, criticized or drawn attention to. In their discussion of the phrase *friendly fire* Teubert and Čermáková (2004: 146) point out that references to something as a 'term' or 'phrase' together with a paraphrase often occur when a new unit of meaning enters the discourse. Although SD is not exactly a neologism in 2002, because of the topicality of the World Summit a definition may seem useful since not all readers may be aware of the concept as it was outlined at previous conferences and discussed in newspapers. An example of such a definition was given by example 3 above.

The examples in the 'SD means' group (G10) also suggest a negative semantic prosody of the phrase that relates to its meaninglessness. The meaninglessness can be due to the fact that SD has to cover too many things; it is *a catch-all phrase* as in the following example:

(5) The idea is to improve social, environment and economic advancement all in one go, under *the catch-all phrase of sustainable development.*

The vagueness of the phrase seems to be linked to the many debates and meetings on SD. It appears that SD is mainly talked about but does not have real implications:

(6) Sadruggin Aga Khan, the former UN Commissioner for Refugees, was unhappy about the prospects for the natural world, and dismissed the phrase '*sustainable development*'. He said it had been adopted as a convenient mantra, but it was a delusion.

The emptiness of the debates is explicitly criticized when the World Summit is referred to as a *talking shop*. The article from which example (5) above is taken has the headline 'The biggest talking shop in history or a mass gathering to save the world?' and we read:

(7) The conference, seen by many as a *talking shop* and too unwieldy to produce concrete results, takes place . . .

Such examples point to the relationship between the groups 'SD means' (G10) and 'Talking about SD' (G9). The existence of the latter is to some extent evidence of the many discussions about SD. Examples of 'SD means' may also relate to the largest meaning group 'Working towards SD' (G6). Although the patterns in the immediate context of SD include words such *promote, achieve, commitment to* that indicate efforts to achieve SD, only further context can give information on the likeliness of the success, and thus on what SD actually means for the society.

Although more data would be needed to make strong claims, it seems that in feature articles the criticism of SD can be more blatant:

(8) As the world prepares for next month's world summit on social development (WSSD) in Johannesburg, the Rio rhetoric is back on the airwaves. Northern governments are treating us to painful cover versions of the old *sustainable development* classics, and marketing them with more hype than that surrounding the launch of Will Young.

In feature articles, sarcasm, irony and allusions are not uncommon. In the following example, the *triumphantly enshrined* suggests that SD is about big events, documents and the celebration of these, but not about real results.

(9) Yet it was believed that the solution to the great clash between ecology and economy had been discovered in the 1980s: this was the idea of '*sustainable development*', *triumphantly enshrined* in the Rio declaration.

In newspapers' sections that are expected to have a more factual tone, critical opinions on SD can appear in the form of quote, for instance:

(10) He added: '*Sustainable development* is not yet a central concern for this government. [sic] At best it's a "very now and then" kind of thing, to be run occasionally and ostentatiously up the flagpole just to show willing; at worst it's an irritating pressure point that cuts across more "mainstream" agendas.'

The above example is from a Home News article with the headline 'Earth Summit 2002: Blair adviser attacks Labour's record'. The criticism of the Labour approach thus is part of the political issue, the verbal attack, presented in the article. In such cases negative opinions on SD satisfy the news value of negativity that makes a good story.

Finally, we turn to the examples from Obituaries. Table 7.3 shows that each of the four examples from Obituaries belong to different functional groups. They are listed below (11 and 12 are from the same article):

(11) Anil Agarwal, who has died aged 54 of cancer, was one of the world's most important environmentalists, campaigning from a developing country – India – at a time when many of the international debates around *sustainable development* were dominated by the west.

(12) . . . he was one of the first campaigners to talk about what became known as *sustainable development.*

(13) Under his leadership, the trust spearheaded the setting up of LSx, the London Sustainability Exchange, promoting *sustainable development* and dedicated to improving the environment of London.

(14) Barraclough became head of UNRISD, specialising in '*sustainable development*'.

Example (11) illustrates the meaning group 'Talking about SD' (G9), example (12) belongs to 'SD means' (G10). Example (13) illustrates the group 'Working towards SD' (G6), and example (14) is a case of 'Approaches to SD' (G4) describing systematic ways of dealing with SD. Although the narrow context around SD is different in all four examples, thus all of them belong to different meaning groups, what they have in common is that they provide positive information on the person who died. All three people held leading positions and their involvement with SD is a positive fact to be mentioned in their obituaries. In this sense SD seems to have a positive semantic prosody when it occurs in obituaries. That the semantic prosody of the term is not necessarily positive, was illustrated above by the examples from the group 'SD means' (G10).

7 Returning to the corpus linguistic starting point

The groups that result from the concordance analysis in section 4 are partly based on similarities of features on the textual surface. For some groups it is possible to find clear collocational patterns, as in the group 'Working towards SD' (G6) where the verb *promote* occurs repeatedly. To some extent it can be argued that examples in the same group share semantic preferences: the label 'Working towards SD' reflects that the examples in the group are all about efforts to achieve progress on SD. Similarly, the group 'Talking about SD' (G9) puts examples such as *debate, message* and *talk* together that share semantic features. In this group we also find colligation of SD with prepositions (*about, around*). But for the present purpose the type of similarities that hold between the examples in a group need not be described in detail. The *ad hoc* labels aim to give an indication of the grounds on which the examples are grouped together.

The concordance analysis highlights meanings of SD that are important to a society in the sense that they are discussed in newspapers. These meanings can relate to specific events, which is illustrated by references to the World Summit (G1 Conferences), but they also reflect aspects of the social organization when institutions are described that are in place to deal with SD issues (G2 Organizations). The social structure becomes visible in systematic approaches to SD (G4 Approaches), in the education system that has to deal with socially important issues (G3 Education), as well as in the relationship of SD to other social factors around it (G5 SD requires) and to concepts on the social and political agenda (G11 And SD). Newspapers are interested in dynamic processes and developments. Activities and progress (or hampered progress) are described in group 6 (G6 Working towards SD), and specific activities are the debates about SD (G9 Talking about SD). With activities there are also actors and the efforts by different politicians or countries can be compared (G7 Leading in SD). Other important aspects of society are the opinions and evaluations that are expressed on an issue. SD can be regarded as something that is necessary (G8 The need for SD), but it can also be regarded as a concept whose meaning needs to be explained, redefined and criticized (G10 SD means).

The meanings identified in the present study highlight what makes SD newsworthy or what the *Guardian* regards as socially relevant. The examples illustrate events and activities taking place in the life of a society. Instead of 11 groups, we could try to identify fewer groups. The first three, for instance (G1 Conferences, G2 Organizations, G3 Education), could be put together on the grounds that they all deal with 'institutions'. Such a general characterization, however, loses some of the detail that is relevant to the textual point of view. We have seen that specialist sections in newspapers can focus on a particular aspect of meaning (the section Education) and evaluative meanings can appear stronger depending on the section in which the example occurs (the examples of Obituaries). We also looked at differences between newspaper sections that refer to characteristics that seem to be more typical of hard news or more typical of features. Thus the examples illustrate a number of local textual functions of SD.

Except group 10 (SD means) all groups illustrate usage meanings of SD, whereas group 10 presents paraphrases, i.e. instances where attention is drawn to the fact that a meaning is negotiated.[9] On the one hand, SD is a concept that can be defined with reference to official political documents, on the other hand those who use the phrase are criticized for using empty words. Thus group 10 highlights the importance of investigations into local aspects of meaning. This point is further strengthened if we return to Alexander's (2002) study of Shell Reports. Alexander (2002: 248) points out that SD is used by both business people to promote their industrial operations and by environmentalists who campaign against the fatal exploitation of global resources. However, unlike Alexander (2002) the description in the present study would not view such differing uses as evidence of the term becoming 'meaningless' (cf. section 3). Instead, the different uses are seen as evidence of how meanings are created in a discourse community and group 10 highlights specific forms of this negotiation.

The present chapter emphasizes the context-dependency of meanings and the concept of local textual functions is put forward to broaden the description of lexical items in text. Although wider in scope than Alexander's (2002) work, the present study is still limited to small numbers of examples. More data, for instance, across different periods of time, may support or refine tendencies described in the present chapter and can investigate how the meanings associated with SD develop over time. In the following chapter, the concept of local textual functions is further developed and employed in the study of literary text in the context of corpus stylistics.

Acknowledgements

I would like to thank Anna Čermáková, Matthew Brook O'Donnell and Wolfgang Teubert for reading and commenting on earlier versions of this chapter; all remaining errors are entirely my own.

Notes

1. *budge* is discussed in Sinclair (2004: 142 ff.) and often quoted to illustrate his concept of the lexical item.
2. Ways in which people are talked about are also illustrated by the group of 'people nouns' discussed in Mahlberg (2005).
3. Sinclair (2004) is a collection of key papers reflecting Sinclair's work over a period of 20 years.
4. Note that only the core and the semantic prosody are obligatory categories in Sinclair's (2004: 141) model.
5. Alexander (2002: 248) finds support for his arguments in Hobsbawm (1994).
6. UN Department of Economic and Social Affairs, Division for Sustainable Development, www.un.org/esa/sustdev/ (accessed September 2006).
7. For a more detailed discussion of *ad hoc* labels see Mahlberg (2005: 58 ff., 81 f.).

8. Information on the source of the examples quoted in the present chapter is provided in the Appendix.
9. For a more detailed discussion of meaning as 'usage' and meaning as 'paraphrase' see Teubert and Čermáková (2004: 127 ff.), and Mahlberg (2005: 162 f.).

References

Adolphs, S. (2006) *Introducing Electronic Text Analysis. A Practical Guide for Language and Literary Studies.* London: Routledge.
Alexander, R. J. (2002) 'Everyone is talking about "sustainable development". Can they all mean the same things? Computer discourse analysis of ecological texts', in A. Fill, H. Penz and W. Trampe (eds), *Colourful Green Ideas. Papers from the Conference 30 Years of Language and Ecology, Graz, 2000, and the Symposium Sprache und Ökologie, Passau, 2001.* Bern: Peter Lang, pp.239–54.
Baker, P. (2006) *Using Corpora in Discourse Analysis.* London: Continuum.
Baker, P. and McEnery, T. (2005) 'A corpus-based approach to discourses of refugees and asylum seekers in UN and newspaper text'. *Journal of Language and Politics,* 4,2: 197–226.
Bell, A. (1991) *The Language of News Media.* Oxford and Massachusetts: Blackwell.
Brundtland, G. H. (1987) *Our Common Future.* Oxford and New York: Oxford University Press.
Firth, J. R. (1957) *Papers in Linguistics 1934–51.* London: Oxford University Press.
Fowler, R. (1991) *Language in the News. Discourse and Ideology in the Press.* London: Routledge.
Garzone, G. and Santulli, F. (2004) 'What can Corpus Linguistics do for Critical Discourse Analysis', in A. Partington, J. Morley and L. Haarman (eds), *Corpora and Discourse.* Bern: Peter Lang, pp. 351–68.
Hobsbawm, E. (1994) *Age of Extremes. The Short Twentieth Century 1914–1991.* London: Michael Joseph.
Hoey, M. (2005) *Lexical Priming. A New Theory of Words and Language.* London: Routledge.
Hunston, S. (2002) *Corpora in Applied Linguistics.* Cambridge: Cambridge University Press.
Hunston, S. and Francis, G. (2000) *Pattern Grammar. A Corpus-driven Approach to the Lexical Grammar of English.* Amsterdam: John Benjamins.
Koller, V. and Mautner, G. (2004) 'Computer Applications in Criticial Discourse Analysis', in C. Coffin, A. Hewings and K. O'Halloran (eds), *Applying English Grammar. Functional and Corpus Approaches.* London: Arnold, pp. 216–28.
Louw, B. (2004) 'Unravelling the ideological from the authentic'. *Guardian Weekly,* Thursday 20 May 2004, http://education.guardian.co.uk/tefl/story/0,,1220377,00.html. (Accessed August 2006.)

Mahlberg, M. (2005) *English General Nouns: a Corpus Theoretical Approach.* Amsterdam: John Benjamins.

—— (2006) '*but it will take time* . . . points of view on a lexical grammar of English', in A. Renouf and A. Kehoe (eds), *The Changing Face of Corpus Linguistics.* Amsterdam: Rodopi, pp. 377–90.

Partington, A. (2003) *The Linguistics of Political Argument. The Spin-doctor and the Wolf-pack at the White House.* London: Routledge.

Scott, M. (2002) 'Picturing the key words of a very large corpus and their lexical upshots or getting at the *Guardian*'s view of the world', in B. Kettemann and G. Marko (eds), *Teaching and Learning by Doing Corpus Analysis. Proceedings of the Fourth International Conference on Teaching and Language Corpora, Graz 19–24 July, 2000.* Amsterdam: Rodopi, pp. 43–50.

—— (2004) *WordSmith Tools. Version 4.0.* Oxford, OUP.

Sinclair, J. M. (2004) *Trust the Text. Language, Corpus and Discourse.* London: Routledge.

—— (2005a) 'Meaning in the framework of corpus linguistics', in W. Teubert and M. Mahlberg (eds), *The Corpus Approach to Lexicography. Thematic Part of Lexicographica. Internationales Jahrbuch fuer Lexikographie*, 20, 2004. Tübingen: Niemeyer, pp. 20–32.

—— (2005b) 'Corpus and Text – Basic Principles', in M. Wynne (ed.), *Developing Linguistic Corpora. A Guide to Good Practice.* Oxford: Oxbow Books, pp. 1–16.

Stubbs, M. (1996) *Text and Corpus Analysis.* Oxford: Blackwell.

—— (2001) *Words and Phrases. Corpus Studies of Lexical Semantics.* Oxford: Blackwell.

—— (2006) 'Corpus analysis: the state of the art and three types of unanswered questions', in G. Thompson and S. Hunston (eds), *System and Corpus. Exploring Connections.* London and Oakville: Equinox, pp. 15–36.

Teubert, W. (2001) 'A Province of a Federal Superstate, Ruled by an Unelected Bureaucracy – Keywords of the Euro-Sceptic Discourse in Britain', in A. Musolff, C. Good, P. Points and R. Wittlinger (eds), *Attitudes towards Europe: language in the unification.* Burlington: Ashgate, pp. 45–86.

—— (2004) 'Language and corpus linguistics', in M. A. K. Halliday, C. Yallop, W. Teubert and A. Čermáková, *Lexicology and Corpus Linguistics. An Introduction.* London: Continuum, pp. 73–112.

—— (2005) 'My version of corpus linguistics', *International Journal of Corpus Linguistics*, 10, 1: 1–13.

Teubert, W. and Čermáková, A. (2004) 'Directions in corpus linguistics', in M. A. K. Halliday, C. Yallop, W. Teubert and A. Čermáková, *Lexicology and Corpus Linguistics. An Introduction.* London: Continuum, pp. 113–65.

Tognini-Bonelli, E. (2001) *Corpus Linguistics at Work.* Amsterdam: John Benjamins.

Tribble, C. (2006) 'What counts in current journalism. Keywords in newspaper reporting', in M. Scott and C. Tribble, *Textual Patterns. Key Words and Corpus Analysis in Language Education.* Amsterdam: John Benjamins, pp. 161–77.

White, P. (1997) 'Death, disruption and the moral order: the narrative impulse in mass-media "hard news" reporting', in F. Christie and J. R. Martin (eds), *Genre and Institutions. Social Processes in the Workplace and School.* London and New York: Continuum, pp. 101–33.

Wierzbicka, A. (1997) *Understanding Cultures Through Their Key Words.* New York and Oxford: Oxford University Press.

Williams, R. (1983) *Keywords: a Vocabulary of Culture and Society* (2nd edn). London: Fontana.

Appendix

Examples quoted from the *Guardian*

For all examples: Copyright Guardian News and Media 2007

(1) 'Education: Earth diplomats', 18 June 2002, John Vidal

(2) 'Letter: New Conservatives take up arms', 16 January 2002, Tony Baldry

(3) 'Society: Time for the big push', 3 July 2002, Derek Osborn

(4) 'Society: Environment: Earth summit: Freed is good', 24 July 2002, Kevin Watkins

(5) 'The biggest talking shop in history or a mass gathering to save the world?', 6 August 2002, Paul Brown

(6) 'Society: Sermon on the cruise ship: Religions of the world collaborate to warn against environmental destruction', 19 June 2002, Paul Brown

(7) 'The biggest talking shop in history or a mass gathering to save the world?', 6 August 2002, Paul Brown

(8) 'Society: Environment: Earth summit: Freed is good', 24 July 2002, Kevin Watkins

(9) 'Comment & Analysis: Sustainable development is a hoax: we cannot have it all', 5 August 2002, Jeremy Seabrook

(10) 'Earth Summit 2002: Blair adviser attacks Labour's record', 26 August 2002, Nicholas Watt

(11) 'Obituary: Anil Agarwal: India's leading environmental campaigner', 11 January 2002, Tony Juniper

(12) 'Obituary: Anil Agarwal: India's leading environmental campaigner', 11 January 2002, Tony Juniper

(13) 'Obituary: Peter Rigby: Life of service that helped to change the landscape', 18 April 2002, Clare Thomas

(14) 'Obituary: Solon Barraclough', 31 December 2002, Richard Gott

8   Corpus stylistics: bridging the gap between linguistic and literary studies

Michaela Mahlberg

Introduction

The term 'corpus stylistics' is becoming increasingly popular, but it is still difficult to delimit a field or discipline. What seems to be characteristic of corpus stylistics is that it combines different approaches. The present chapter views corpus stylistics as a way of bringing the study of language and literature closer together. It is argued that corpus stylistics can make use of innovative descriptive tools that not only fit into linguistic frameworks but also leave room to account for individual qualities of texts and thereby link in with literary interpretation. The present chapter therefore broadens the corpus theoretical context of the previous chapter to include the study of literary texts. Section 1 begins by identifying a common ground between literary stylistics and corpus linguistics, before section 2 discusses the role of the concept of collocation in literary stylistics. Section 3 looks at the applicability of local textual functions as corpus stylistic tools and introduces clusters as pointers to local textual functions. The examples that are discussed in the present chapter are from a corpus of Dickens texts. Section 4 starts with 'long' clusters, section 5 introduces five functional groups of clusters for the description of stylistic features in Dickens, and section 6 applies these functional categories to the analysis of *Bleak House*.

1   Corpus linguistics + (literary) stylistics = corpus stylistics?

There are a number of publications that illustrate applications of corpus linguistic concepts and methods to the study of literature. Louw (1997) gives examples of how a corpus can help to test intuitions and how symbolism can be discussed in terms of collocations. Culpeper (2002), and also Scott and Tribble (2006) analyse *Romeo and Juliet* in terms of key words. Adolphs and Carter (2002) study semantic prosodies in Virginia Woolf (cf. also Adolphs 2006). Semino and Short (2004) investigate speech and thought representation. Stubbs (2005) explores a number of quantitative methods to study Conrad's *Heart of Darkness*; and Starcke (2006) looks at three-word sequences in Austen's *Persuasion*. Although this list can only give examples it is obvious that corpus approaches to literature can come in a variety of forms. However, as Wynne (2006: 223, 225) observes, the potential of corpora is only tentatively exploited in the field of literary stylistics. In order to get a clearer picture of what could be regarded as characteristic features of a discipline called 'corpus stylistics', it will be useful to have a look at both corpus linguistics and stylistics.

'Style', the object of study in stylistics, can be defined in very general terms, as referring to 'the way in which language is used in a given context, by a given person, for a given purpose, and so on' (Leech and Short 1981: 11). Thus when the focus is on variation according to situation, instead of style we also talk about 'register'. When we take a sociolinguistic perspective, stylistic variation relates to degrees of formality. When the focus is on literary texts, we can talk about 'literary stylistics' and distinctions can be made with regard to the style of a particular work, a particular author, a period, and so on. Whatever the point of view, an important aspect of style is, as Wales (2001: 371) points out, that it is regarded as 'distinctive: in essence, the set or sum of linguistic features that seem to be characteristic: whether of register, genre, or period, etc'. To describe characteristic features of a piece of language, stylistics has to draw on linguistic categories. Thus when studying literary texts, stylistics seems to border on two disciplines: it 'can sometimes look like either linguistics or literary criticism, depending upon where you are standing when you are looking at it' (Short 1996: 1). This position, however, makes it possible for literary stylistics to come under attack from two camps: literary critics may find that stylistics does not leave enough room for interpretation because of the systematic linguistic framework that it employs; linguists, on the other hand, may find stylistic analyses not systematic enough, because they apparently incorporate too much interpretation (cf. also Short 1996: 1).

With literary stylistics already giving rise to controversial opinions, the situation does not become any easier when we introduce a corpus linguistic point of view. Basic methods of corpus linguistics cover the generation of quantitative information, the display of words in their contexts to make patterns visible, and the handling of annotation. Such corpus linguistic methods can be applied in a variety of fields with a variety of aims and theoretical implications so that corpus approaches can be viewed as more or less corpus-driven (cf. also the previous chapter). However, in their book with the title *Corpus Stylistics*, Semino and Short (2004: 8) suggest a cooperative approach for the use of corpus linguistic methodology for the study of style. They point out the need to combine corpus methodology with more intuition-based approaches. Thus it seems to be a useful starting point to look at joint interests of corpus linguistics and literary stylistics.

In the previous chapter, I discussed local textual functions as a tool extending the corpus-driven approach to a more textual dimension, and summarized what I regard as the main points that can shape a corpus theoretical framework. Against this background, a link between corpus linguistics and literary stylistics can be seen in the following way. Both are interested in the relationship between meaning and form. Stylistics puts an emphasis on <u>how</u> we say what we say and corpus linguistics also claims that what we say depends on form, i.e. the patterns which are attested in corpora. The focus of interest of the two disciplines, however, tends to be different. Stylistics focuses on what makes a text, or a group of texts, distinctive, and it investigates deviations from linguistic norms that trigger artistic effects and reflect creative ways of using language. Corpus linguistics, on the other hand, mainly focuses on repeated and typical uses that do not only hold in one text, but are found across a number of texts in a corpus. Although specialized and purpose-built small corpora are used in corpus linguistics, the focus is still on repeated patterns. We can see a link between corpus linguistics and literary stylistics in that 'creativity' can only be recognized as such when there is a language norm against which the 'creative' language comes to stand out. A crucial question is then how to measure, describe and handle this creativity. We cannot simply assume that large general corpora constitute what makes 'ordinary' language so that we can contrast it with 'creative' language that stands out in an individual text compared to the large corpus, and that makes a piece of language 'literary' as opposed to 'ordinary'. The following point by Leech and Short (1981) is central to the corpus stylistic approach of the present article:

> Every analysis of style [. . .] is an attempt to find the artistic principles underlying a writer's choice of language. All writers, and for that matter, all texts, have their individual qualities. Therefore the features which recommend themselves to the attention in one text will not necessarily be important in another text by the same or a different author.
>
> (Leech and Short 1981: 74)

What corpus stylistics can do beyond the obvious provision of quantitative data, is help with the analysis of an individual text by providing various options for the comparison of one text with groups of other texts to identify tendencies, intertextual relationships, or reflections of social and cultural contexts. As Carter (2004: 69) points out when he dismisses the distinction between literary and non-literary language as unhelpful: literary language should be seen as a continuum, 'a cline of literariness in language use with some uses of language being marked as more literary than others in certain domains and for certain judges within that domain'. To talk about such a cline implies various points for comparison that corpus linguistics can provide through different sets of reference corpora. Such comparisons can then help to find the features that recommend themselves for closer analysis in an individual text.

Another aspect of corpus stylistics is that it can help to develop descriptive tools to identify and characterize the features that make a text distinctive. Stylistic categories draw on the tools provided by linguists to describe features of language. Leech and Short (1981), for instance, give an overview of useful categories which may be used as a checklist for a stylistic analysis. These categories build on linguistic concepts: a stylistic analysis may refer to the high number of adjectives in a text, or the predominance of simple sentences, the fact that nouns tend to be postmodified by prepositional phrases, and so on. If corpus linguistic evidence suggests that our linguistic descriptions need to be revised critically, this revision will also have implications for the stylistic categories that are used. A central descriptive category to characterize the association between meaning and form is the concept of collocation describing the tendency of words to co-occur. The concept of collocation is not new to stylistics. Corpus stylistics, however, assigns it a new role.

2 Collocations and style

An example of a large-scale study of collocations as stylistic features is Hori's (2004) investigation of Dickens' style.[1] Hori (2004) uses a corpus of 23 Dickens texts, and comparative data from eighteenth- and nineteenth-century fiction, as well as native informant tests, and information from the *Oxford English Dictionary*. Hori (2004) finds support for stylistic approaches to collocation as early as in the work of Firth (1957). One of Hori's (2004) claims is that:

> [t]he study of usual collocations with high frequencies in the corpus of writers' whole texts may reveal their predilection for particular collocations; and repeated usual collocations in their works could be considered the characters' idiolects
>
> (Hori 2004: 12)

Hori is also interested in unusual collocations or 'creative' collocations, which he examines under eight categories. For instance, *glorious spider, aristocratic slowness* or *wrathful sunset* are examples of 'metaphorical' collocations according to his categories (Hori 2004: 57 ff.). Another type of creative collocations are 'oxymoronic' collocations, as in *old infant*, or *comfortable wickedness* (Hori 2004: 77 ff.).

Although Hori (2004: 26) highlights the advantages of a computer-assisted approach, he stresses that his approach is nevertheless different from statistical stylistics as represented, for instance, by the work of Hoover (2001). Hori (2004) aims to give stronger emphasis to the qualitative study of collocation and draws on native informant tests to complement his corpus analysis. Hori (2004) focuses on collocations of content words, such as combinations of adjectives and nouns. He explicitly excludes function words and a number of other words from his data (cf. Hori 2004: 33), arguing that these are words which are very frequent and 'show no distinctive features among particular texts' (Hori 2004: 33).[2] Frequency, however, is a not a straightforward issue. I do not want to attempt a comprehensive discussion of the factors involved in frequency analysis, but will merely highlight two points here.

Firstly, frequency is relative, and an important factor in corpus work is comparison. A corpus tool that is very useful for the comparison of frequencies is Mike Scott's *KeyWords Tool* of the software *WordSmith* (Scott 2004). *KeyWords* compares the frequencies of words in one text (or a group of texts) with the frequencies of the words in a larger reference corpus. This makes it possible to identify 'key words', i.e. words which are unusually frequent (or infrequent) in a text as compared to the reference corpus. There are typically three types of key words: proper nouns, content words that give an indication of the aboutness of the text, and function words. Scott (2004–2006: 116) points out that the function words thrown up by *KeyWords* may indicate stylistic features. The importance of function words for style is also shown in the work of Burrows (1987) who illustrates stylistic nuances of function words such as *the* and *and* in Jane Austen. These points suggest that deliberately excluding function words from a stylistic analysis will result in a partial picture.

Secondly, collocations describe how words tend to occur together. Consequently, frequencies of individual words have to be seen in relation to words in their contexts. Even though function words are very frequent and can co-occur in a variety of texts, we can still identify collocational tendencies and see how frequent words have their own patterns. Similarly, when we describe collocational patterns of content words, there will be function words in their contexts that affect their patterns. To see how frequent words play a role in collocations, it is useful to extend the notion of collocation to cover not only the co-occurrence of two words, but also the co-occurrence of words in a sequence. The sequences, or 'clusters', *out of the, as if he were, as if he had been* are the most frequent three, four and five-word clusters in the Dickens corpus (the corpus will be discussed in more detail in the following section). Each of these sequences is made up of function words, and each of these sequences can be analysed with regard to stylistic features. In a short chapter on collocations and characters in *Bleak House*, Hori's (2004) examples occasionally include sequences such as *my dear friend, by my soul, Discipline must be maintained*, but the nature of these patterns deserves to receive more attention. The following section focuses on clusters. It is suggested that clusters are pointers to local textual functions and thus to stylistic features.

3 Clusters as pointers to local textual functions in a Dickens corpus

In literary stylistics we assume that the artistic effect of a text is something that is noticeable. Literary appreciation and linguistic analysis are not independent. In fact, they can be described as being in cyclic motion (cf. Leech and Short 1981: 13). A central concept in stylistic analysis is the foregrounding that results from the deviation from linguistic norms, i.e. the psychological effect that the linguistic deviation has on the reader. So it seems reasonable that Hori (2004) wants to give special attention to unusual collocations, and unusual collocations of content words seem to be even more striking than unusual collocations involving function words. However, linguistic norms and deviations from these norms cannot necessarily be described in terms of sharp contrasts, a point that is stressed by Carter (2004), who suggests a cline of literariness. Even though we may notice a special effect in a text, it may be difficult to describe which factors contribute to its creation. The multifunctionality of words and the flexibility with which words can enter into textual relationships with other words enable various linguistic effects. Furthermore, linguistic norms may be as difficult to identify as deviations from norms. Corpora can reveal typical and repeated uses of language that are so common that they do not strike us as important. Thus corpus stylistics can make an important contribution to the investigation of the interplay between conventional, idiosyncratic and creative patterns of language use. Corpus stylistics also highlights that intuition and automatic processes should work together and that the descriptive categories that are applied to the analysis of style should be flexible enough to account for meanings in texts.

The definition of local textual functions is necessarily flexible: local textual functions characterize (a group of) lexical items with regard to the functions they fulfil in (a group of) texts (cf. Mahlberg 2005; previous chapter). The definition is relational and the amount of descriptive detail depends on the choice of the texts and/or lexical items. Localness can be of different types. In the previous chapter, I looked at a purpose-built corpus containing newspaper articles. In this chapter, the focus is on local textual functions in a Dickens corpus. The present work is part of an ongoing project in corpus stylistics dealing with Dickens' style. The corpus that I use for my studies was designed to mirror the corpus used by Hori (2004) to allow for cross-references to be drawn. The corpus covers 23 texts and contains about 4.5 million words. At the time of writing Hori's Dickens corpus was not publicly available, so I use texts from Project Gutenberg. The fact that Project Gutenberg does not follow consistent standards for the preparation of electronic texts can raise issues about the quality of the texts, but for studies like the present one, these problems are not too damaging.[3] In addition to the Dickens texts, I use a corpus of 29 novels by 18 authors from the nineteenth century; again the texts are from Project Gutenberg. This nineteenth-century corpus (19C) contains about 4.5 million words, roughly the same amount of words as the Dickens corpus. Although the majority of texts in the Dickens corpus are novels, not all of the texts belong clearly to this type.

Like the previous chapter, this chapter builds on a claim that is central to corpus linguistic investigations: units of meaning are not equivalent to single words. The study of the previous chapter starts with the core *sustainable development* to identify links between lexical and textual features. The examples in the present chapter start from the texts and aim to identify local textual functions as stylistic features of texts in the Dickens corpus, and specifically in one novel by Dickens, *Bleak House*. To identify local textual functions in this way the claim by Leech and Short (1981: 74) about the 'individual qualities' of each text is crucial (see section 1). Leech and Short (1981: 74 f.) stress that '[t]here is no infallible technique of selecting what is significant. We have to make ourselves newly aware, for each text, of the artistic effect of the whole, and the way linguistic details fit into this whole'.

From a corpus stylistic perspective, clusters can be taken as pointers to meanings and textual functions. 'Clusters' are repeated sequences of words. Other terms that have been used are, for instance, 'n-grams' or 'lexical bundles' (e.g. Biber et al. 1999). The hypothesis is that the occurrence of clusters reflects the functional relevance of these sequences in texts. Related arguments can be found, for instance, in Conrad and Biber (2005) for the interpretation of discourse functions of lexical bundles, in Mahlberg (2005) with regard to textual functions of high-frequency nouns, and in Stubbs (present volume). However, units of meaning are not equivalent to fixed sequences either. Patterns of words display various degrees of flexibility. It is this flexibility that makes it possible for patterns of words to link in with other patterns to form cohesive texts.[4] Clusters can only be an initial step towards finding meanings in texts and identifying local textual functions.

The local point of view in the present chapter sees one text in relation to other similar texts. The fact that the concept of local textual functions is 'relational' means that the analysis of clusters in *Bleak House* can be more detailed if it is linked to observations in other works by Dickens and further nineteenth-century data. The local point of view also affects the type of clusters, i.e. the length of repeated sequences, that are taken into account. When we look at the three-word clusters in the Dickens corpus the most frequent clusters are the following (with the frequencies given in brackets[5]): *out of the* (1,210), *as if he* (1,158), *there was a* (1,091), *it was a* (1,050), *one of the* (1,008), *I don't know* (1,001), *that he was* (959), *the old man* (941), *that it was* (853), *that he had* (809). As the length of clusters increases their frequency decreases: the most frequent five-word clusters are *as if he had been* (90) and *his hands in his pockets* (90). Additionally, the length of clusters relates to their distribution across texts. Whereas out of the 25 most frequent three-word clusters, for instance, 20 clusters occur in all 23 texts, none of the 25 most frequent five-word clusters occur in all texts, but at most in 20 texts. The literature on cluster analysis and their distributions across different texts suggests that a useful cluster length is generally three to five or six words, (the upper limit of *WordSmith* at the time of writing this chapter was eight-word clusters[6]). When we look at clusters in Dickens, however, it is also useful to take longer clusters into consideration.

4 Long clusters

Table 8.1 contains the first 25 of 51 eight-word clusters in the Dickens corpus that occur a minimum of five times. With eight-word clusters the link of longer clusters to particular texts becomes clearly visible. For

Table 8.1 The first 25 of 51 8-word clusters in Dickens that occur five times or more

		Freq.	Texts
1	WITH THE AIR OF A MAN WHO HAD	15	9
2	NOT TO PUT TOO FINE A POINT UPON	14	1
3	TO PUT TOO FINE A POINT UPON IT	14	1
4	WITH HIS HANDS IN HIS POCKETS AND HIS	11	7
5	THE YOUNG MAN OF THE NAME OF GUPPY	10	1
6	WHAT HAVE YOU GOT TO SAY TO ME	9	5
7	THE WAITER WHO OUGHT TO WAIT UPON US	8	1
8	WHAT SHALL I DO WHAT SHALL I DO	7	4
9	HIM REMEMBER IT IN THAT ROOM YEARS TO	7	1
10	LET HIM REMEMBER IT IN THAT ROOM YEARS	7	1
11	REMEMBER IT IN THAT ROOM YEARS TO COME	7	1
12	MONOTONY OF BELLS AND WHEELS AND HORSES FEET	7	1
13	IT WAS AS MUCH AS I COULD DO	6	4
14	THE UNITED KINGDOM OF GREAT BRITAIN AND IRELAND	6	3
15	HE HAD HAD SOMETHING THE MATTER WITH HIS	6	2
16	HOT MUFFIN AND CRUMPET BAKING AND PUNCTUAL DELIVERY	6	1
17	IMPROVED HOT MUFFIN AND CRUMPET BAKING AND PUNCTUAL	6	1
18	METROPOLITAN IMPROVED HOT MUFFIN AND CRUMPET BAKING AND	6	1
19	MUFFIN AND CRUMPET BAKING AND PUNCTUAL DELIVERY COMPANY	6	1
20	UNITED METROPOLITAN IMPROVED HOT MUFFIN AND CRUMPET BAKING	6	1
21	OF ALL THE KING'S KNIGHTS TIS THE FLOWER	6	1
22	THE ANGLO-BENGALEE DISINTERESTED LOAN AND LIFE ASSURANCE COMPANY	6	1
23	VILLAGE OF DOTHEBOYS NEAR GRETA BRIDGE IN YORKSHIRE	6	1
24	I'M A DEVIL I'M A DEVIL I'M A	6	1
25	A DEVIL I'M A DEVIL I'M A DEVIL	5	1

instance, the cluster *not to put too fine a point upon* occurs 14 times in one novel, *Bleak House*, and is associated with the character Mr Snagsby. The clusters *not to put too fine a point upon* and *to put too fine a point upon it* are related: there is a nine-word cluster *not to put too fine a point upon it* that occurs 14 times in *Bleak House*. A concordance of *too fine a point* will also find a variant of this cluster: *not to put too fine a point on it*, where *on* appears instead of *upon*. This cluster occurs just once. All of the 15 occurrences, however, are associated with Mr Snagsby. In 14 cases it is Mr Snagsby who uses the phrase himself, as in the example below:

> 'About a year and a half ago,' says Mr. Snagsby, strengthened, 'he came into our place one morning after breakfast, and finding my little woman (which I name Mrs. Snagsby when I use that appellation) in our shop, produced a specimen of his handwriting and gave her to under-stand that he was in want of copying work to do and was, *not to put too fine a point upon it*,' a favourite apology for plain speaking with Mr. Snagsby, which he always offers with a sort of argumentative frankness, 'hard up! My little woman is not in general partial to strangers, par-ticular – *not to put too fine a point upon it* – when they want anything. But she . . .
>
> (*Bleak House*, Chapter 11)

The phrase is repeated within a short space and the narrator even draws attention to it by describing it as a *favourite apology for plain speaking with Mr Snagsby*. The fact that this phrase is characteristic of Mr Snagsby is also highlighted when the narrator later on in the same chapter alludes to Snagsby's habit again:

> It is anything but a night of rest at Mr. Snagsby's, in Cook's Court, where Guster murders sleep by going, as Mr. Snagsby himself allows – *not to put too fine a point upon it* – out of one fit into twenty.
>
> (*Bleak House*, Chapter 11)

Numbers 16 to 20 in Table 8.1 also illustrate a 'longer' cluster. In *Nicholas Nickleby* we find the 12-word cluster *United Metropolitan Improved Hot Muffin and Crumpet Baking and Punctual Delivery Company* six times, and five of these occurrences are 13-word clusters with the definite article as first word. Below is the one example without the definite article:

> 'Pretty well!' echoed Mr Bonney. 'It's the finest idea that was ever started. "*United Metropolitan Improved Hot Muffin and Crumpet Baking and Punctual Delivery Company*. Capital, five millions, in five hundred thousand shares of ten pounds each." Why the very name will get the shares up to a premium in ten days.'
>
> (*Nicholas Nickleby*, Chapter 2)

It seems that not only did Mr Bonney know the value of a selling name, but Dickens also was aware of the potential of names or functions of tags like Mr Snagsby's favourite phrase, that are associated with characters. Hori

(2004) could be criticized for looking at the obvious when he investigates unusual collocations, the investigation of 'long' clusters might also be subject to similar criticism. When we identify such phrases the question is: Do we need the computer for this? A phrase like Mr Snagsby's favourite expression is aimed to be prominent, and such phrases have been the subject of critical analyses. The relationship between repetition and functional relevance is described, for instance, by Brook (1970):

> Dickens was never afraid of making excessive use of a way of writing that happened to appeal to him. [. . .] A phrase, either descriptive or conversational, once associated with a particular character, will be repeated at intervals throughout a novel whenever that character is introduced.
>
> (Brook 1970: 36)

Repeated phrases are also seen in relation to humour and the cumulative effect of laughter; they create a snowball effect or cause a sense of anticipation that develops with the entrance of a specific character:

> Our memory builds up associations which can act reflexively and set us laughing without apparent local cause. Dickens appeals to this reflexive laughter most obviously in his use of tags to accompany so many characters.
>
> (Kincaid 1971: 16)

The fact that corpus linguistic methods draw attention to similar findings as those identified by literary critics is not a problem as such. Stubbs (2005) points out:

> [E]ven if quantification only confirms what we already know, this is not a bad thing. Indeed, in developing a new method, it is perhaps better not to find anything too new, but to confirm findings from many years of traditional study, since this gives confidence that the method can be relied on.
>
> (Stubbs 2005: 6)

The important point is that corpus linguistic observations do not start with too many restrictions determined by previous assumptions, thus a strength of corpus stylistics can lie in the potential of corpus linguistics and literary stylistics complementing each other.

5 Functional groups of five-word clusters

In a comparison of texts, longer clusters tend to point more clearly to individual texts, while shorter clusters can reveal more general functional tendencies found across texts. These tendencies can then form a basis for a detailed study of a single text. The study of *Bleak House* in the following section builds on and develops five functional groups of clusters that seem to be particularly relevant to Dickens' style:

1. labels
2. speech clusters
3. body part clusters

4. *as if* clusters
5. time and place clusters

These groups of clusters have been identified by comparing five-word clusters in the Dickens corpus with five-word clusters in 19C (see section 3). With the help of *WordSmith*, Mahlberg (forthcoming) identified 66 positive key clusters and classified them into functional groups. Most of the key clusters are covered by the first four groups above. Although there are time and place clusters found among the key clusters, group 5 mainly accounts for the fact that the time and place clusters are frequent in both Dickens and 19C. Mahlberg (forthcoming) provides the details of how of these groups have been identified. In the present chapter, the five categories of clusters are applied to the study of *Bleak House*. The following is a brief general characterization of each functional group.

The first group, 'labels', covers clusters such as *Mr Pickwick and his friends*, *the Lady of the caravan*, or *man with the wooden leg*. Labels contain a name of a person (or place), or a nominal expression used to refer to a person, for instance, *one of the young ladies*. A cluster can also count as a label, if it is specific to one text only, as Mr Snagsby's phrase discussed in section 4. Parts of this phrase are found in five-word clusters such as *not to put too fine* or *put too fine a point* (cf. also section 6). The 'speech' clusters in group 2 contain a first- or second-person personal pronoun or possessive, which are interpreted as signals of interaction. Examples are *do me the favour to*, *all I can say is*. In addition to pronouns and possessives, signals of interaction that characterize speech clusters are imperative forms and terms of address. If a cluster contains features of both labels and speech, the label overrules the category speech. Clusters in the 'body part' group (group 3) contain at least one noun referring to a part of the human body as in *with his hand to his*. In this group the presence of a body part noun overrules criteria of speech clusters. Group 4 contains clusters beginning with *as if*, e.g. *as if he would have*. The final group, 'time and place' clusters, collects clusters such as *a quarter of an hour*, *at the bottom of the*, *the other side of the*, or *up and down the room*. Clusters of this group contain a time or place expression often in the form of a noun, but there are also prepositions as in *up and down the room*. A preposition as such does not necessarily reflect an adverbial function, but it can also introduce a postmodification as in the case of *of* in *the other side of the*. The classification, however, does not go into grammatical detail.

The criteria that are outlined here are still broad, and the grounds on which borderline cases are assigned to one group or the other are only starting points. The categories provide an initial stage for the classification of clusters across the 23 texts of the Dickens corpus. The key point is that the five functional groups seem to be able to account for most clusters in the texts of the Dickens corpus and they provide a useful basis for more detailed studies. At this initial stage the groups characterize broad functions: naming and referring to characters (labels), interaction between characters (speech), description of looks and movements of characters (body part), creation of a textual world by comparison (*as if*), and references to time and place (time and place). On the basis of these groups we can investigate at least two types of questions. On the one hand, we can take individual texts and look at the groups in more detail in order to identify the textual functions of the clusters that are 'local' to a specific text. On the other hand, we can compare clusters in Dickens with other fiction to explore functional and distributional differences. Thus the five functional groups are a starting point to zoom in and out of different degrees of localness. The remainder of the present chapter focuses on the local view of a single novel, *Bleak House*.

6 Analysing five-word clusters in *Bleak House*

Bleak House is a very complex novel with two main plot lines: the Chancery suit of Jarndyce and Jarndyce, which has been dragging on for years and whose estate is eventually eaten up by the costs, and the story around the mystery of Esther Summerson's parentage. The narration is divided between two narrators, a third-person narrator and Esther, with complicated links between the two narrations. Ada and Richard are wards of Court and live together with Esther at Bleak House, the home of John Jarndyce, who is a descendant of the suitor in the Jarndyce case. A number of characters are involved with aspects of the court case and Esther's mysterious past. Lady Dedlock, who is now married to Sir Leicester, turns out to be Esther's mother. Lady Dedlock's secret is investigated by her lawyer Mr Tulkinghorn and Inspector Bucket. At the same time Mr Guppy, a law clerk, who wants to marry Esther, discovers a link between Esther and Lady Dedlock. In addition to the complex network of characters that has been discussed extensively by critics, the novel is famous for the picture it provides of problematic issues of the time.

I will start with an overview of the functional groups outlined in section 5. *Bleak House* contains about 350,000 words and *WordSmith* returns 97 cluster types that occur a minimum of five times in the novel. The cut-off point of five was set to obtain a manageable sample. Table 8.2 shows how the 97 clusters are distributed across the five functional groups. The group 'Other' collects those examples that do not fit easily into one of the five groups. Table 8.4 in the Appendix lists all clusters together with the categories to which they are assigned.

Table 8.2 Distribution of cluster types

Labels (L)	Speech (S)	Body parts (BP)	*as if* (AI)	Time and place (TP)	Other (O)
59	17	3	2	10	6

The initial overview presented in Table 8.2 follows the broad criteria outlined in section 5, but there are also further issues to be taken into account due to the local point of view. When the Dickens corpus is compared to 19C the five groups above were in the first place identified on the basis of surface features of the clusters and their distribution across texts (the distribution played a role when a cluster was classified as label because it occurred in one novel only). With the focus on one novel, the classification incorporates more detail based on the analysis of concordances of the clusters. Labels make up the biggest group of clusters. Labels that contain names are for instance *of the name of Guppy, old girl says Mr Bagnet,* or *Sir Leicester Dedlock Baronet and.* Also counted as labels are clusters such as *never own to it before,* when they are associated with a specific person. The five-word cluster *never own to it before* is in five of six cases part of the cluster *But I never own to it before her. Discipline must be maintained.* In one of the cases we find *the old girl* instead of *her* in the cluster: *But I never own to it before the old girl. Discipline must be maintained.* All of these occurrences characterize Mr Bagnet's relationship with his wife.

With the focus on one novel, clusters that would be counted as speech or body part clusters in a more general overview can be classified as labels. For instance, *when we came to the* is on the surface a speech cluster going by the criterion that the cluster has to contain a first- or second-person pronoun, but in *Bleak House* it is a label as it is associated with Esther only. In contrast to *not to put too fine,* which is associated with Mr Snagby, *when we came to the* is not restricted to *Bleak House* only, but is also found once in *Great Expectations,* which has a first person narrator, too. Another example is *I ask your pardon sir,* which could be classified as a speech cluster on the grounds of the pronoun *I* and the fact that the cluster is not restricted to *Bleak House.* It occurs in three other texts as well. In *Bleak House,* however, all six occurrences belong to Mr George, who uses the phrase. Among the clusters that appear on the surface as body part clusters we also find two labels: *his head against the wall* and *with his head against the.* Both occur in texts other than *Bleak House:* the first cluster occurs in four other texts, the second cluster in three other texts, where the second cluster is not in each case followed by *wall* but also once by *parlour wall* and once by *bars.* The clusters are, however, more frequent in *Bleak House,* and in each case refer to Mr Jellyby, as in the following example:

> Poor Mr. Jellyby, who very seldom spoke and almost always sat when he was at home *with his head against the wall,* became interested when . . .
> (*Bleak House,* Chapter 30)

The examples show that the category labels does not only contain expressions with names, but also clusters that contribute to the creation of characters. Thus the high number of labels compared to the other groups of clusters is not surprising. The following discussion therefore focuses on labels.

Labels such as those of Mr Snagsby, Mr Bagnet and Mr Jellyby are prominent and do not escape the attention of the reader. Not only are these phrases repeated, but it is also possible that the narration draws attention to them explicitly, for instance, when Esther comments on Jellyby's habit:

> Her father released her, took out his pocket handkerchief, and sat down on the stairs *with his head against the wall.* I hope he found some consolation in walls. I almost think he did.
>
> (*Bleak House*, Chapter 30)

Such characteristic expressions have been discussed by literary critics, and the question is now what insights we can gain from a corpus linguistic approach. One point is that the computer can help us track the expressions through the novel in order to analyse them in more detail. Additionally, the cluster analysis highlights different ways of characterizing members of the cast and relationships between them. Snagsby, Bagnet and Jellyby appear as more comic or even unidimensional characters and this characterization goes together with more striking labels. The Reverend Chadband is another character of this group. Clusters associated with Chadband illustrate that a label does not necessarily have to be long to be prominent, but it can also attract attention when it is repeated in a short sequence, as is the case for the cluster *right that I should be*: all five occurrences belong to Chapter 19, four of them appearing in the following example of Chadband's hypocritical sermonizing:

> 'My friends,' says Mr. Chadband with his persecuted chin folding itself into its fat smile again as he looks round, 'it is *right that I should be* humbled, it is *right that I should be* tried, it is *right that I should be* mortified, it is *right that I should be* corrected. I stumbled, on Sabbath last, when I thought with pride of my three hours' improving. The account is now favourably balanced: my creditor has accepted a composition. O let us be joyful, joyful! O let us be joyful!'
>
> (*Bleak House*, Chapter 19)

Important aspects of characterization are relationships between characters. A famous example is again Mr Bagnet and his wife (cf. Budd 1994), but there are also other relationships. The clusters *my friend in the city* and *your friend in the city* are used by Grandfather Smallweed and Mr George respectively when they talk about Smallweed's friend. Mr Guppy's link to Lady Dedlock is reflected by the cluster *your ladyship says Mr Guppy*. This link becomes even more prominent when we take the occurrences of *your ladyship* into account as well. The two-word cluster *your ladyship* occurs 77 times in three chapters altogether (Chapters 29, 33, 55); in all cases it is used by Guppy talking to Lady Dedlock.

Another link between characters is visible through the cluster *Sir Leicester Dedlock Baronet I*, which is used by Bucket when he talks to Sir Leicester. This cluster illustrates that Bucket likes to stress the title *Baronet*. The cluster can be seen in relation to another cluster: *Inspector Bucket of the Detective*, showing that Bucket puts emphasis on his own title, too. Of the five occurrences of this cluster, four are part of Bucket's speech when he introduces or refers to himself. One of the clusters shows how the narrator picks up on Bucket's conscious approach to titles, when Chapter 55 starts with the following sentence:

> *Inspector Bucket of the Detective* has not yet struck his great blow, as just now chronicled, but is yet refreshing himself with sleep preparatory to his field-day, when through the night and along the freezing wintry roads a chaise and pair comes out of Lincolnshire, making its way towards London.
>
> (*Bleak House*, Chapter 55)

The clusters *your ladyship says Mr Guppy* and *Sir Leicester Dedlock Baronet I* show that some clusters containing names are not only a label because of the name they include, but also because of the person who uses the cluster. A further example is the way in which Bucket defines himself through his relationship to Sir Leicester. Bucket uses the cluster *by Sir Leicester Dedlock Baronet* when alluding to the fact that he has business relations with Sir Leicester. Below are the five examples of this cluster, all found in the speech of Bucket:

> . . . I tell you plainly there's a reward out, of a hundred guineas, offered *by Sir Leicester Dedlock, Baronet*. You and me have always been pleasant together; but I have got a duty to discharge; and if that hundred guineas is to be made, it may as well be made by me as any other man. . . .
>
> (*Bleak House*, Chapter 49)

> 'That is, I am deputed *by Sir Leicester Dedlock, Baronet*, to consider (without admitting or promising anything) this bit of business,' says Mr. Bucket . . .
>
> (*Bleak House*, Chapter 54)

> 'Very good,' says Mr. Bucket. 'Now I understand you, you know, and being deputed *by Sir Leicester Dedlock, Baronet*, to look into this little matter . . .
>
> (*Bleak House*, Chapter 54)

> Now, Mr. Jarndyce, I am employed *by Sir Leicester Dedlock, Baronet*, to follow her and find her, to save her and take her his forgiveness.
>
> (*Bleak House*, Chapter 56)

> 'Then you keep up as good a heart as you can, and you rely upon me for standing by you, no less than *by Sir Leicester Dedlock, Baronet*. Now, are you right there?'
>
> (*Bleak House*, Chapter 57)

The examples also show how clusters can be fixed reference points for more flexible patterns. Bucket does not repeat exactly the same words, but uses *I am deputed* or *being deputed*, but also *I am employed*, or other paraphrases (in the first and the last of the examples) to refer to his relationship to Sir Leicester.

The flexibility of the way in which clusters fit into their context can also account for the distribution of clusters across the speech of different characters. Examples are the clusters *as well as anything else*, and *do as well as anything*, which are associated with Richard. Five of the six occurrences of *as well as anything else* occur in Chapter 17, which cover all five instances of *do as well as anything else*. The following section shows how the phrase is introduced.

> 'Well enough?' I repeated.
> 'Yes,' said Richard, 'well enough. It's rather jog-trotty and humdrum. But it'll *do as well as anything else!*'
> 'Oh! My dear Richard!' I remonstrated.
> 'What's the matter?' said Richard.
> '*Do as well as anything else!*'
> 'I don't think there's any harm in that, Dame Durden,' said Ada, looking so confidingly at me across him; 'because if it will *do as well as anything else*, it will do very well, I hope.'
>
> (*Bleak House*, Chapter 17)

First it is Richard, who uses the phrase, then it is taken up by Esther and eventually by Ada. In this way Richard's indifferent and careless attitude is highlighted. Although the cluster is not restricted to Richard's speech it still characterizes him in this situation, and the other three occurrences of *as well as anything else* are then spoken by Richard, two in Chapter 17 again, and one in Chapter 37. The cluster reflects Richard's ongoing problem of finding the right profession for him.

The examples of Mr Snagsby's phrase and *Inspector Bucket of the Detective* discussed above are examples that illustrate how the narrator can come in and add a different point of view, thus implicitly commenting on the characters. Through the narrator the use of labels to indicate links between characters can become rather complex, which is of particular relevance for the link between Guppy, Lady Dedlock and Tulkinghorn. A cluster that belongs to Guppy is *of the name of Guppy* which occurs 13 times, and in four chapters: nine times in Chapter 29, twice in 33, once in 48, and once in 55. Chapters 29, 33 and 55 are the same chapters as those in which the 77 instances of *your ladyship* occur that relate to conversations between Guppy and Lady Dedlock. The instance of *of the name of Guppy* that appears in Chapter 48 reminds the reader of previous conversations between Guppy and Lady Dedlock:

> My Lady sits in the room in which she gave audience to the young man *of the name of Guppy*. Rosa is with her and has been writing for her and reading to her.
>
> (*Bleak House*, Chapter 48)

When the cluster *of the name of Guppy* first appears in Chapter 29 it is used by Mercury, a servant of Lady Dedlock, to announce Guppy's visit. The cluster is linked to the other clusters *man of the name of, young man of the name, the young man of the*, but not in each case are the words exactly repeated. There can be a definite or indefinite article, or it is possible that not all of the words appear in a sequence. The extract below illustrates five examples that contain the cluster *of the name of Guppy*. In Mercury's introduction (1) *The young man, my lady, of the name of Guppy*, the sequence is interrupted by *my lady*. In the sentence that follows, the phrase (2) *The young man of the name of Guppy* is taken up by Sir Leicester, before the narrator then picks up on it as well (3). At this point the phrase is felt to add unnecessary detail and thus receives prominence, which is continued when Sir Leicester speaks again (4) and when the narrator describes how Mercury looks at (5) *the young man of the name of Guppy*.

> Sir Leicester is reading with infinite gravity and state when the door opens, and the Mercury in powder makes this strange announcement, '(1) *The young man, my Lady, of the name of Guppy*.'
> Sir Leicester pauses, stares, repeats in a killing voice, '(2) *The young man of the name of Guppy?*'
> Looking round, he beholds (3) *the young man of the name of Guppy*, much discomfited and not presenting a very impressive letter of introduction in his manner and appearance.
> 'Pray,' says Sir Leicester to Mercury, 'what do you mean by announcing with this abruptness (4) *a young man of the name of Guppy?*'
> 'I beg your pardon, Sir Leicester, but my Lady said she would see the young man whenever he called. I was not aware that you were here, Sir Leicester.'
> With this apology, Mercury directs a scornful and indignant look at (5) *the young man of the name of Guppy* which plainly says, 'What do you come calling here for and getting ME into a row?'
> (*Bleak House*, Chapter 29)

By presenting Guppy in this way, a comic element is introduced, but also options opened that can be exploited in the development of the conversation. Guppy speaks more than Lady Dedlock, who appears rather mysterious with short replies or her responses presented in an indirect way, for instance in the following:

> '. . . Consequently, I rely upon your ladyship's honour.'
> My Lady, with a disdainful gesture of the hand that holds the screen, assures him of his being worth no complaint from her.
> 'Thank your ladyship,' says Mr. Guppy;
> (*Bleak House*, Chapter 29)

When the narrator then indicates how Lady Dedlock struggles to keep her self-control, the cluster highlights the special relationship between Lady Dedlock and Guppy. The narrator shares Lady Dedlock's point of view, whose time is wasted by the intrusion of Guppy, and his inappropriate behaviour seems to be reflected by the unnecessarily long term of address:

> *Young man of the name of Guppy*! There have been times, when ladies lived in strongholds and had unscrupulous attendants within call, when that poor life of yours would NOT have been worth a minute's purchase, with those beautiful eyes looking at you as they look at this moment.
>
> (*Bleak House*, Chapter 29)

In Chapter 33, when Guppy arrives at Lady Dedlock's house, the reader is reminded of the relationship between Lady Dedlock and Guppy:

> . . . *the young man of the name of Guppy* presents himself at the town mansion at about seven o'clock in the evening and requests to see her ladyship.
>
> (*Bleak House*, Chapter 33)

When Guppy leaves again, a parallel to Tulkinghorn is drawn. What both men have in common is that they are investigating Lady Dedlock's secret, and the link between them is highlighted with the help of the cluster *the young man of the name of Guppy* which is contrasted with *an old man of the name of Tulkinghorn*:

> And she rings for Mercury to show *the young man of the name of Guppy* out.
>
> But in that house, in that same moment, there happens to be *an old man of the name of Tulkinghorn*. And *that old man*, coming with his quiet footstep to the library, has his hand at that moment on the handle of the door – comes in – and comes face to face with *the young man* as he is leaving the room.
>
> (*Bleak House*, Chapter 33)

The examples of clusters and characterization that we have seen so far illustrate that the characterization can have different degrees of complexity, and it is important to note that the clusters are only pointers to more detailed questions of analysis; clusters alone provide an incomplete picture. The patterns of which they are part can be very flexible and blend in with their contexts in various ways. Thus it is clear that the classification in Table 8.2 is to some extent due to practical decisions aiming to find systematic criteria. It is not an indication of clear boundaries between functions of clusters. On the basis of the examples we have looked at, the criteria for classifications can now be more clearly seen. The biggest group, labels, basically contains three types of labels. There are clusters which contain names or expressions used to refer to people. These clusters which are defined by surface criteria can function as characterization in two ways: the cluster is always used to characterize the same person or situation, or the cluster can be used for characterization but at the same time occur in other uses. For instance, *now Sir Leicester Dedlock Baronet* always occurs with Bucket, whereas *Sir Leicester Dedlock Baronet and* is used in Bucket's typical way, but also found in the speech of Boythorn, for instance. Finally, there are labels that do not contain a name, but the expressions are nevertheless typical of only one character, as in the case of *not to put too fine* or *his head against the wall*. These criteria yield the following list (Table 8.3) of characters that are associated with label clusters for which each occurrence of the cluster adds to an aspect of characterization or specifies a relationship with other characters. Where names are used in different situations and not clearly as characterization, e.g. *Mr Jarndyce of Bleak House*, the clusters are not included in the list. Labels that refer to places and things, e.g. *the rag and bottle shop*, are not included in the list either.

The table shows that an analysis of five-word clusters in *Bleak House* provides information on 16 characters in the novel. In addition to the labels in Table 8.3, we find more subtle characteristics when we look at the group of speech clusters. A case in point is the characterization of Esther. In Table 8.3 Esther gets two labels: *I thought it best to* and *when we came to the*. Although they only characterize Esther, they are more subtle as they can be

Table 8.3 Characters and labels associated with them

Character	Clusters associated with the character
Mr Snagsby	NOT TO PUT TOO FINE PUT TOO FINE A POINT TO PUT TOO FINE A FINE A POINT UPON IT TOO FINE A POINT UPON
Mr Guppy	MAN OF THE NAME OF OF THE NAME OF GUPPY YOUNG MAN OF THE NAME THE YOUNG MAN OF THE CIRCUMSTANCES OVER WHICH I HAVE OVER WHICH I HAVE NO WHICH I HAVE NO CONTROL YOUR LADYSHIP SAYS MR GUPPY
Mr Bagnet	OLD GIRL SAYS MR BAGNET BUT I NEVER OWN TO I NEVER OWN TO IT NEVER OWN TO IT BEFORE BEFORE HER DISCIPLINE MUST BE HER DISCIPLINE MUST BE MAINTAINED IT BEFORE HER DISCIPLINE MUST OWN TO IT BEFORE HER THE OLD GIRL SAYS MR TO IT BEFORE HER DISCIPLINE

Continued

Table 8.3 *Continued*

Character	Clusters associated with the character
Mr Jellyby	HIS HEAD AGAINST THE WALL WITH HIS HEAD AGAINST THE
Mr Bucket	SIR LEICESTER DEDLOCK BARONET I BY SIR LEICESTER DEDLOCK BARONET NOW SIR LEICESTER DEDLOCK BARONET INSPECTOR BUCKET OF THE DETECTIVE
Mr George	YOUR FRIEND IN THE CITY I ASK YOUR PARDON SIR
Richard	AS WELL AS ANYTHING ELSE DO AS WELL AS ANYTHING ELSE
Esther	I THOUGHT IT BEST TO WHEN WE CAME TO THE
Mr Vholes	IN THE VALE OF TAUNTON
Mr Jarndyce	HAVE SOMETHING TO SAY ABOUT SOMETHING TO SAY ABOUT IT WILL HAVE SOMETHING TO SAY
Miss Flite	I EXPECT A JUDGMENT SHORTLY
Charley	IF YOU PLEASE MISS SAID
Chadband	IN A SPIRIT OF LOVE RIGHT THAT I SHOULD BE YOU ARE TO US A
Grandfather Smallweed	MY FRIEND IN THE CITY TO LOOK AFTER THE PROPERTY
Krook	MY NOBLE AND LEARNED BROTHER
Jo	WOS WERY GOOD TO ME

completed in various ways and are not part of fixed 'longer' clusters. On the surface these labels look like speech clusters. We find further subtle features of Esther with the clusters *I don't know what I,* and *I don't know how it;* in both cases two of the five occurrences appear in Esther's speech. This observation fits in with the picture that is created of Esther as someone who is very considerate and tries to do her best, but may not always be very confident. In this sense *I don't know what I* and *I don't know how it*[7] are similar to the label *I thought it best to.*

A closer look at Esther's speech clusters that are not counted as labels suggests a tentative hint at the relationship between Esther and Lady Dedlock. Lady Dedlock uses the cluster *I don't know how it* once, and of the five occurrences of *you will allow me to* three are used by Lady Dedlock and one by Esther. This evidence so far can only be taken as indication for directions of further research, but it may well be that the characterization of the more complex and mysterious characters goes together with a more complex network of clusters. Support for this claim comes from the description of the character Tulkinghorn. On the basis of the present analysis none of the five-word clusters strikingly characterize Tulkinghorn,[8] but we have seen a link with Guppy already. Tulkinghorn is a quieter and more mysterious character and clusters that seem to point towards his characterization are *his hands behind him* and *his hands in his pockets*. Six of the eight occurrences of *his hands behind him*, and two of the five occurrences of *his hands in his pockets* describe Tulkinghorn. A more detailed investigation will be necessary to see how different patterns work together to characterize Lady Dedlock's lawyer.[9]

Within the space of the present chapter, the analysis has to focus on selected points, but we can already see wider implications for corpus stylistic work. The five categories of clusters (labels, speech clusters, body part clusters, *as if* clusters, time and place clusters) sketch basic groups for the description of local textual functions in Dickens. The example of *Bleak House* shows how the focus on one novel leads to the identification of more specific functions. In *Bleak House* the biggest group of clusters are labels that seem to play an important role for characterization. It is important to stress that such an approach cannot claim to provide a comprehensive picture of a novel. What it can do is highlight features that are made visible with the help of corpus linguistic tools and that can then form the basis for more detailed critical discussion. The results of the present study suggest interesting links to post-structuralist readings of *Bleak House*, as proposed in Miller's (1971) influential essay. Miller (1971) points to correspondences between characters, and the resemblances and cross-references between scenes and themes. Correspondences between characters can to some degree be identified with the help of a cluster analysis. And the fact that clusters are by definition repetitions links in with the textual readings of the novel that discuss cross-references and links between scenes. It would be interesting to investigate in further detail how the recurrences that have been identified by literary critics correspond to local textual functions as they can be identified with the help of clusters. Moreover, further work is needed to relate findings of individual novels to general tendencies in Dickens and to works by other authors.

Conclusions

The relationship between meaning and form plays a crucial role in both corpus linguistics and literary stylistics. The present chapter emphasizes that corpus stylistics can do more than simply apply computer method-ology to the study of literature. Corpus stylistics can contribute to the exploration and development of descriptive tools that aim to characterize meanings in texts. For the analysis of a work of literature the individual qualities of the text and relationships with other texts play a role. The concept of local textual functions provides possibilities to explore textual features from various points of view. With functional groups of clusters and the examples from *Bleak House* I hope to have shown the applicability and potential of local textual functions in the growing field of corpus stylistics.

Acknowledgements

I would like to thank Anna Čermáková and Matthew Brook O'Donnell for reading and commenting on earlier versions of this chapter, and Mike Scott in particular for invaluable advice and discussions about *WordSmith* questions. I am also grateful for the support from the British Academy to present initial findings of this chapter at ICAME 27, 2006, in Helsinki.

Notes

1. For further corpus linguistic work on Dickens see also the publications by Tomoji Tabata, e.g. Tabata (2002).
2. For a more detailed discussion of Hori (2004) see Mahlberg (2007a).
3. General information on the creation of Project Gutenberg texts can be found at www.gutenberg.org/howto/spd-howto. For a survey of free eBooks see Berglund et al. (2004).
4. For an example of a corpus linguistic approach to the analysis of cohesive features in a single text see Mahlberg (2006).
5. When frequencies are given it is important to note that in the course of further research typos or other textual issues of individual Project Gutenberg texts may be discovered. Some of these findings may have an impact on the precision of the quantitative information provided here, e.g. if typos have prevented a repetition to be counted. Typos and other issues of the quality of texts can occur in all corpora, but the effects will be more serious in smaller corpora. Still, for the conclusions drawn in the present article, the impact of potential quantitative adjustments is not too damaging.
6. *WordSmith* is continuously developing and by the time this book went into print the limit for the cluster size had gone up to 12.
7. The way in which clusters are generated does not account for punctu-ation, and one of the *I don't know how it* examples contains a comma: *I don't know how, it.*
8. It may be that there are clusters which occur fewer than five times, and that occur only with Tulkinghorn, but then they could still be regarded

as less striking in the sense that they occur fewer times than those discussed in the present chapter.

9. For more detail on patterns with the core *his hands . . . pockets*, see Mahlberg (2007b).

References

Adolphs, S. (2006) *Introducing Electronic Text Analysis. A Practical Guide for Language and Literary Studies*. London: Routledge.

Adolphs, S. and Carter, R. (2002) 'Point of view and semantic prosodies in Virginia Woolf's *To the Lighthouse*'. *Poetica*, 58: 7–20.

Berglund, Y., Morrison, A., Wilson, R. and Wynne, M. (2004, Online) 'An investigation into free eBooks'. www.ahds.ac.uk/litlangling/ebooks/report/FreeEbooks.html. (Last accessed December 2005.)

Biber, D., Johansson, S., Leech, G., Conrad, S. and Finegan, E. (1999) *Longman Grammar of Spoken and Written English*. Harlow: Longman.

Brook, G. L. (1970) *The Language of Dickens*. London: Andre Deutsch.

Budd, D. (1994) 'Language Couples in *Bleak House*'. *Nineteenth-Century Literature*, 49, 2: 196–220.

Burrows, J. F. (1987) *Computation into Criticism. A study of Jane Austen's Novels and an Experiment in Method*. Oxford: Clarendon.

Carter, R. (2004) *Language and Creativity. The Art of Common Talk*. London: Routledge.

Conrad, S. and Biber, D. (2005) 'The frequency and use of lexical bundles in conversation and academic prose', in W. Teubert and M. Mahlberg (eds), *The Corpus Approach to Lexicography. Thematic Part of Lexicographica. Internationales Jahrbuch fuer Lexikographie*, 20, 2004, pp. 56–71.

Culpeper, J. (2002) 'Computers, language and characterisation: An analysis of six characters in Romeo and Juliet', in U. Melander-Marttala, C. Östman and M. Kytö (eds), *Conversation in Life and in Literature*. Uppsala: Universitetstryckeriet, pp. 11–30.

Firth, J. R. (1957) 'Modes of meaning', in *Papers in Linguistics, 1934–51*, London: OUP, pp. 190–215.

Hoover, D. (2001) 'Statistical stylistics and authorship attribution: an empirical investigation'. *Literary and Linguistic Computing*, 16: 421–44.

Hori, M. (2004) *Investigating Dickens' Style. A Collocational Analysis*. Basingstoke: Palgrave Macmillan.

Kincaid, J. R. (1971) *Dickens and the Rhetoric of Laughter*. London: Oxford University Press.

Leech, G. and Short, M. (1981) *Style in Fiction. A Linguistic Introduction to English Fictional Prose*. Harlow: Pearson Education.

Louw, B. (1997) 'The role of corpora in critical literary appreciation', in A. Wichman, S. Fligelstone, T. McEnery and G. Knowles (eds), *Teaching and Language Corpora*. Addison Wesley Longman: Harlow, pp. 240–51.

Mahlberg, M. (2005) *English General Nouns: a Corpus Theoretical Approach.* Amsterdam: John Benjamins.

—— (2006) 'Lexical cohesion: corpus linguistic theory and its application in ELT'. *International Journal of Corpus Linguistics,* 11, 3: 363–83.

—— (2007a). 'Review of M. Hori. 2004. Investigating Dickens' Style: A Collocational Analysis'. *Language and Literature,* 16, 1: 93–6.

—— (2007b). 'Corpora and translation studies: textual functions of lexis in *Bleak House* and in a translation of the novel into German', in V. Intoni, G. Todisco and M. Gatto (eds), *La Traduzione. Lo Stato dell'Arte. Translation. The State of the Art.* Ravenna: Longo, pp. 115–35.

—— (forthcoming). 'Clusters, key clusters and local textual functions in Dickens'. *Corpora.*

Miller, J. H. (1971) 'Interpretation in *Bleak House*'. Reprinted in *Victorian Subjects,* 1991. Durham, NC: Duke University Press, pp. 179–99.

Project Gutenberg (2003–2006) www.gutenberg.org/. (Last accessed July 2006.)

Scott, M. (2004) *WordSmith Tools. Version 4.0.* Oxford: OUP.

—— (2004–2006). *WordSmith Tools. Version 4.0. Manual.* Oxford: OUP.

Scott, M. and Tribble, C. (2006) *Textual Patterns. Key Words and Corpus Analysis in Language Education.* Amsterdam: John Benjamins.

Semino, E. and Short, M. (2004) *Corpus Stylistics. Speech, Writing and Thought Presentation in a Corpus of English Writing.* London: Routledge.

Short, M. (1996) *Exploring the Language of Poems, Plays and Prose.* Harlow: Pearson Education.

Starcke, B. (2006) 'The phraseology of Jane Austen's *Persuasion*: phraseological units as carriers of meaning'. *ICAME Journal,* 30: 87–104.

Stubbs, M. (2005) 'Conrad in the computer: examples of quantitative stylistics methods'. *Language and Literature,* 14, 1: 5–24.

Tabata, T. (2002) 'Investigating stylistic variation in Dickens through correspondence analysis of word-class distribution', in T. Saito, J. Nakamura and S. Yamazaki (eds), *English Corpus Linguistics in Japan.* Amsterdam: Rodopi, pp. 165–82.

Wales, K. (2001) *A Dictionary of Stylistics.* Harlow: Pearson Education.

Wynne, M. (2006) 'Stylistics: corpus approaches', in Brown, K. (ed-in-chief), *The Encyclopedia of Language and Linguistics.* Oxford: Elsevier, pp. 223–6.

Appendix

Table 8.4 Five-word clusters in *Bleak House* that occur five times and more (L = Labels, S = Speech, BP = Body parts, AI = *as if*, TP = Time and place, O = Other)

Rank	5-word cluster	Freq.	Chapters	Funct. Group
1	NOT TO PUT TOO FINE	15	8	L
2	PUT TOO FINE A POINT	15	8	L
3	TO PUT TOO FINE A	15	8	L
4	FINE A POINT UPON IT	14	8	L
5	TOO FINE A POINT UPON	14	8	L
6	MAN OF THE NAME OF	13	4	L
7	OF THE NAME OF GUPPY	13	4	L
8	YOUNG MAN OF THE NAME	12	4	L
9	BE SO GOOD AS TO	11	11	S
10	IN THE COURSE OF THE	10	9	TP
11	THE YOUNG MAN OF THE	10	4	L
12	AS IF IT WERE A	9	8	AI
13	OLD GIRL SAYS MR BAGNET	9	3	L
14	AS IF HE WERE A	8	8	AI
15	HIS HEAD AGAINST THE WALL	8	4	L
16	WITH HIS HANDS BEHIND HIM	8	6	BP
17	IS RIGHT THAT I SHOULD	7	3	S
18	IT IS RIGHT THAT I	7	3	S
19	SIR LEICESTER DEDLOCK BARONET AND	7	5	L
20	SIR LEICESTER DEDLOCK BARONET I	7	3	L
21	THE FACE OF THE EARTH	7	6	O
22	THE MISTRESS OF BLEAK HOUSE	7	4	L
23	WITH HIS HEAD AGAINST THE	7	4	L
24	YOUR FRIEND IN THE CITY	7	3	L
25	AS WELL AS ANYTHING ELSE	6	2	L
26	BUT I NEVER OWN TO	6	4	L
27	CIRCUMSTANCES OVER WHICH I HAVE	6	3	L
28	DON'T KNOW BUT WHAT I	6	3	S
29	HA HA HA HA HA	6	2	S

Continued

Table 8.4 *Continued*

Rank	5-word cluster	Freq.	Chapters	Funct. Group
30	HEARD OF SUCH A THING	6	6	O
31	I ASK YOUR PARDON SIR	6	4	L
32	I DON'T KNOW BUT WHAT	6	4	S
33	I NEVER OWN TO IT	6	4	L
34	I THOUGHT IT BEST TO	6	6	L
35	IN THE VALE OF TAUNTON	6	4	L
36	MY DEAR MISS SUMMERSON SAID	6	3	L
37	NEVER HEARD OF SUCH A	6	6	O
38	NEVER OWN TO IT BEFORE	6	4	L
39	OVER WHICH I HAVE NO	6	3	L
40	SIR LEICESTER AND LADY DEDLOCK	6	4	L
41	THE BRILLIANT AND DISTINGUISHED CIRCLE	6	1	L
42	THE RAG AND BOTTLE SHOP	6	5	L
43	WHAT DO YOU SAY TO	6	3	S
44	WHEN WE CAME TO THE	6	5	
45	WHICH I HAVE NO CONTROL	6	3	L
46	YOUR LADYSHIP SAYS MR GUPPY	6	2	L
47	A QUARTER OF AN HOUR	5	4	TP
48	A YEAR AND A HALF	5	2	TP
49	AM MUCH OBLIGED TO YOU	5	5	S
50	AT THE CORNER OF THE	5	5	TP
51	AT THE TOP OF THE	5	5	TP
52	BEFORE HER DISCIPLINE MUST BE	5	3	L
53	BY SIR LEICESTER DEDLOCK BARONET	5	4	L
54	DO AS WELL AS ANYTHING	5	1	L
55	EARLY IN THE MORNING AND	5	5	TP
56	FOR A MINUTE OR TWO	5	5	TP
57	GALAXY GALLERY OF BRITISH BEAUTY	5	3	L
58	HAD THE PLEASURE OF SEEING	5	5	O
59	HAVE SOMETHING TO SAY ABOUT	5	1	L

Table 8.4 *Continued*

Rank	5-word cluster	Freq.	Chapters	Funct. Group
60	HER DISCIPLINE MUST BE MAINTAINED	5	3	L
61	HIS HANDS IN HIS POCKETS	5	4	BP
62	HOW DO YOU DO MR	5	5	S
63	I AM GLAD TO HEAR	5	4	S
64	I AM MUCH OBLIGED TO	5	5	S
65	I AM NOT AT ALL	5	4	S
66	I DON'T KNOW HOW IT	5	5	S
67	I DON'T KNOW WHAT I	5	5	S
68	I EXPECT A JUDGMENT SHORTLY	5	3	L
69	I MADE UP MY MIND	5	4	S
70	IF YOU PLEASE MISS SAID	5	4	L
71	IN A SPIRIT OF LOVE	5	3	L
72	IN COOK'S COURT CURSITOR STREET	5	4	L
73	IN THE MIDDLE OF THE	5	5	TP
74	INSPECTOR BUCKET OF THE DETECTIVE	5	3	L
75	IT BEFORE HER DISCIPLINE MUST	5	3	L
76	LEANING BACK IN HIS CHAIR	5	3	O
77	MR JARNDYCE OF BLEAK HOUSE	5	2	L
78	MRS PIPER AND MRS PERKINS	5	3	L
79	MY DEAR SAID MR JARNDYCE	5	4	L
80	MY FRIEND IN THE CITY	5	2	L
81	MY NOBLE AND LEARNED BROTHER	5	2	L
82	NOW SIR LEICESTER DEDLOCK BARONET	5	1	L
83	ON THE OTHER SIDE OF	5	5	TP
84	OWN TO IT BEFORE HER	5	3	L
85	RIGHT THAT I SHOULD BE	5	1	L
86	SOMETHING TO SAY ABOUT IT	5	1	L
87	THE GREATER PART OF THE	5	5	O
88	THE OLD GIRL SAYS MR	5	3	L
89	THE OTHER SIDE OF THE	5	5	TP

Continued

Table 8.4 *Continued*

Rank	5-word cluster	Freq.	Chapters	Funct. Group
90	TO IT BEFORE HER DISCIPLINE	5	3	L
91	TO LOOK AFTER THE PROPERTY	5	1	L
92	WILL HAVE SOMETHING TO SAY	5	1	L
93	WITH HIS BACK TO THE	5	5	BP
94	WOS WERY GOOD TO ME	5	3	L
95	YOU ARE TO US A	5	1	L
96	YOU BE SO GOOD AS	5	4	S
97	YOU WILL ALLOW ME TO	5	5	S

Name Index

Adolphs, S. 196, 219
Aitchison, J. 142
Alexander, R. 198, 215
Allan, G. 78
Anscombe, E. 140
Aquinas, Thomas 96, 101, 104–6
Austin, J. L. 145, 150, 153

Bacon, F. 135
Baker, P. 196–7
Bakhtin, M. 71, 78, 82
Barthes, R. 82
Bell, A. 37, 206, 208
Berger, P. 66
Berkeley, G. 135
Bhaskar, R. 148
Biber, D. 225
Bloomfield, L. 70, 136, 179
Bloor, M. 32
Bloor, T. 32
Boeckh, A. 82
Botha, R. P. 131, 150
Brocker, M. 96
Brook, G. L. 228
Brundtland, G. H. 198
Burrows, J. F. 155, 223
Busse, Ditrich 77

Canfora, L. 73
Carr, P. 142
Carroll, L. 7, 10–17
Carter, B. 131
Carter, R. 27, 219, 221, 224
Čermáková, A. 211
Chomsky, N. 74–5, 16, 28, 31, 127, 129, 133–4, 140, 146, 150, 155, 179
Conrad, S. 225
Croft, W. 148, 173, 182

Cruse, A. 148
Culpeper, J. 219

Darnton, A. 38
Dennett, D. 60
Descartes, R. 128, 133–4, 142
Detjen, J. 123–4

Engels, F. 90
Evert, S. 178

Fagiani, F. 100
Fairclough, N. 59
Fillmore, C. 97
Firth, J. R. 133, 137, 192
Fletcher, W. 166
Foucault, M. 57, 73, 74, 75, 82
Fowler, R. 206
Fox, G. 171
Francis, G. 35, 131, 155, 163, 173, 180, 192
Frank, M. 81
Fries, C. C. 136

Gadamer, H. G. 82–3, 85
Garzone, G. 196
Goldberg, A. 179
Goody, J. 64
Grice, H. P. 146, 153

Halliday, M. A. K. 32, 37, 128, 130, 133, 136–8, 148, 153, 155, 180
Hardy, G. H. 141
Harris, R. 60, 62, 65, 151
Hasan, R. 137, 180
Heierle, W. 91
Hermanns, F. 81
Hoey, M. 7–8, 21, 31–2, 34, 38, 63, 148, 192, 194

Subject Index

aboutness 196
ad hoc category 199, 214
agency 146, 150
attested data 130

Bank of English 195
behaviourism 134, 136
British National Corpus (BNC) 10, 129, 156, 163, 183

canonical use (pattern) 168, 172, 176, 179, 181–2
Centesimus annus 90, 92, 93, 94, 111–16, 119–121
children's fiction 16
cluster 223, 225
cognitive linguistics 57, 67
cohesion 15, 169
colligation 8, 13, 15, 19, 24–7, 31, 33, 35, 37, 39, 44, 47, 51–53, 163, 167, 178–9, 194–5
collocation 7–8, 11, 15, 21, 24–7, 31, 33–4, 39–50, 163, 167, 178–9, 194–5, 222–3
    temporary collocation 48–49
communicative competence 143, 146
competence 134, 137, 140, 146, 147, 149, 150, 153
compositional meaning 164, 165
concordance 131, 154, 163, 177
construction grammar 182
constructionism 57
corpus 144, 155, 195–6
    corpus-based 192
    corpus-driven 177, 180, 192–3
    corpus theoretical 193, 195
creativity 16, 31–32, 53, 221–2
critical discourse analysis (CDA) 59, 196
cultural key word 197

De iustitia in mundo 93
deduction 132–3, 135
deictics 32
denotation 164–5
diachronic corpus linguistics 89, 90
discourse 145, 147, 150, 153, 196–7
    discourse prosody 178
discovery method 169
dualism 134, 137, 139, 141, 150, 177

emergent phenomenon 128, 149
empiricism (empirical evidence) 127, 130–2, 144, 146, 155, 163, 168, 177, 182
entrenchment 127, 148
episode 38
epistemology 131, 132–3, 153
evaluative meaning 165, 173, 182, 213
extended lexical unit 182 *see also* unit of meaning

fairy tales 16
features (feature articles) 209, 214
fixed phrase 163, 169, 172
folk tales 16
frequency 127, 130, 138, 196, 222
functional group 199

Gaudium et spes 93, 119
grammar 31–2, 35–6, 193
    grammar, acquisition of 47–55
    grammatical category 35–6
    grammatical function 36
grammaticalization 148
Gricean maxims 61

hermeneutics 57, 75, 80–3
homunculus 60